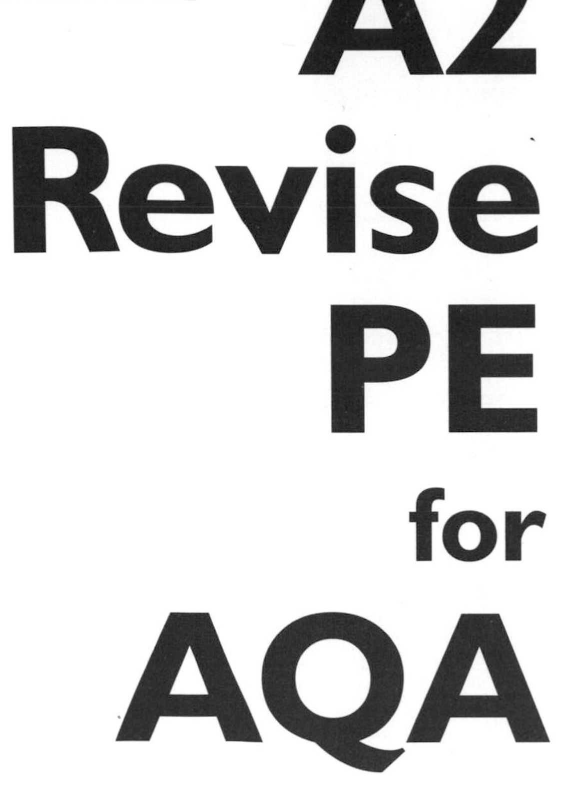

A2 UNIT 3 PHED1

Optimising performance and evaluating contemporary issues within sport

by

Dennis Roscoe
Bob Davis
Jan Roscoe

JRP

A2 Revise PE for AQA

by

Dennis Roscoe
Bob Davis
Jan Roscoe

Jan Roscoe Publications

Published as 978-1-901424-57-7 in 2010 by Jan Roscoe Publications.

'Holyrood'
23 Stockswell Road
Widnes
Cheshire
WA8 4PJ
United Kingdom

tel: 0151 420 4446
fax: 0151 495 2622
e-mail: sales@jroscoe.co.uk

A Catalogue record for this book is available from the British Library

ISBN Published as 978-1-901424-57-7

Cover designs by Helen Roscoe.

Published via Adobe InDesign CS4, Adobe Illustrator 9.0, Smartdraw 6.0

Printed and bound by

Poplar Services
Poplar House
Jackson Street
St Helens
WA9 3AP

tel: 01744 23363
fax: 01744 451242

www.poplarservices.com

INTRODUCTION

Examination courses in Physical Education have now become established within the post-16 curriculum and are a very popular and successful part of school, college or higher education.

This new student book has been written to address the change in content and style of the AQA A2 Physical Education syllabus which commenced in September 2009 (first examination 2010).

This Physical Education course is multidisciplinary in nature, developing a knowledge and understanding of applied physiology, biomechanics, psychological aspects, and contemporary influences on physical education. These subject areas have generated a substantial quantity of specialist literature each with its own specific language. At times you may be overwhelmed by the amount of material covered in such a one year examination course. 'A2 Revise PE for AQA' addresses the problem of dealing with copious notes by summarising the content of the subject matter and attempting to explain in simple language what are sometimes complicated concepts or issues. Practice questions are provided at the end of each chapter, with answers provided on a CD-ROM. The answers will amplify the subject matter and provide clues as to how the exam itself should be approached. A new feature this time is the requirement that the final exam questions on each section of the syllabus shall include an essay type answer. This allows students to express their ability and knowledge in the context of properly written language (prose) with attention to grammar and punctuation.

Materials are presented in a concise and visual approach for effective and efficient revision. Modern terminology, nomenclature and units have been used wherever possible. At the end of the book there is a comprehensive index available for easy reference.

Note that the AS course provides the foundation for study of the A2 programme, so students need to refer to 'AS Revise PE for AQA' ISBN: 978 1 9014242 56 0 for background support.

HOW TO USE THIS REVISION GUIDE

The ideal use of this Revision Guide would be to purchase it at the start of the course and relate each of the summary pages to the specific areas of the syllabus as an aide memoire. The inclusion of specific questions and full answers (see below) provide a means of self-testing. Don't be tempted to find out the answers before attempting a question.

In reality, whole examination questions contain a much broader content than those given in this guide. Examiners will attempt to examine more than one small area of the syllabus within the context of one full question and therefore it is important that you revise all aspects of your syllabus.

The main use of the Revision Guide should be during the final revision period leading up to your examinations, as it should help you to understand and apply concepts i.e. link summary content with examination question.

The aim of this book is to provide an aid that enhances syllabus analysis, and to raise your level of success in examinations.

ANSWERS TO QUESTIONS

The CD-ROM enclosed with this book includes answers to all the questions in the text by chapter. You will have noticed that the AS version of this book included the answers in the main text. Feedback from teachers tells us that students have a habit of looking at the answers before actually attempting to derive their own answers as part of the revision process. Hence, people will now have the option of removing or delaying the answers provided by us - to give students a chance to undertake the revision process properly. Note also that although our answers are presented in bullet format, some questions will require to be answered in prose format as mentioned above.

To access the information on the CD-ROM, if it does not autorun to bring up a list of chapters, then the main CD directory should be accessed from 'my computer' and the programme 'run.bat' double clicked. This will bring up the list of chapters. Each answer chapter is in pdf format.

THE QUALITY OF AUTHOR

We are an expert team of writers, who have considerable experience in teaching 'A' Level Physical Education, who have written past and current examination syllabuses, who have set and marked examination questions within this subject area and taught at revision workshops throughout the UK. Much of the material within this book has been thoroughly student tested.

We hope that this Revision Guide will prove useful to staff and students. Jan Roscoe Publications will welcome any comments you would wish to make about the book's utility or layout. Thank you for using our work.

Dennis Roscoe
Jan Roscoe

ACKNOWLEDGMENTS

We would like to thank Bob Davis for his co-operation and adherence to our demanding deadlines, and Pete Rich for his painstaking proofing of the text. We thank Poplar Services for their patience in linking our work to their computers, and JRP staff member Linda Underwood for working hard in the background while I put this book together. We thank Helen Roscoe for her contribution as cover designer and photographer and Lois Cresswell and Jenny Pacey for their patience as photographic models. We thank members of the Belgian Olympic Athletics Squad for permission to use their images, and Vicky Griffiths for her help in formulating an athlete's diet.

Dennis Roscoe
Editor

ACKNOWLEDGMENTS FOR GRAPHICS

Figure

1.8	Physical Education and the Study of Sport 5e, ISBN: 9780 72343375 0
3.1	Physical Education and the Study of Sport 5e, ISBN: 9780 72343375 0
3.2	Physical Education and the Study of Sport 5e, ISBN: 9780 72343375 0
3.8	istockphoto/Damir Spanic
3.9	istockphoto/nikada
4.6	istockphoto/Yuri Maryunin
5.2	The Stretching Institute
5.15	Wikimedia Commons/Charles J Sharp
6.5	istockphoto/Ben Blankenburg
6.9	istockphoto/Rich Legg
7.2	Wikimedia Creative Commons 3.0/Jim Lamberson
7.10	Physical Education and the Study of Sport 5e, ISBN: 9780 72343375 0
10.2	Wikimedia Creative Commons/John the scone
11.5	GNU free documentation/Ian Thorpe
11.7	Sport Development Centre, Loughborough University
11.10	Wikimedia Creative Commons/Brett Weinstein/Nrbelex
13.5	Shutterstock/Albo
13.6	LTA Wimbledon
14.2	Wikimedia Commons/Yann Caradec/Flickr
15.2	Getty Images/AFP/Stringer
15.4	Shutterstock/Vladmir Wrangel
15.7	Getty Imagwes/David Rogers
16.5	London2012
16.6	GNU free documentation/Rocky Biggs CC-BY-SA-3.0
19.4	Wikimedia Commons/GNU free documentation/Pilise Gabor
20.4	Wikimedia Commons/Flickr
20.5	Shutterstock.com/Hanzrussell
20.8	Wikimedia Commons/GNU free documentation
20.10	Wikimedia Creative Commons 2.0/Flickr/Elvar Palsson/Coda Coza
20.11	LTA Wimbledon

Helen Roscoe is the author of the following graphics:
1.1/4.3/5.13/6.8/6.11/12.4/13.7(part)/20.14
All other graphics are by Helen Roscoe, Jan Roscoe, Bob Davis and Dennis Roscoe.

For September 2008 syllabuses onwards

HIGH QUALITY PHOTOS

REVISION SUMMARY NOTES

Fiedler's Contingency Model (1967)

According to **Fiedler**, the **effectiveness** of a leader is dependent on 2 factors:

- **The personality coach.**
- **The situation.**

The personality of the leader is **measured** using **The Least Preferred Co-worker Scale (LPC)**. The test records whether a leader is **task-orientated** (concerned with achievement) or **person-orientated** (concerned with the members of the group).

The **type of situation** is said to determine which type of leader will be most successful.

According to Fiedler:

- A **task-orientated** leader is most successful in the most favourable and least favourable situations.
- A **person-orientated** leader is most successful in the most favourable and least favourable situations.

QUALITY GRAPHS

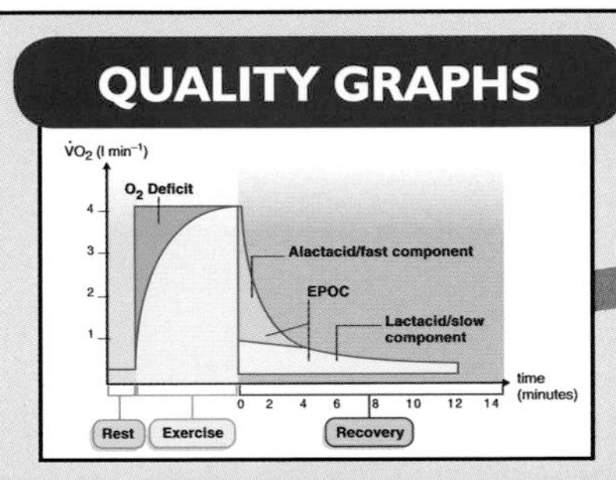

REVISION SUMMARY CHARTS

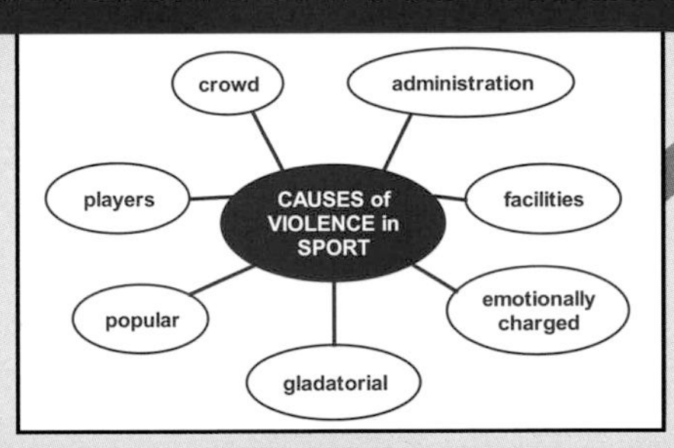

PRACTICE QUESTIONS & ANSWERS

6) How has modern technical developments influenced performance in sport today? *5 marks*

Answer

- *Equipment such as the javelin allows it to be thrown farther.*
- *All-weather surfaces allow games to be played when grass would not and improves performance.*
- *Athletic tracks are faster today producing higher standards.*
- *The timing of races is now more accurate improving confidence.*
- *Better media communications have stimulated interest.*
- *In car racing, modern cars are faster, but safer.*
- *Specialised footwear for athletics and climbing.*
- *Research into swimming and water resistance.*
- *TV evidence used in cricket and rugby.*
- *Fitness suites for improving strength and mobility.*

ROSCOE et al
AS Revise PE for AQA
ISBN 978-1-901424-56-0

This Revise Series covers all aspects of the examinable AS PE AQA syllabus that commenced in September 2008. The book consists of student notes, full colour illustrations, photographs, exam questions and full answers. Key concepts are clearly defined with examples that can be used in answers to exam questions, thus enabling the student to self-test. This student revision guide supports a comprehensive revision plan and will enhance student grades.

HOW TO ORDER

tel **+44(0)151 420 4446**
(open every day 9am-5pm)

fax **+44(0)151 495 2622**
(open 24 hours a day)

email **sales@jroscoe.co.uk**

by post to: **Jan Roscoe Publications, 'Holyrood', 23 Stockswell Road, Widnes, Cheshire WA8 4PJ, United Kingdom**

For **full listings** see the **JRP Catalogue** or visit **www.jroscoe.co.uk**

A2 Revise PE for AQA

A2 UNIT 3 PHED1: Opportunities for and the effects of leading a healthy and active lifestyle

UNIT 3 – SECTION A

APPLIED PHYSIOLOGY TO OPTIMISE PERFORMANCE

A2 Revise PE for AQA

A2 UNIT 3 PHED1: Opportunities for and the effects of leading a healthy and active lifestyle

CONTENTS

A2 Revise PE for AQA

A2 UNIT 3 PHED1: Opportunities for and the effects of leading a healthy and active lifestyle

UNIT 3 – SECTION C

EVALUATING CONTEMPORARY INFLUENCES

SECTION A: APPLIED PHYSIOLOGY TO OPTIMISE PERFORMANCE

CHAPTER 1 – ENERGY SYSTEMS

Energy definitions

Energy is the capacity to do work, and work has a mechanical definition, namely **work = force x distance** moved in the direction of the force. Energy and work are measured in joules (J).

Chemical energy is energy that is produced by a complex series of chemical reactions, which can then be made available as **kinetic energy** (energy due to movement which results from muscular contractions), or **potential energy** which is stored energy due to gravity.

Power is the **rate** at which energy is used, or the energy used per second which is measured in watts (W).
Power can be calculated using the formula:

$$\text{power} = \frac{\text{energy (in joules)}}{\text{time (in seconds)}} \quad \text{answer in watts}$$

Energy sources and systems

We derive our energy from food, namely carbohydrates (CHO), fats, and to a lesser extent proteins. Table 1.1 summarises the details of the major contributions from our diet to the provision of **energy** for exercise, how these contributions are absorbed, and where this energy is stored within the body.

Table 1.1 – **summary of carbohydrate, fat and protein utilisation**

type of food / sources	function as a food fuel - how it is used	energy content ($kJ\,g^{-1}$)	percentage in a balanced diet
carbohydrate (CHO) sugars, rice, potatoes, pasta	**Main energy supply**. Absorbed as glucose in small intestine. Transported around body as blood glucose. Available for immediate energy. Excess stored as muscle and liver glycogen and as fat.	17	60 %
fats butter, oil, pastry, fried food	**Secondary energy supply**. Absorbed as fatty acids and glycerol (called free fatty acids, FFAs) in the small intestine. Stored as triglycerides in adipose tissue. Triglycerides conveyed to the liver via the circulatory system. In the liver they are converted to glucose. Available as delayed (20 minutes delay) energy source for long duration low intensity aerobic exercise.	39	20-25 %
proteins meat, eggs, milk, cheese, nuts	Absorbed as amino acids in the small intestine. Used for growth and repair by all tissues. Used as an energy source when the body is depleted of CHO and fat. Excess protein not needed for tissue repair is broken down and used as an energy supply. Protein can supply between 5 and 10% of energy needed to sustain prolonged exercise.	23	10-15 %

The energy derived from carbohydrates, fats and proteins is stored in bodily tissues in the form of a high energy compound called **adenosine triphosphate** (ATP).

ATP - adenosine triphosphate

ATP is the compound which stores energy and is therefore the energy currency linked to **intensity** and **duration** of physical activity. ATP exists in every living tissue and its breakdown gives energy for all life functions - this includes the action of the liver and the brain for example, as well as the contraction of muscle tissue. All muscular activity requires the availability and breakdown of ATP (figure 1.1).

figure 1.1 – all muscle action uses ATP

The energy released during tissue respiration is stored in the chemical bonds in ATP, and this energy is released during the reaction: **ATP → ADP + P_i + energy**

where ADP is adenosine diphosphate, and P_i is a free phosphate radical. **ATPase** is an enzyme which facilitates this reaction, which is **exothermic** - it releases energy.

The energy stored within ATP is only available as long as ATP is retained within the cells using it. In muscle cells during intense (flat-out) exercise, the stored ATP only lasts about 2 seconds. Therefore the ATP must be replaced as soon as possible so that exercise can continue. There are **three** processes by which this can happen:

- The **ATP-PC** system (also called the alactic anaerobic system).
- The **lactic acid** system (which is also anaerobic).
- The **aerobic** system.

Resynthesis of ATP from ADP uses the reaction: **energy + ADP + P_i → ATP**

This is an **endothermic** reaction since energy is **given** to the molecule to enable the reaction to happen. This energy will be derived from **food fuels**.

Anaerobic energy systems

The ATP-PC system

This system of replenishing of ATP from ADP is the predominant one for activity which lasts between 3 and 10 seconds, which means for high intensity maximum work, for example, flat out sprinting - the 100m sprint.

No oxygen is needed - the process is anaerobic. The chemical reactions within this system are a **coupled reaction** in which ATP is resynthesised via **phosphocreatine** (PC) stored in muscle cell sarcoplasm.

The following reactions take place: **PC → P_i + C + energy**

energy + ADP + P_i → ATP

The two reactions together are called a **coupled reaction** and are facilitated by the enzyme **creatine kinase** (CK).

The net effect of these two coupled reactions is:

PC + ADP → ATP + C

STUDENT NOTE

This process does not directly require glucose as an energy source - but the re-creation of PC during recovery will do so.

PC is re-created in muscle cells during the recovery process, which requires energy and is an **endothermic** reaction.

During intense exercise, peak anaerobic power is attained within the first 5 seconds, and depletion of PC occurs between 7 and 9 seconds.

figure 1.2 – changes in muscle ATP and PC

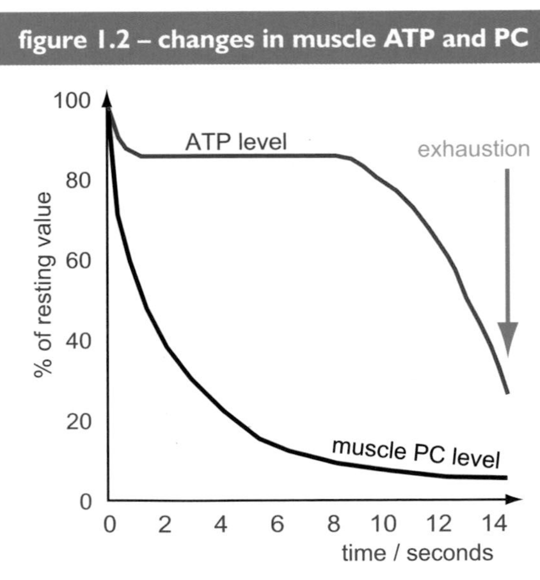

Look at the graph in figure 1.2 showing changes in muscle ATP and PC. After an initial small fall, the ATP level is maintained, then falls as the PC is used up because the energy from PC is being used to resynthesise ATP.

This causes PC levels to fall rapidly to zero after about 10 seconds. The capacity to maintain ATP production at this point depends on the lactic acid system.

The lactic acid system

This system depends on a chemical process called **glycolysis** which is the incomplete breakdown of sugar. Figure 1.3 (see overleaf) shows the schematic layout of glycolysis.

The lactic acid system

figure 1.3 – the lactic acid system

glucose $C_6H_{12}O_6$
glycolytic enzymes (GPP, PFK)
2ATP
pyruvic acid
LDH
lactic acid

- **Carbohydrate** from food you have eaten is stored as **glycogen** (in the muscles and liver).
- This glycogen is converted into **glucose** by the hormone **glucagon** released when blood glucose levels fall (when glucose is used during tissue respiration).
- The breakdown of glucose provides the energy to rebuild ATP from ADP.
- This is facilitated by enzymes such as **glycogen phosphorylase** (GPP) and **phosphofructokinase** (PFK).
- The whole process produces **pyruvic acid**.
- **Glycolysis is anaerobic**.
- It takes place in the **sarcoplasm** of the muscle cell.
- No oxygen is needed, and the end product of this reaction (in the absence of oxygen) is lactic acid.
- The enzyme facilitating the conversion from pyruvic acid to lactic acid is **lactate dehydrogenase** (LDH).

As work intensity increases, lactic acid starts to accumulate above resting values, which produces **muscle fatigue** and pain. The resultant low pH inhibits enzyme action and cross-bridge formation, hence muscle action is inhibited and physical performance deteriorates.

The lactic acid system is the predominant one used to resynthesise ATP in sport or activities in which the flat-out effort lasts up to 30-60 seconds. For example, a 400m run or a 100m swim.

After exercise stops, extra oxygen is taken up to remove lactic acid by changing it back into pyruvic acid - this is the **EPOC** (**Excess Post-exercise Oxygen Consumption**, sometimes called the oxygen debt), see page 18 below for the details of EPOC.

The aerobic system

The aerobic energy system releases stored energy from muscle glycogen, fats and proteins.

Figure 1.4 is a graphic of some of the details of the aerobic system showing how between 32 and 34 ATP molecules are resynthesised from one molecule of glucose - which is the food fuel created from the food we eat. This process will continue indefinitely until energy stores run out - or the exercise stops.

Stage one - glycolysis

This process takes place in the **muscle cell sarcoplasm** and is identical to the lactic acid system (anaerobic).
ATP regenerated = 2ATP per molecule of glucose.

Stage two - Kreb's cycle (citric acid cycle)

This stage occurs in the **presence of oxygen**, and takes place in the **muscle cell mitochondria** within the inner **fluid filled** matrix. Here, 2 molecules of **pyruvic acid** combine with **oxaloacetic acid** (4 carbons) and **acetyl coA** (2 carbons) to form citric acid (6 carbons). The cycle produces H^+ and electron pairs, and CO_2 and 2 ATP. Also, free fatty acids (from body fat) facilitated by the enzyme **lipoprotein lipase**, or protein (keto acids - from muscle), act as the fuel for this stage.

figure 1.4 – the aerobic system

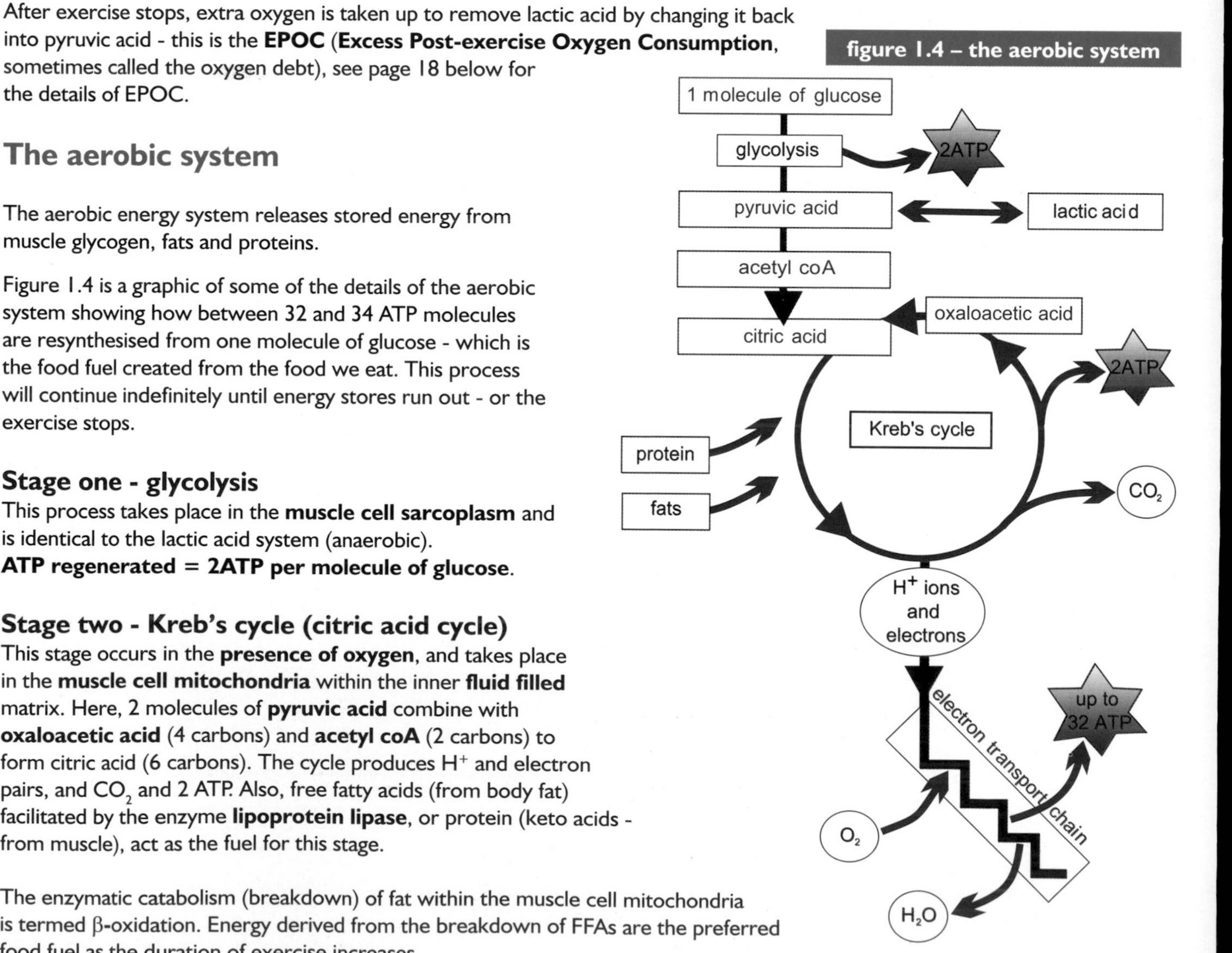

The enzymatic catabolism (breakdown) of fat within the muscle cell mitochondria is termed β-oxidation. Energy derived from the breakdown of FFAs are the preferred food fuel as the duration of exercise increases.

Stage three - the electron transport chain

The electron transport chain occurs in the presence of oxygen within the **cristae** (inner part) of the **muscle cell mitochondria**. **Hydrogen ions** and **electrons** have potential energy which is used to produce the ATP which is then released in a controlled step-by-step manner. Oxygen combines with the final H^+ ions to produce water and 32 ATP.

Aerobic respiration

In summary, the total effect of aerobic respiration is that it is an **endothermic** reaction:

$$\textbf{glucose} + 36ADP + 36P_i + 6O_2 \rightarrow 6CO_2 + 36ATP + 6H_2O$$

Fat fuels produce 2 ATP less than glucose.

Short-term response to aerobic activity

The aerobic system requires carbohydrate in the form of **glucose** which is **derived from glycogen** stored in muscle cells (mostly slow twitch - SO type I) or in the liver.

The graph in figure 1.5 shows how the rate of usage of muscle glycogen is high during the first 30 minutes of steady exercise - which has to be replaced if a sportsperson is to continue at the same rate. Hence consumption of energy drinks and bananas during a long tennis match.

figure 1.5 – change in muscle glycogen during low intensity exercise

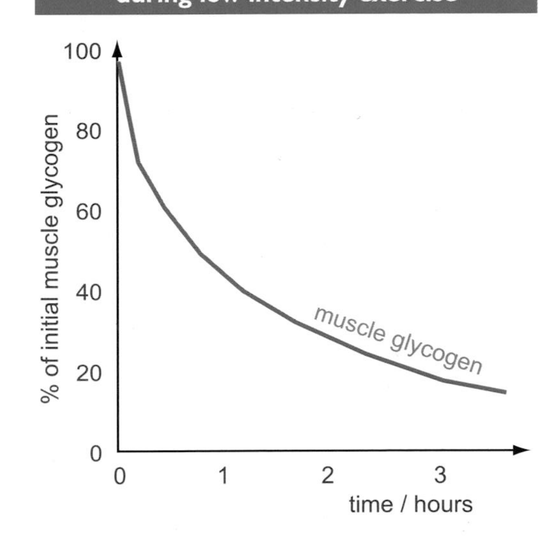

Endurance athletes can utilise FFAs during prolonged exercise sooner than untrained people. This training adaptation enables the trained athlete to not use glycogen up immediately, but save it for later on in an exercise effort, or when the intensity of exercise increases. This is called **glycogen sparing** and is illustrated in figure 1.6.

The energy continuum

This describes the process by which ATP is regenerated via the different energy systems depending on the **intensity** and **duration** of exercise. Although **all** the systems contribute to ATP regeneration during any activity, one or other of the energy systems usually provides the major contribution for a given activity. Table 1.2 shows approximate proportions of ATP resynthesised via aerobic and anaerobic pathways for some sporting activities.

Table 1.2 – **percentage contribution of the aerobic and anaerobic energy systems to different sports**

sport or event	aerobic %	anaerobic (all) %
100m sprint	0	100
200m sprint	10	90
100m swim	20	80
boxing	30	70
800m run	40	60
hockey	50	50
2000m rowing	60	40
4000m cycle pursuit	70	30
3000m run	80	20
cross country run	90	10
marathon	100	0

figure 1.6 – contribution of CHO and fats for trained and untrained people

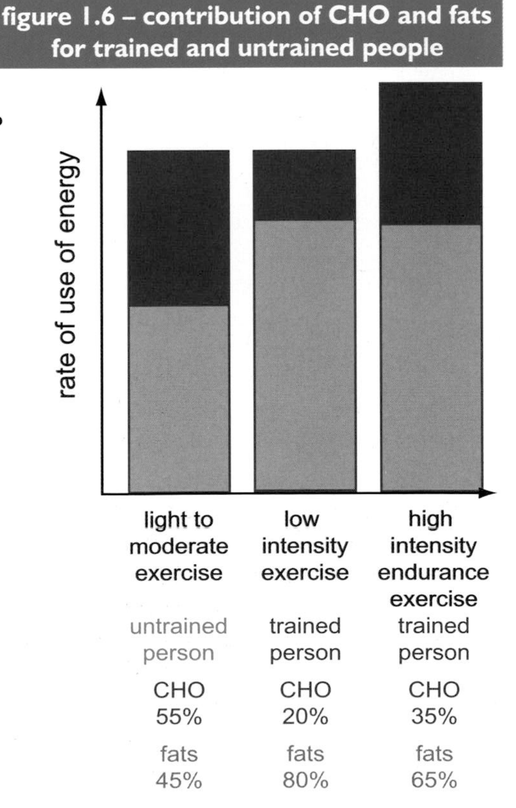

The graph in figure 1.7 overleaf shows how the different energy systems contribute resynthesis of ATP during flat-out exercise. Obviously, at reduced intensity of exercise, the contributions will be slightly different. But note that **all systems** are contributing from the start of exercise, only it takes some time for the lactic acid and aerobic systems to get going.

Short-term responses - thresholds

The concept of a **threshold** applies to the time at which one particular system of ATP regeneration takes over from another as the major regenerator of ATP during flat out exercise - marked as T in figure 1.7.

- For example, **ATP muscle stores** are depleted **within 2 seconds**, and towards the end of this period the ATP-PC system has risen enough to be able to provide the ATP necessary for the exercise.
- **Peak anaerobic power** is attained within the first 5 seconds of flat-out exercise, but depletion of PC occurs between 7 and 9 seconds.
- At this point, the lactic acid system has risen enough to be able to provide the ATP required for the next 40 seconds or so.

Hence the **threshold** between **ATP-PC and lactic acid** systems occurs between 7 and 9 seconds after the start of an exercise period.

figure 1.7 – variation in contribution of energy systems

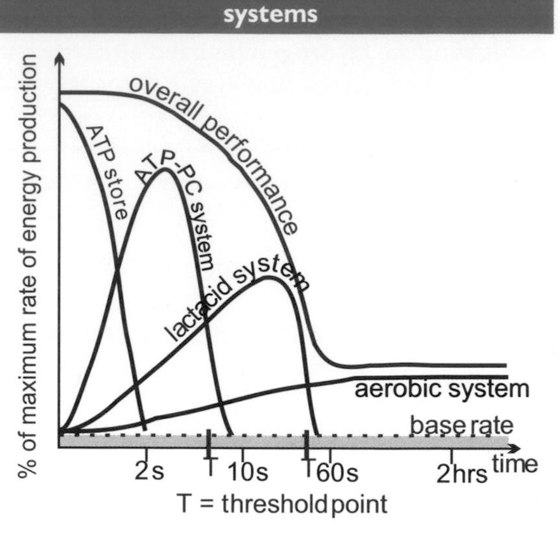

Long-term training effects - thresholds

It is found that thresholds are **delayed** by training, so that the trained individual has a greater capacity for ATP-PC, has a greater lactic acid toleration, and more efficient ATP regeneration than the untrained person.

Other factors affecting the proportions of energy systems

- The **level of fitness** (whether adaptations to training have included enhancement of relevant enzymes - which would for example postpone levels of lactate accumulation).
- The **availability of O_2 and food fuels**. For example, a high CHO diet would assist replenishment of glycogen stores which would then be available for glycolysis.

Practice questions

1) Define energy, and briefly describe how energy is released from food in the body. 5 marks

2) a) Identify the only form of usable energy in the body. 1 mark

b) What is meant by an exothermic reaction? Illustrate this definition with an example. 2 marks

c) What is meant by an endothermic reaction? Illustrate this definition with an example. 2 marks

3) Explain the specialist role of mitochondria in energy production. 4 marks

4) a) An elite cyclist wants to discover her maximum output when sprinting. A load of 85 newtons is applied to the wheel of a cycle ergometer. The cyclist then sprints for 10 seconds and records a distance travelled of 200m. Assuming that no other force is acting on the cycle, calculate the power output of the cyclist. Show each stage of your calculation. 4 marks

b) Name the predominant energy system that would be utilised during this activity and describe how ATP is re-created within this system. 4 marks

5) a) An elite swimmer performs a flat-out 100 metre freestyle swim in 50 seconds. Describe how most of the ATP is regenerated during the swim. 4 marks

b) Sketch a graph, which shows the use of the appropriate energy systems against time during the swim. 4 marks

6) a) Taking part in a triathlon involves swimming, cycling and running. Briefly describe how the aerobic energy system within the cell mitochondria supports this endurance event. 6 marks

b) Construct a graph, which illustrates the food fuel usage against time during a triathlon race lasting 2 hours. 2 marks

7) Compare the relative efficiency of ATP production via the aerobic and anaerobic routes. Explain your answer. 3 marks

8) Describe the predominant energy system being used in the following activities: shot put, 200 metres breaststroke, a game of hockey, 100 metres hurdles race, gymnastics vault, modern pentathlon. 6 marks

Table 1.3 – **table of activities**

activity	energy system
shot-put	
200 metres breaststroke	
a game of hockey	
100 metres hurdles race	
gymnastics vault	
modern pentathlon	

figure 1.8 – energy blocks for a variety of sports

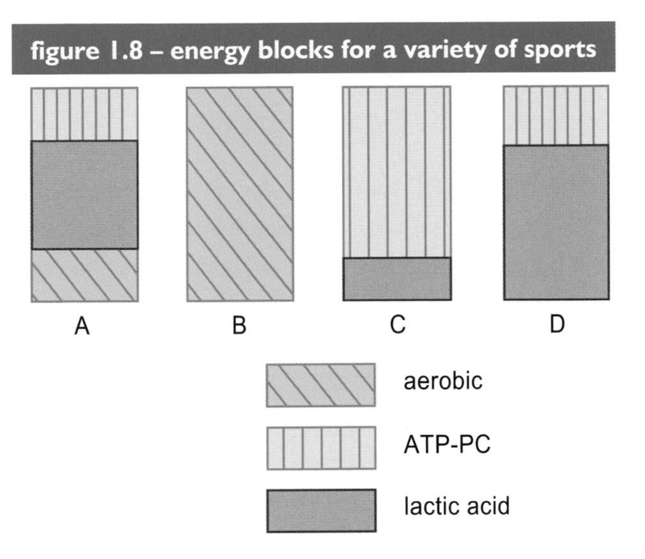

9) Figure 1.8 represents the energy systems used during the following athletic events: 100 metres, 400 metres, 1500 metres and marathon, but not necessarily in that order.

a) Identify each event with an energy block and comment briefly on the reasons for your choice. 8 marks

b) Using the same key, complete a block to show the approximate proportions of aerobic/anaerobic work during a basketball game. 2 marks

figure 1.9 – variation in contribution of energy system

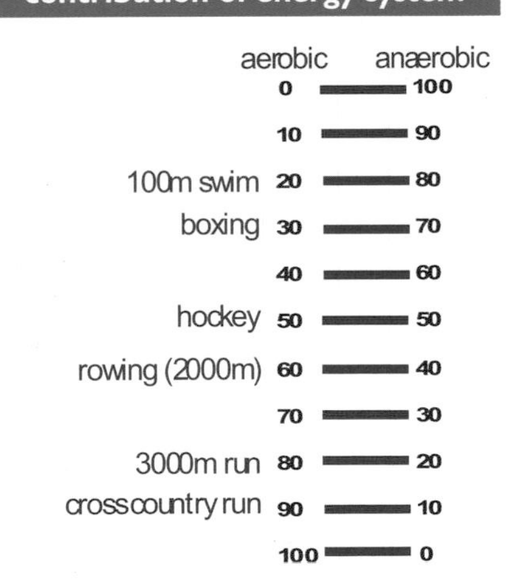

10) The diagram in figure 1.9 is an energy continuum in relation to a variety of sports activities.

a) Explain the concept 'the energy continuum'. 2 marks

b) At each end of the continuum examples of sporting activities have been omitted. Give one example of a sporting activity that is predominantly anaerobic and one example of a sporting activity that is predominantly aerobic. 2 marks

c) Suggest two factors that need to be considered in evaluating sports activities on the basis of their relative position on the energy continuum. 2 marks

d) Explain, using specific examples, why a game of hockey has aerobic and anaerobic components. 4 marks

CHAPTER 2 – FATIGUE AND RECOVERY

Fatigue

Effects of fatigue on performance

Performance can be affected by muscle fatigue, the depletion of energy stores in muscle (and the liver). Various factors contribute to this.

Muscle fatigue

Muscle fatigue can be described as a reduction of muscular performance, and an inability to maintain expected power output. Performance can often be continued at quite a high level in spite of fatigue, but the outcome of 'jelly legs' or 'jelly shoulders' will be well known to all sportspeople after an exhausting performance has been completed.

Depletion of energy stores

- Depletion of **PC** (phosphocreatine) and muscle and liver **glycogen** stores will be the major cause of fatigue.
- Fatigue in marathon runners is due to depletion of **muscle glycogen** in both ST and FT muscle fibres.
- **FT muscle fibres** have low aerobic capacity and therefore **quickly fatigue** during maximal activity. This is because stored ATP and PC are quickly used up (in under 7 seconds) during this sort of activity (weight training, sprinting for example).

Metabolic accumulation

During intense exercise lasting longer than 7 seconds and under 45 seconds, **accumulation of lactic acid** and **CO_2** in muscle cells causes extreme fatigue and complete loss of muscle function. This is because increase in H^+ ions (decrease in pH due to the lactic acid acidity) inhibits both aerobic and anaerobic enzyme activity required for ATP regeneration.

Body fluid balance and dehydration

- Fluid loss **decreases plasma volume** which reduces blood pressure and hence produces a reduction in blood flow to skin and muscles.
- This means that the heart has to work harder, body temperature rises, and **fatigue** occurs.
- Hence **fluid intake is important** during endurance activities.

figure 2.1 – factors contributing to EPOC

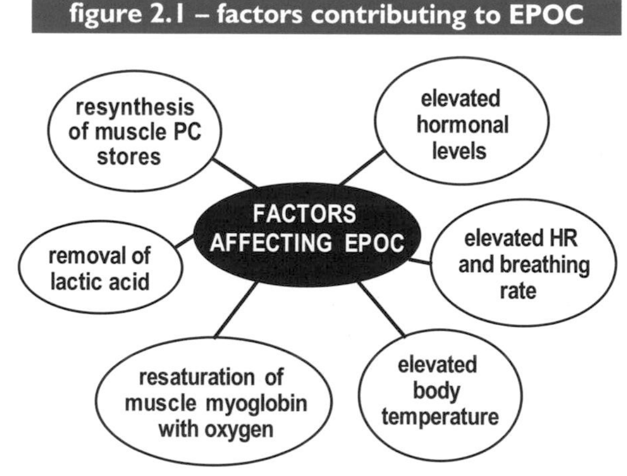

Recovery

Bodily processes do not immediately return to resting levels after exercise ceases. The time taken for this to occur is called the **recovery period**. The recovery period is dependent on the intensity and duration of the exercise.

Excess post-exercise oxygen consumption (EPOC)

After every strenuous exercise (figure 2.1), there are **four** tasks that need to be completed before the exhausted muscle can operate at full efficiency again:

- **Replacement of ATP and phosphocreatine** (fast replenishment component).
- **Removal of lactic acid** (slow replenishment component).
- **Replenishment of myoglobin** with oxygen.
- **Replacement of glycogen**.

The first three require oxygen in substantial quantities, hence the need for rapid breathing and high pulse rate to carry oxygen to the muscle cells.

The need for oxygen

The need for oxygen to rapidly replace ATP and remove lactic acid is known as the oxygen debt. The more modern term for oxygen debt is **excess post-exercise oxygen consumption** (EPOC) or oxygen recovery. This represents the elevation of the metabolic rate above resting values which occurs after exercise during the recovery period.

figure 2.2 – oxygen consumption during exercise and recovery

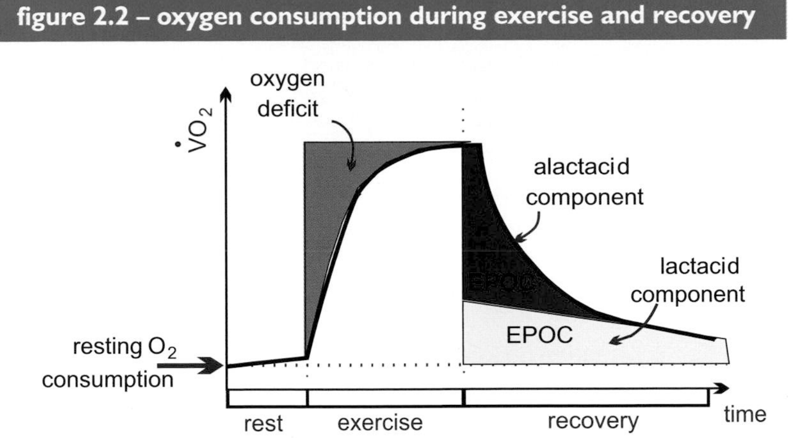

EPOC is the excess O_2 consumed following exercise needed to provide the energy required to resynthesise ATP used and remove lactic acid created during previous exercise. EPOC has **two** components (figure 2.2):

- **Alactic or alactacid**.
- **Lactic or lactacid**.

The **oxygen deficit** is the difference between the oxygen required during exercise and the oxygen actually consumed during the activity. The graph in figure 2.2 shows the relationship between oxygen consumption and the time before, during and after exercise.

The alactacid component

This component involves the **conversion of ADP back into PC and ATP**, and is known as **restoration of muscle phosphagen**. This is a very rapid process (120 seconds to full restoration - see figure 2.3) and is of size 2 to 3.5 litres of O_2.

Phosphagen Recovery

Phosphagen recovery (figure 2.3) is achieved via **three** mechanisms:

- There is **aerobic** conversion of carbohydrates into CO_2 and H_2O to resynthesise ATP from ADP and P_i.
- Some of the ATP is immediately utilised **to create PC** using the coupled reaction: **ATP + C → ADP + PC**.
- A small amount of ATP is **resynthesised via glycogen,** producing small amounts of lactic acid.

figure 2.3 – phosphagen recovery

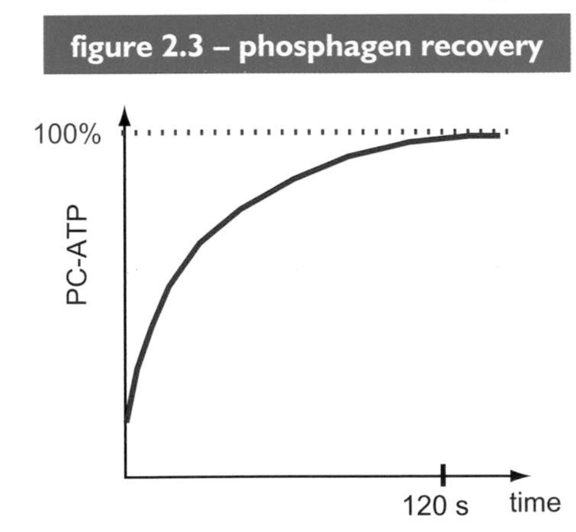

Continuous oxygen recovery

During the **post-exercise period**, oxygen recovery is continuous.

This is because:

- Muscle myoglobin recovers.
- Temperature falls.
- Hormone levels fall.

During the **recovery period**, temperature and hormone levels are higher than normal (although falling), which:

- Keeps metabolic rate high.
- Keeps respiratory rate high.
- Keeps heart rate high.
- Requires more oxygen than normal.

Hence EPOC increases.

The implications for interval training

- If there is only a short interval between bouts of exercise, the level of phosphagen stores gradually reduces (see figure 2.4) thereby reducing the energy available for the later bouts.
- This stresses the ATP and PC storage and forces the muscle cells to adapt by storing more of these quantities.
- Also, cells will adapt by improving their ability to provide O_2, and hence increase the possible size of the alactic component.

- Anaerobic interval training studies have shown that 30 second bouts of exercise increase the activities of **glycolytic enzymes**, such as phosphorylase, phosphofructokinase and lactate dehydrogenase, from around 10% to 25%.
- This increase in **glycolytic capacity** will allow the muscle to develop greater tension for a longer period of time as the muscle tissue increases its **tolerance to lactate**.

See further information on long-term adaptations on page 28 onwards.

figure 2.4 – phosphagen recovery during interval training

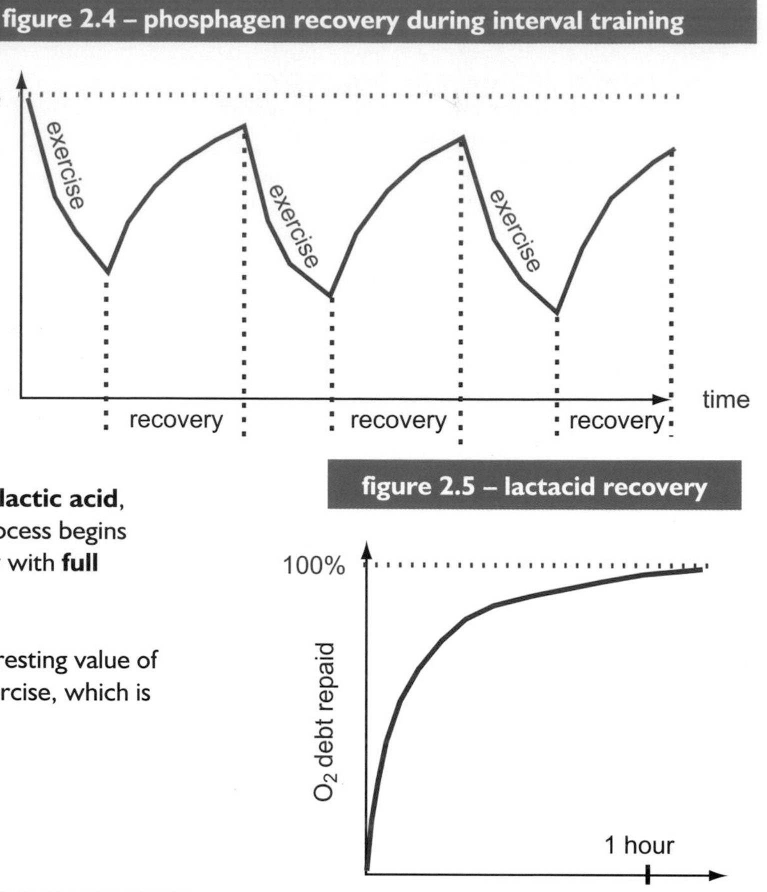

Lactacid oxygen recovery

High intensity exercise up to about 60 seconds creates **lactic acid**, and **oxygen is needed** to remove this lactic acid. This process begins to restore muscle and liver glycogen, and is relatively slow with **full recovery** taking up to 1 hour (figure 2.5).

Relatively large amounts of lactic acid (15 to 20 times the resting value of 1 to 2 mmol litre^{-1}) are produced during high intensity exercise, which is removed according to the proportions listed in table 2.1

Removal of the lactic acid

Table 2.1 – **removal of the lactic acid**

oxidation into CO_2 + H_2O	65%
conversion into glycogen then stored in muscle and liver (Cori cycle)	20%
conversion into protein	10%
conversion into glucose	5%

The lactate shuttle

During the recovery process after intense exercise, a small proportion of the lactic acid produced is recycled back into glucose in the muscle cell. This is the reverse process to glycolysis and requires energy from ATP breakdown.

Buffering

A **blood buffer** is a chemical substance which resists abrupt changes in hydrogen ion (H^+) concentration. For example, when H^+ concentration increases as a result of intense exercise, H^+ reacts with oxyhaemoglobin (buffer) to form haemoglobinic acid. These ions are released when H^+ concentration falls. So this is a temporary solution to rapid changes in acidity or alkalinity which would otherwise cause rapid fatigue symptoms.

figure 2.6 – blood lactate concentration after exercise

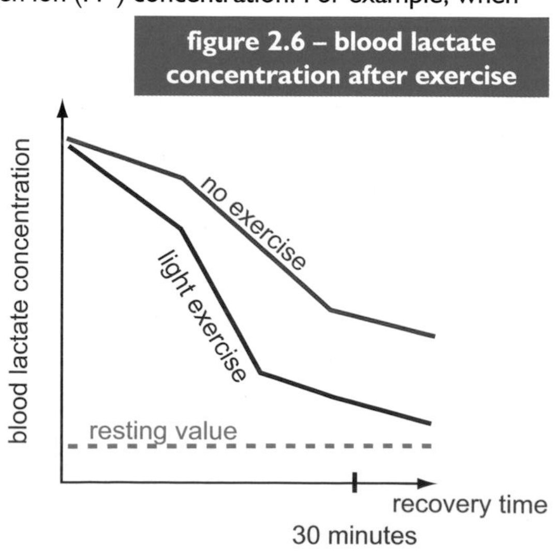

Cool-down following exercise

Cool-down (the process of continuing low level exercise immediately after the end of a high intensity exercise bout) **continues to provide oxygen** to skeletal muscle. This therefore **enhances oxidation of lactic acid** and ensures that less lactic acid remains in tissue. Hence there is less muscle soreness (**less DOMS**).

Figure 2.6 shows how blood lactate falls after exercise, and that when an active cool-down is undertaken less lactate remains in muscle tissue.

Restoration of muscle glycogen stores

- During short duration high intensity exercise, restoration of glycogen takes up to 2 hours, and after prolonged low intensity aerobic exercise, restoration can take days.
- A **high carbohydrate diet** speeds up the glycogen recovery process, and there is a need for the athlete to restore stores as soon as possible after activity, with for example, a high CHO loaded drink immediately following exercise.

Restoration of myoglobin

Muscle myoglobin (an iron protein molecule located in skeletal muscle similar to haemoglobin) serves as a storage site for O_2, and has a temporary but greater affinity for O_2 than haemoglobin. Hence it acts as a **carrier of O_2** from HbO_2 (in blood) to mitochondria (in a muscle cell). Myoglobin is reoxygenated within 2 minutes.

Restoration of muscle myoglobin is important for recovery from high intensity exercise.

figure 2.7 – oxygen uptake as exercise intensity increases

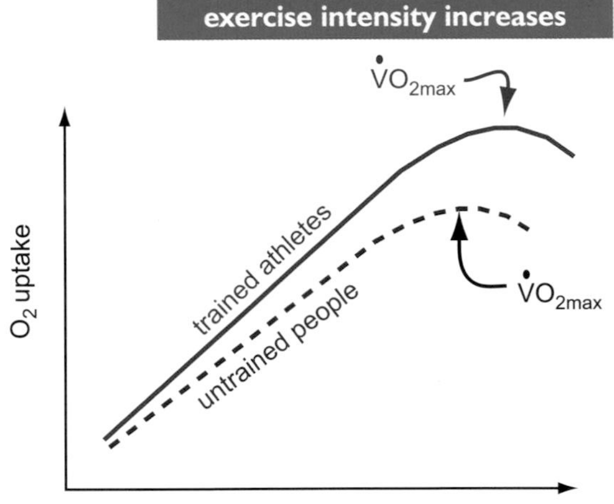

Oxygen uptake - $\dot{V}O_2$

The amount of oxygen consumed per unit of time (usually 1 minute) is expressed as $\dot{V}O_2$, and the mean value of $\dot{V}O_2$ at rest = 0.2 to 0.3 litres min^{-1}.

$\dot{V}O_2$ increases proportionally to work intensity (see figure 2.7) up to a maximum value - called $\dot{V}O_{2max}$.

You can see from figure 2.7 that $\dot{V}O_{2max}$ is bigger for trained athletes. This is an adaptation produced by aerobic training, which means that the athlete can work harder for longer.

$\dot{V}O_{2max}$ is therefore a key component of aerobic endurance and is called **aerobic power** or **maximum oxygen uptake**, and so represents an accurate indicator of an athlete's fitness.

STUDENT NOTE

For details of long-term training adaptations that have a direct impact on $\dot{V}O_{2max}$ values, refer to pages 36 and 48 of 'AS Revise PE for AQA' ISBN: 978 1 901424 56 0.

$\dot{V}O_{2max}$ tests as a measure of aerobic endurance

- A $\dot{V}O_{2max}$ test assesses the maximum amount of oxygen that a person can consume per minute during a progressive exercise test to exhaustion.
- $\dot{V}O_{2max}$ is assessed directly when using closed-circuit spirometry.
- Simple **predicted $\dot{V}O_{2max}$** tests are used as indicators of aerobic fitness or stamina, and include the Physical work capacity test (PWC170), the Cooper run/walk test, the Multi-stage shuttle run test, and the Queen's College step test.
- Elite marathon athletes run at optimal percentages of their $\dot{V}O_{2max}$ in order to achieve world class performances.

STUDENT NOTE

The details of submaximal tests are outlined on page 78 of 'AS Revise PE for AQA' ISBN: 978 1 901424 56 0.

Values for oxygen uptake - $\dot{V}O_2$

$\dot{V}O_{2max}$ mean values are:	males (20 yo)	= 3.5 litres min^{-1}
		= 40 ml kg^{-1} min^{-1} (for average male body mass 87.5 kg)
	females (20 yo)	= 2.3 litres min^{-1}
		= 35 ml kg^{-1} min^{-1} (for mean female body mass 66 kg)
	endurance athletes	= 4 to 6 litres min^{-1}
		= 60 to 90 ml kg^{-1} min^{-1} (for mean body mass 66 kg)

Recovery

There is improved oxygen recovery as a result of long-term aerobic training because of **better muscle capillarisation**. If an efficient cool-down is used, **lactic acid removal** is improved, hence there is a reduction in **DOMS** (delayed onset muscle soreness).

OBLA (Onset of Blood Lactate Accumulation)

As **work intensity** increases, **lactic acid** starts to **accumulate** above resting values. At a certain point (called the OBLA point) this produces muscle fatigue and pain, since the resultant low pH (high acidity) inhibits enzyme action and cross-bridge (see page 24 below) formation. This means in turn that muscle action is inhibited and **physical performance deteriorates**.

figure 2.8 – onset of blood lactate

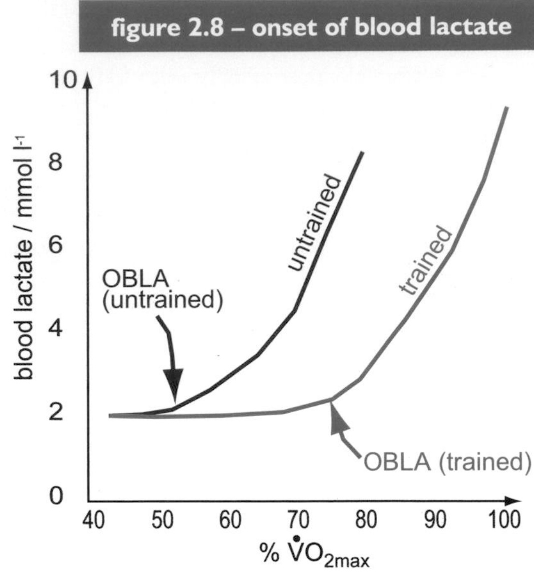

OBLA can be expressed as a percentage of $\dot{V}O_{2max}$ as shown in figure 2.8.

This point governs the **lactic aerobic threshold**.

- In the graph (figure 2.8), as exercise intensity increases and $\dot{V}O_2$ increases, untrained people have blood lactate which increases sharply at about 50% of $\dot{V}O_{2max}$.
- But trained athletes can exercise up to 70% of $\dot{V}O_{2max}$ before lactate concentration in the blood increases markedly.
- Hence **trained athletes** begin **OBLA at higher work intensities** - especially since trained athletes have higher values of $\dot{V}O_{2max}$ than untrained people in the first place.
- All this means that the **lactic-aerobic threshold** moves to **higher values of $\dot{V}O_{2max}$**.

Practice questions

1) a) What is muscle fatigue? 2 marks

   b) Describe the possible causes of fatigue during maximal exercise lasting 2 to 10 seconds. 3 marks

2) During intense exercise, athletes can experience a large increase in lactic acid.

   a) Explain the effect of lactic acid build up on muscle function. 4 marks

   b) Suggest strategies that athletes could use to increase their tolerance to lactic acid. 4 marks

3) What do you understand by lactate threshold and how the lactate threshold relates to $\dot{V}O_{2max}$? 4 marks

4) Describe the possible causes of fatigue during submaximal exercise lasting between 2 and 4 hours. 4 marks

5) Explain what you understand by the term 'buffer'. How does the blood buffer lactic acid? 3 marks

6) a) State where and in what conditions lactic acid is commonly found in relatively large amounts. 2 marks

   b) There are several ways by which lactic acid can be removed from active muscles. Identify the major pathway for the removal of lactic acid and the organs and tissues involved. 4 marks

   c) Identify the three other ways, with approximate percentages, in which lactic acid is disposed of in the body. 3 marks

   d) How does light exercise influence lactate removal? 3 marks

7) Explain why cool-down is important within an exercise regime. 4 marks

8) Figure 2.9 shows oxygen uptake of an elite games player undertaking exercise followed by a recovery period.

a) Using the appropriate letters, identify the oxygen deficit and Excess Post Oxygen Consumption (EPOC). 3 marks

b) Why does the elite player incur an oxygen deficit during exercise? 2 marks

c) Excess Post Oxygen Consumption (EPOC) is considered to have two components. State two aims of the first component and explain how this component is achieved. 4 marks

d) Describe the process of ATP production that restores the oxygen debt or EPOC. 6 marks

figure 2.9 – oxygen consumption during exercise and recovery

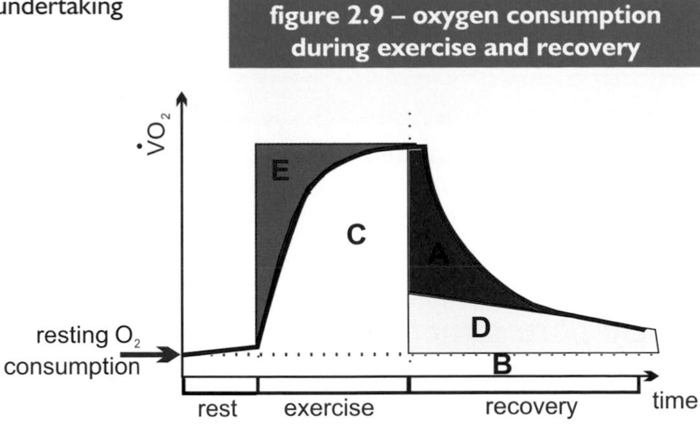

9) An elite games player performs an interval training session during which the rate of muscle phosphagen levels during the recovery period was recorded. The results from this training session are given in table 2.2.

a) Using the results in table 2.2, plot a graph of recovery time against the percentage of muscle phosphagen restored. 3 marks

b) What resting value would you recommend for a full recovery, and what would be the effect of restarting the exercise after 30 seconds? 2 marks

c) Part of the recovery mechanism after anaerobic exercise involves myoglobin. Explain the function of myoglobin during the recovery process. 3 marks

Table 2.2 – **muscle phosphagen during recovery**

recovery time / s	muscle phosphagen restored / %
10	10
30	50
60	75
90	87
120	93
150	97
180	99
210	101
240	102

10) How could information on oxygen debt recovery be of use to an athlete and coach in designing training sessions? 5 marks

11) a) Define the term $\dot{V}O_{2max}$ and describe two main factors which limit $\dot{V}O_{2max}$. 3 marks

b) Describe a field test used to estimate a person's $\dot{V}O_{2max}$. 3 marks

12) a) Figure 2.10 shows variation in $\dot{V}O_{2max}$ between three different sports. Suggest reasons for variations in $\dot{V}O_{2max}$ between these three sports. 3 marks

b) Explain the potential physiological advantages for endurance athletes having a high $\dot{V}O_{2max}$. 2 marks

figure 2.10 – $\dot{V}O_{2max}$ for different sports

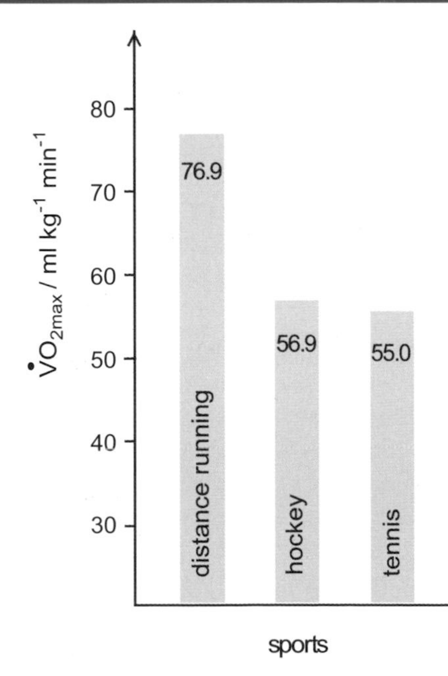

CHAPTER 3 – MUSCLES

STUDENT NOTE

An introduction to the anatomy of the human muscular system can be found on page 57 onwards of 'AS Revise PE for AQA' ISBN: 978 1 901424 56 0. This segment also explains agonists and antagonists, the types of muscular contraction, and an analysis of which muscles are used in various activities as outlined in the AS syllabus.

Muscle fibre structure

There are three types of muscle tissue in the human body.

- **Involuntary** or smooth or visceral muscle, which is found within the walls of blood vessels (the tunica media) and the alimentary canal.
- **Cardiac** muscle, which forms the walls of the heart – the myocardium.
- **Skeletal** muscle, which is the muscle type concerned with human movement and activity.

figure 3.1 – structure of skeletal muscle

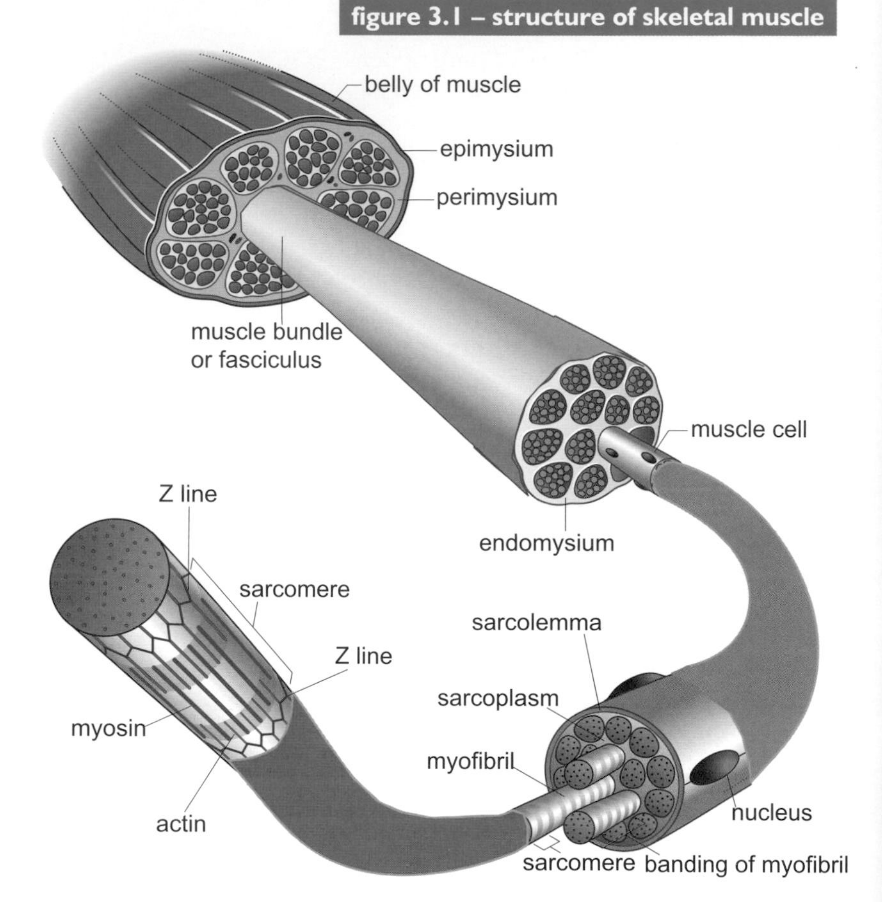

Skeletal muscle tissue

Skeletal muscle (also called striated voluntary muscle because microscopic bands or striations can be seen) attaches to bone and is responsible for the following functions:

- **Producing** movement by exerting force on its origin and insertion.
- **Maintaining** body posture and changing body shape.
- **Generating** heat to keep us warm.
- **Storage** of glycogen for energy.

Figure 3.1 shows the basic structure of a muscle from the muscle belly down to the individual sarcomere. Each myofibril consists of filaments of actin (thin filaments) and myosin (thick filaments), the forces between which enable a muscle to shorten its length and hence contract and exert forces on its origin and insertion.

Muscle contraction

- The process of muscle contraction is initiated when a **neural action potential** (electrical impulse form the brain) travels via a **motor neurone** to the **motor end-plate**, which creates a **muscle action potential** (see page 27 below) over the muscle fibre's **sarcoplasm**, and inward along the **'T' tubules**.
- This triggers the release of **Ca^{++}** ions from 'T' vesicles (located within SR - Sarcoplasmic Reticulum) into the sarcoplasm, where it binds to a **troponin** molecule on an actin filament (troponin is a globular protein with a high affinity for Ca^{++}).
- Then **tropomyosin** molecules (thread-like protein which winds around the surface of actin) on the thin **actin** filaments move, exposing actin's active sites, and energised **myosin cross-bridges** bind to actin's active sites.
- Hence their energy (released from ATP via the enzyme **myosin-ATPase**) is used to pull the thin **actin** filaments towards the centre of the sarcomere (called the power stroke), causing the H zone within the sarcomere to disappear (figure 3.2).
- This attach, detach, reattach of cross-bridges is called the **ratchet mechanism**.
- The cycle repeats itself as long as ATP is available.

Hence during a muscle contraction, the **thin actin filaments** are drawn in between the **thicker myosin filaments** (this is called **Huxley's sliding theory of muscle contraction**). The greater the overlap of filaments the stronger the contraction.

Figure 3.2 shows the basic structure of actin/myosin filaments within the sarcomere in a relaxed and contracted state.

figure 3.2 – actin/myosin structure within the sarcomere

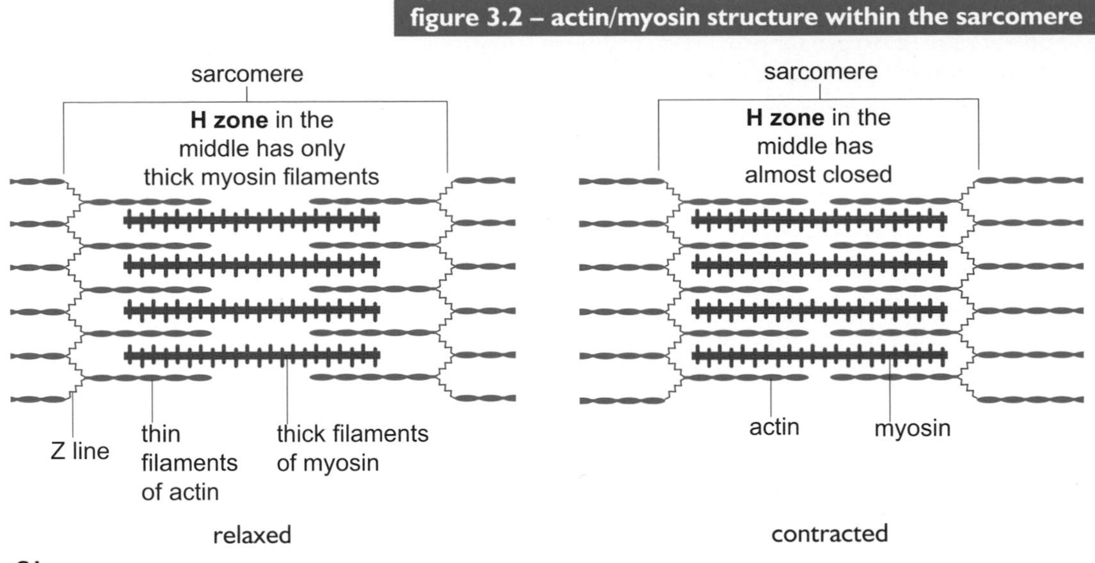

Muscle fibre types

Muscle fibres

Not all skeletal muscle fibres have identical functional capabilities. Some muscle fibres contract quickly and fatigue quickly (known as **fast twitch** muscle fibres) whereas others contract more slowly and are resistant to fatigue (known as **slow twitch or type I or Slow Oxidative** (**SO**) fibres). Fast twitch fibres are classified into 2 groups – **fast twitch type IIa or Fast oxidative-Glycolytic** (**FOG**) and **fast twitch type IIb or Fast glycolytic** (**FG**) muscle fibres.

Table 3.1 – **major structural and functional differences between slow oxidative (SO type I), fast oxidative glycolytic (FOG type IIa) and fast glycolytic (FG type IIb) muscle fibre types.**

	SO – type I	FOG – type IIa	FG – type IIb
structural differences			
colour	red	red to pink	white
fibre diameter	small	medium	large
fibres per motor unit	10-80	300-800	300-800
sarcoplasmic reticulum development	low	high	high
myoglobin content	high	high	low
capillary density	high	midway/high	low
mitochondrial density	many	midway	few
energy stores (phosphocreatine (PC)/ glycogen/ATP content)	low	high	high
functional differences			
myosin ATPase activity	low	high	high
glycolytic enzyme activity	low	high	high
oxidative enzyme activity	high	midway	low
motor unit strength	low	high	high
recruitment order	first	second	third
contractile strength	low	high	high
contractile time	long	midway	short
fatigue resistance	low	midway	high
aerobic capacity	high	moderate	low
anaerobic capacity	low	high	high
primary function	maintaining posture/ endurance-based activities	running/sprinting	high intensity or rapid activity

STUDENT NOTE

The **metabolism** of the different types of cell/fibre differs depending on the different way in which ATP is regenerated following dissociation to produce energy. The fast twitch muscle fibres tend to be anaerobic and do not require oxygen for production of energy. They have high storage of phosphocreatine but low myoglobin content. The slow twitch muscle fibres tend to be aerobic and have low phosphocreatine but high myoglobin content. The myoglobin (see page 21 above) contains an immediate source of oxygen which is transferred from blood haemoglobin, across the cell wall, to the mitochondrion for abundant energy release.

Short-term responses to exercise

Fibre type recruitment and force production

Fibre type usage (**recruitment**) is based on the intensity of exercise.

- **At low intensity, slow twitch** (ST or SO – slow oxidative) motor units are recruited first.
- **At higher intensity fast oxidative glycolytic** (FOG) type **IIa** motor units are recruited.
- **At greatest intensity fast glycolytic** (FG) type **IIb** motor units are recruited to produce powerful fast muscle contractions.

All available fibres are recruited for all high power activities as seen in the graph (see figure 3.3).

figure 3.3 – fibre type recruitment

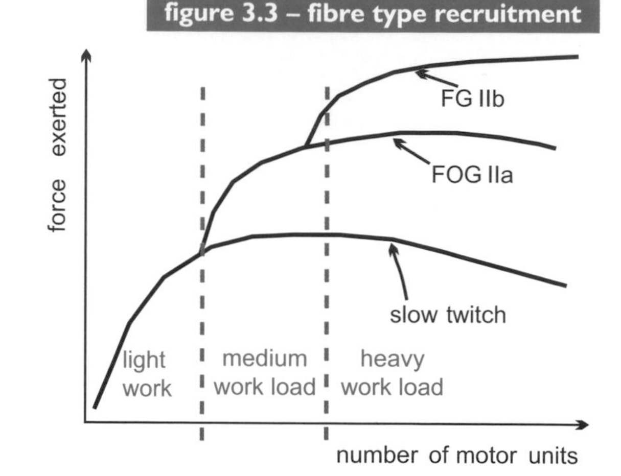

Differences within individual muscles

The proportion of muscle fibre type differs within individual muscles. Most muscles have both fibre types, however the large postural muscles contain a high proportion of slow twitch fibres because postural muscles need to produce low forces over a long period of time.

The arms tend to consist of more fast twitch muscle fibres as they need to move quickly but over shorter periods of time. The percentage type of muscle fibres found in the legs determines whether the athlete is more suited to sprinting or endurance running.

Differences in fibre type distribution between different individuals

The average fibre type distribution within **sedentary** men and women and young children is between 45% and 55% slow twitch fibres, with fast twitch equally distributed between type IIa and IIb subdivisions. However, individual variation is large.

Elite sprinters have a greater percentage of fast twitch muscle fibres, whereas elite long-distance runners have a higher percentage of slow twitch muscle fibres in their leg muscles. As might be expected, elite men and women show similar trends.

Long-term adaptations as responses to exercise and training

Endurance training results in **type IIb** muscle fibres being converted to **type IIa**, and increases the aerobic capacity of **slow twitch** muscle fibres. This explains why long steady training results in loss of speed. The efficiency of the blood supply to these muscles will improve with endurance training, enabling slow twitch muscle to function more effectively.

High intensity anaerobic training causes **increase in size** of **fast twitch** muscle fibres (**hypertrophy**), and **number** of **fast twitch** type IIb fibres (**hyperplasia**). Refer to figure 3.4.

Lack of high intensity training causes **atrophy** (loss of size and function) of fast twitch muscle. Therefore, a lot of high intensity training will make a muscle structure bigger and stronger and enabled to apply greater force than before training.

figure 3.4 – fibre type response to training

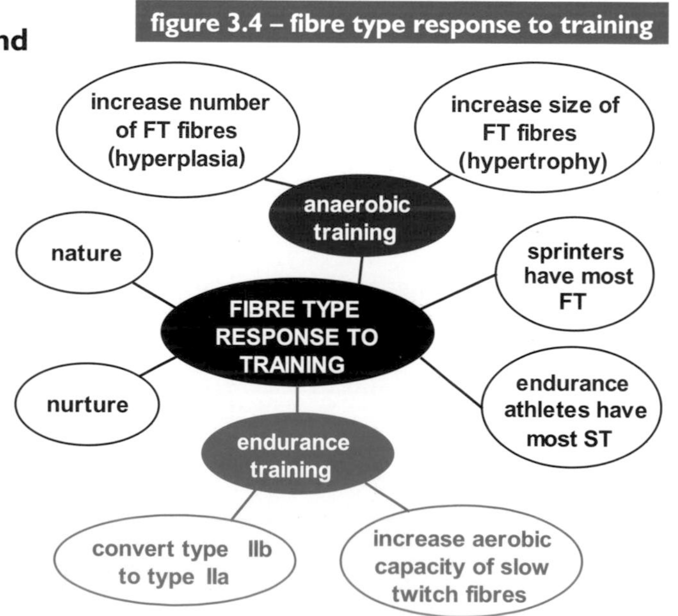

Nature or nurture?

- Proportions of fibre types are **genetically determined**, and this could account for specialisms of individuals such as whether a person becomes good at marathon running or weight lifting.
- On the other hand, research has shown that a knowledge of a person's predominant fibre type is of limited value in predicting the outcome of specific exercise performances.
- This finding is not surprising because performance capacity is the end result of the blending of many physiological, biochemical, neurological and biomechanical 'support systems' – and is not simply determined by a single factor, such as muscle fibre type.
- Men have a greater tendency to be more muscular than women, due to the release of greater amounts of the hormone **testosterone** during adolescence and adulthood. But women can grow muscle in a similar way to men when exposed to high intensity training.

Neuro-muscular structures

Short-term responses of the neuro-muscular system to exercise

Skeletal muscle is caused to contract by **nerve impulses** sent from the **cerebellum** in the brain. These electrical impulses (an electrical nerve impulse is called an action potential) are sent down a specialised nerve called a **motor neurone**.

Further specialised nerves called sensory fibres relay information back to the cerebellum where information about the tension within the muscle and its rate of contraction is received.

The muscle motor unit

A motor neurone will terminate at several synapses (motor end-plates) each linked to a number of muscle fibres. The block of muscle fibres and the nervous system which controls their contraction and relaxation is called a **motor unit**. A motor unit is therefore defined as '**a single block of muscle fibres and its neurone**'. Therefore when a motor neurone is stimulated, all fibres connected to that neurone are activated at once (the '**all-or-none law**'). A single neurone will control muscle fibres of the **same type**, either fast twitch **or** slow twitch. Figure 3.5 shows a simplified diagram of a motor unit.

Each different muscle fibre type (slow twitch or fast twitch) is innervated by a separate and different type of motor neurone. For example, **fast twitch** motor units have **larger diameter neurones**, giving increased conduction of the neural impulse, hence greater speed of contraction.

figure 3.5 – a motor unit

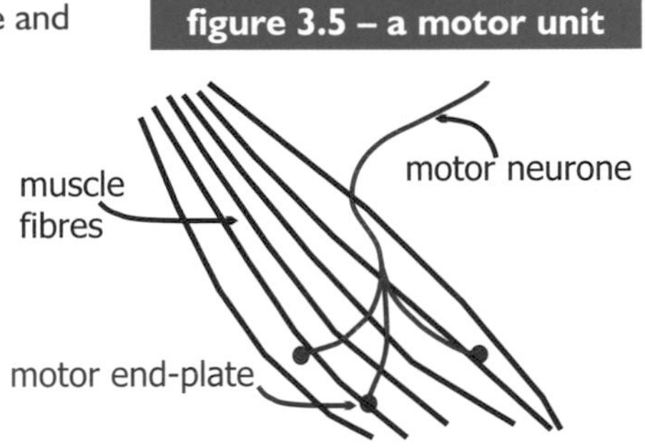

The motor end-plate

The function of the motor end-plate is to transfer an impulse from the motor neurone (see figure 3.5) to the muscle fibre block. This is achieved by the temporary release of neuro-transmitter substances, which enable the electrical nerve impulse to be applied to adjacent muscle fibres (cells). This causes all muscle fibres attached to this end-plate to contract.

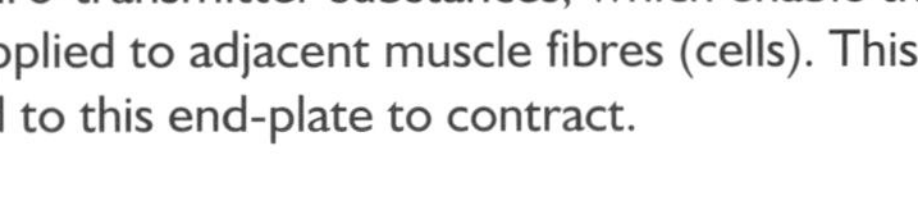

Motor neural firing patterns

In order to control muscle contraction, the cerebellum innervates one or more motor units. Each motor unit controls a number of muscle fibres, so that either **all** the fibres attached to the motor unit are activated at the same time, or **none** of these fibres are activated. This is called the '**all-or-none law**'. Different fibre groups (attached to different motor units) are fired at different times. Each firing produces a fibre '**twitch**'.

The force produced by a single fibre twitch follows the left hand graph in figure 3.6. Note that each twitch only lasts a short length of time, so that in order to prolong the force exerted by a twitch, the fibre group must be fired repeatedly. The build up of force in a single fibre is represented in the right hand graph in figure 3.6. When a fibre is fired repeatedly in this manner, the way in which the force builds up is called '**wave summation**'.

figure 3.6 – force produced by a single fibre twitch

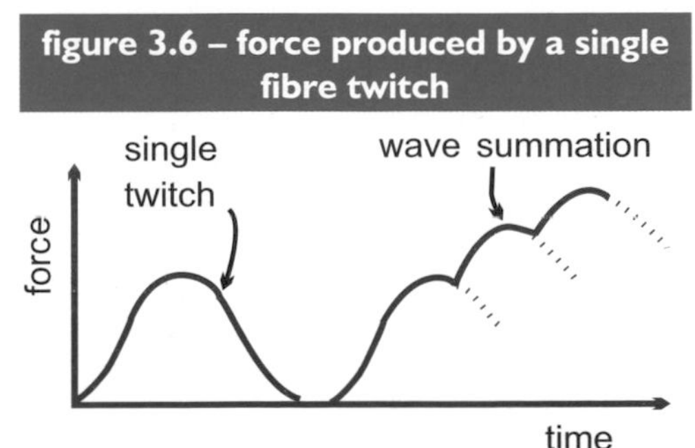

Multiple fibre twitches

In order to activate fibres across a whole muscle body to produce force in a controlled manner, different fibre groups are fired in succession. The total force across the space of a muscle is the sum of the effect of different fibre groups, and is shown in figure 3.7. This is called '**spatial summation**'.

figure 3.7 – force produced across a muscle by multiple fibre twitches

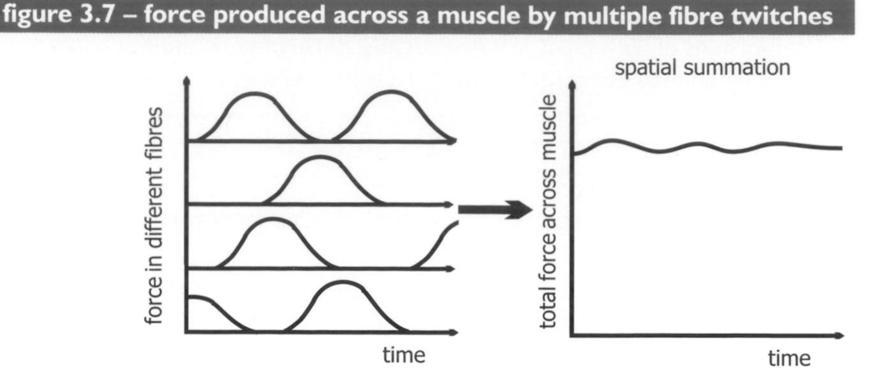

In order to control very fine movements, it is necessary to be able to vary the total force produced by fibre twitches. **Gradation of contraction** refers to the ability of muscle to produce forces varying from very light to maximum force or tension.

Gradation of contraction

This can be achieved in two ways:

- Increasing the frequency of stimulus (wave summation).
- Varying the number of motor units recruited.

For example in hockey, there would be fine control of movement required for a flick, as opposed to the maximum effort required for a full hit.

If there were no time for relaxation between motor unit firing, eventually (after a few seconds) there would be a complete lock up of muscle. This is called '**tetanine contraction**' and happens when a muscle is used at maximum for too long.

The cerebellum

The balance of fine and gross control is under the control of the **cerebellum**. In order to produce smooth co-ordinated movement, the cerebellum compares the intended movement with the actual movement (from sensors within the moving structure – the proprioceptors). If a difference is detected, the cerebellum sends impulses to the appropriate motor units in the spinal cord which would produce a correction. In sport, the cerebellum is involved in the learning of **fine motor skills** (as in archery) or **gross motor skills** (as in weight lifting).

Gross movements use leg and arm muscles having about 1000 muscle fibres associated with one motor unit, whereas fine movements (of the eyes and fingers for example) require muscles with far fewer (10-100) muscle fibres controlled by a single motor unit.

Control is achieved by increasing or decreasing the number of motor units in operation. Different motor units are activated in turn across a muscle and this gradation of contraction across a muscle enables very small forces to be maintained if required. The self-regulation of rhythmic movements between one muscle and its antagonist relies on control of movement which requires relaxation of antagonists during the dynamic activity of an agonist. This process is called '**reciprocal innervation**'.

figure 3.8 – muscle hypertrophy in a body builder

Adaptations to muscle cells produced by exercise – the long-term responses

Tables 3.2 and 3.3 display the adaptations to skeletal muscle cells produced by different types of exercise.

STUDENT NOTE

The increase in muscle mass caused by hypertrophy (see figure 3.8) will increase the proportion of muscle to body fat and help reduce obesity. Increased storage of ATP and phosphocreatine (PC) will increase the strength or efficiency of each fast twitch muscle fibre.

Table 3.2 – **adaptations produced by anaerobic exercise**

adaptations to muscle cells produced by anaerobic exercise
fast twitch muscle **hypertrophy** - increase in size by increased cross sectional area of a muscle
increase in the number of **myofibrils** within each muscle cell
increase in the **sarcoplasmic** volume within each cell
increase in the size and strength of the contractile proteins, **actin and myosin**, leading to increase in the mass of fast twitch fibres
increase in the number of fast twitch muscle fibres (**hyperplasia**), which means that the proportion of type II muscle fibre increases and the proportion of type I decreases
increase in muscle **cell stores** of substances such as ATP, PC, and glycogen, and increase in anaerobic enzymes such as creatine kinase (CK), PFK, GPP, and LDH, which makes the muscle stronger and more powerful
improved toleration of **lactate** in fast twitch fibres, and improved ability to remove lactate from muscle cell into blood - which enhances lactate thresholds and **reduces OBLA**
increased rate of response of **CNS** (Central Nervous System), **recruitment** of additional **fast twitch** fibre motor units, improved co-ordination of fast twitch fibre motor units
toughening of **proprioceptors** so that more force is required to stimulate inhibitory signals, an improved agonist/antagonist response
reduction of **delayed onset muscle soreness** (**DOMS**)

Table 3.3 – **adaptations produced by aerobic exercise**

adaptations to muscle cells produced by aerobic training
body fat proportion is reduced by between 4% and 12%
more **myoglobin** is created in muscle cells
more and bigger **mitochondria** are created in muscle cells
muscle cells have increased **oxidative enzymes** which increases aerobic cell activity
increase in utilisation of **fat** in adipose tissue as an energy source
increase in stores of **glycogen** in muscle which enables more fuel to be available for aerobic work
conversion of type IIb to type IIa fibres, so increasing the proportion of aerobically active muscle cells
better **recruitment** of **slow twitch** fibre motor units making muscle usage more efficient
reduction of **delayed onset muscle soreness** (**DOMS**)

Improved lactate handling enhances alactic/lactate and lactate/aerobic thresholds, and causes a delay in the onset of blood lactate accumulation (**OBLA**). These processes enable an improved capacity of alactic (ATP-PC) and lactic acid systems to resynthesise ATP, and hence to deliver energy more rapidly. Also there would be increases in maximum possible peak power, and the ability to maintain maximal power output for longer. There would be a decrease in delayed onset muscle soreness (**DOMS**), particularly following eccentric training.

The adaptations in which more muscle fibres are recruited within an activity will better utilise fast twitch muscle fibres at their existing level before hypertrophy occurs. Initial measured strength gains are almost exclusively via this process.

figure 3.9 – a female bodybuilder with muscle hypertrophy

STUDENT NOTE

The adaptive response depends on an individual's fitness, cultural norms, gender, psychological preparedness and state of maturation. Given that anaerobic training will have the above effects, the outcomes will vary between individuals. Particularly, female athletes will acquire muscle hypertrophy if exposed to high intensity anaerobic exercise (figure 3.9).

figure 3.10 – fibre type recruitment

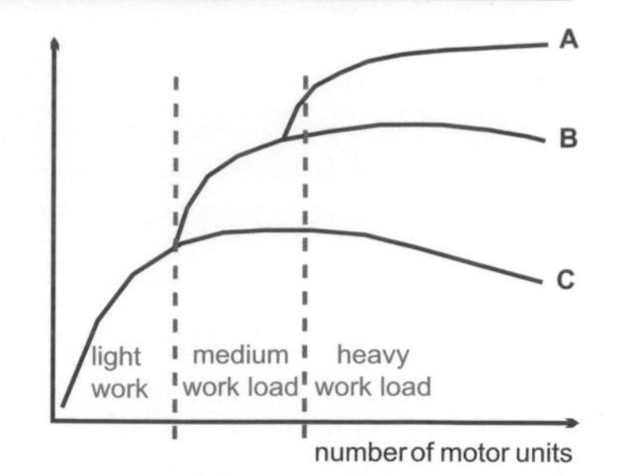

Practice questions

1) a) Skeletal muscle tissue consists of different fibre types. These types are suited to particular intensities of work. Figure 3.10 shows muscle fibre usage for three different work rates. Identify muscle fibre types A, B and C. 3 marks

b) Using the information in figure 3.10 describe the order in which fibre types are recruited as the number of motor units increase. 3 marks

c) How would the motor unit recruitment pattern differ between a weightlifter and an endurance runner? 4 marks

2) Figure 3.11 has been created from a slide of skeletal tissue as seen with a light microscope at a magnification of 800 times. It shows part of two motor units.

a) Use evidence from the drawing to suggest a meaning of the term motor unit. 2 marks

b) Why is it that all the muscle fibres shown will not necessarily contract at the same time? 3 marks

figure 3.11 – muscle motor units

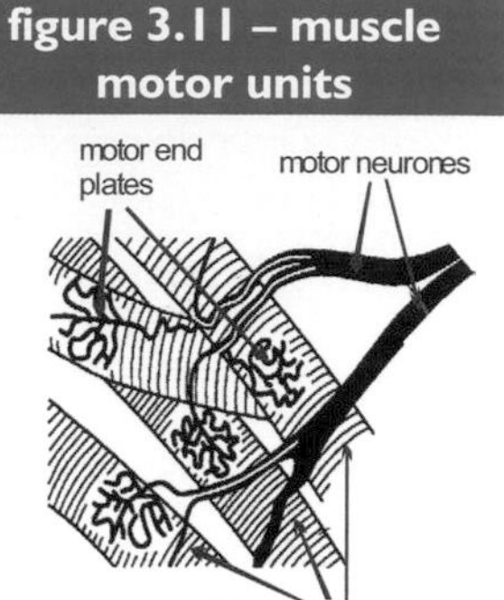

3) A muscle can vary the strength of its contractile response through wave summation. Explain the role of motor units in controlling this response. 4 marks

4) The strength of a muscle contraction involves the use of motor units. How are the motor units used to produce muscle contractions of varying strength in a weight lifting exercise? 3 marks

5) Figure 3.12 shows the thick and thin filaments of a relaxed sarcomere within a skeletal muscle fibre. Draw and label the sarcomere in a state of contraction. Explain how the change from the relaxed to the contracted state is thought to occur. In your answer describe the roles of the nervous system, myosin-ATPase, troponin and tropomyosin molecules. 14 marks

6) Skeletal muscle contains both slow and fast twitch muscle fibres but the proportion of each depends upon the function of a muscle as a whole. Table 3.4 lists some of the differences between slow and fast twitch muscle fibres.

Table 3.4 – **muscle fibre type characteristics**

characteristic	slow twitch type	fast twitch type
contractile time / ms	110	40
mitochondrial density	high	low
glycogen store	low	high
phosphocreatine stores	low	high
capillary density	high	low
sarcoplasmic reticulum	poorly developed	well developed
oxidative enzyme activity	high	low

figure 3.12 – relaxed muscle sarcomere

a) Suggest why the muscles concerned in maintaining the trunk posture of the body of the sprinter might be expected to have a larger percentage of slow twitch muscle fibres. Using table 3.4 explain why fast twitch muscle fibres may build up an oxygen debt during a 400m sprint. 5 marks

b) Account for the difference in the speed of contraction between slow and fast twitch muscle fibre types. Fast twitch muscle fibres are divided into two types, IIa and IIb. Identify the major functional characteristic between these sub groups. In what sporting activities would the adaptation of fast twitch type IIb to type IIa fibres be relevant to a sportsperson? 6 marks

7) Table 3.5 shows the percentage of slow twitch muscle fibres in two muscle groups of elite male (M) and female (F) athletes. The percentage of fast twitch muscle fibre is calculated as the difference between 100% and the percentage of slow twitch fibres.

Table 3.5 – **percentage of slow twitch muscle fibres**

athletic group	shoulder (deltoid)	calf (gastrocnemius)
long distance runners		79% (M) 69% (F)
triathletes	60% (M)	59% (M)
sprinters		24% (M) 27% (F)
shot putters		38% (M)

a) Compare and account for the differences in percentage distribution of slow twitch muscle fibres with respect to long distance runners and sprinters. 3 marks

b) Calculate the percentage of fast twitch muscle fibres for the long distance runners and sprinters. 2 marks

c) Data collected for male triathletes shows a fairly even distribution of slow twitch muscle fibres across both muscle groups. Discuss three possible reasons for this trend. 3 marks

d) For shot putters only the calf muscle is given a value in table 3.5. What percentage distribution of slow twitch muscle fibres would you expect in the deltoid muscle for shot putters. Give a reason to support your answer. 2 marks

8) Identify the physiological adaptations that occur in muscle cells as a result of anaerobic training. 3 marks

9) Describe three changes that occur in muscle cells as a result of endurance training. *3 marks*

CHAPTER 4 – TRAINING

STUDENT NOTE

An introduction to the principles and types of training can be found on page 72 onwards of 'AS Revise PE for AQA' ISBN: 978 1 901424 56 0. This segment also explains fitness, fitness testing, and methods of training as outlined in the AS syllabus.

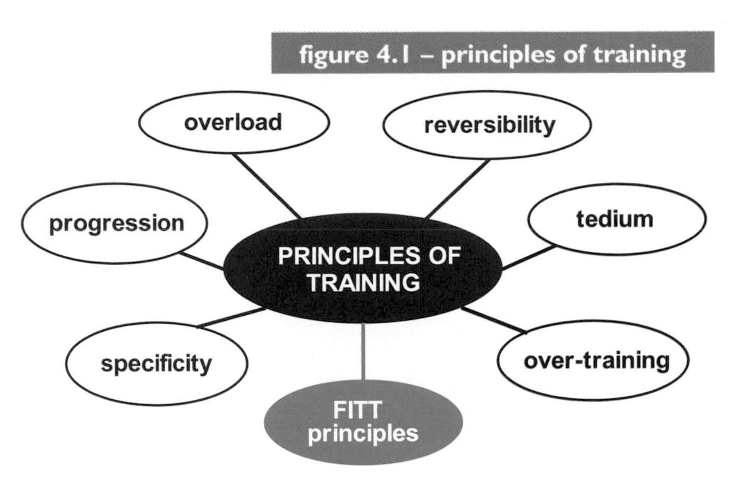

figure 4.1 – principles of training

The principles of training are summarised in figure 4.1. These principles should underline the planning and implementation of a training programme for elite athletes.

Sports supplements as ergogenic aids

An **ergogenic aid** is any substance or method which enhances performance. This includes any method used in training which has this effect including training equipment and nutrition as well as doping and supplementation.

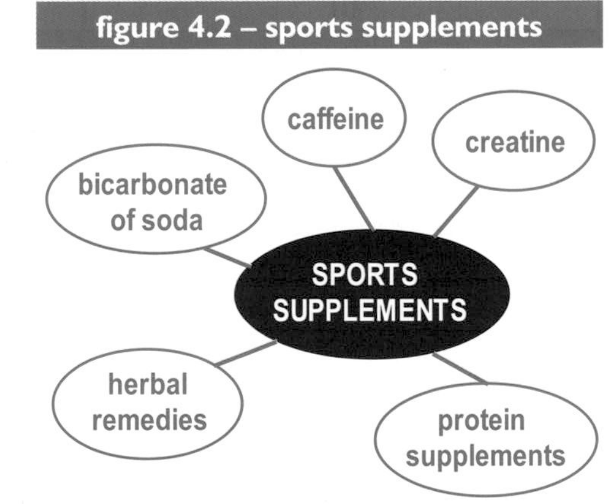

figure 4.2 – sports supplements

Ergogenic aids fall into two main categories, legal and illegal. Figure 4.2 summarises legal sports supplements identified in your syllabus.

Examples of legal physiological supplements, aids or methods

Creatine supplementation

Creatine is a substance found in skeletal muscle and which is stored as **phosphocreatine** (PC). Creatine supplementation (usually together with large amounts of CHO) increases PC levels to enhance the ATP-PC system of ATP resynthesis, thereby delaying the alactic/lactic threshold (see page 13 and 16 above). This is a **legal ergogenic aid**.

Sportspeople use creatine in a way which will help improve anaerobic power and lengthen the time over which they can apply maximal power. It is not a muscle development 'drug', and eating lots of raw white meat (as in fish) would have the same effect. This is because white muscle cells (those not containing lots of myoglobin, which is red in colour and is present in large quantities in slow twitch muscle cells) are predominantly fast twitch in nature and contain creatine in relatively large quantities.

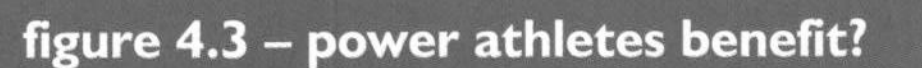
figure 4.3 – power athletes benefit?

Power athletes, such as the pole vaulter in figure 4.3, use in their competitive event a little bit of the ATP-PC system and mostly ATP storage. But almost all the training will be serviced by the ATP-PC system, and therefore creatine supplementation will help the training process.

Creatine supplementation can cause muscle cramps and can be responsible for athlete weight gain.

Protein supplementation

Many athletes regularly consume sports drinks that are designed to supplement the energy, fluid and protein needs of the athlete.
Protein supplements, such as whey protein, are used to increase total protein content of an athletic diet. Sportspeople need more protein than the untrained person to enable muscle hypertrophy and muscle repair following hard training. This particularly applies to sports requiring large muscle mass, as in weight lifting and gymnastics.

Protein supplementation

Within the section on the Athlete's diet on page 35 below, a protein shake is recommended as an important protein supplement for a female 800m athlete, particularly following a high intensity training session.

- A controversial area of research is whether there is need for protein supplementation. This is particularly if the athlete is already consuming a balanced diet that meets all their nutritional requirements. If this is the case protein supplementation becomes a very expensive form of energy food.
- Most protein supplements are legal, but can cause liver and kidney damage if taken in excess.
- **Glutamine** is an **amino acid** forming part of **skeletal muscle** and **immune cells**. Supplementation after exercise therefore reinforces the immune system and **reduces the risk of infection** and therefore enhances the process of glycogen synthesis in recovering muscles. Glutamine supplementation is widely used by athletes.

Herbal remedies

Herbal remedies are derived from plant extracts and are part of the practice of homeopathy and are in the form of tablets, oils or creams and liquids. Intake of a broad range of herbal supplements for ergogenic purposes has expanded considerably over the past decade. Examples include:

- **Ginseng**, which is reported to increase mental alertness, boosts energy levels and the immune system. The controversial use of ginseng was popularised by Chinese women endurance athletes in the 1990s. Little evidence exists to support the effectiveness of ginseng as an ergogenic aid.
- **Glucosamine** is known to reduce joint inflammation and stiffness.
- **Arnica** is used to reduce inflammation, bruising and pain.
- **Camomile** is known to reduce stress, support the immune system, promote tissue repair and assist sleeping.

Many herbal remedies for common conditions such as colds, flu and bronchitis are used to avoid restrictions imposed by doping regulations. This is because there are substances commonly used in the pharmaceutical versions of such remedies, such as codeine or ephedrine, which are against doping regulations.
However, care needs to be taken when using herbal remedies since some herbal remedies contain substances on the doping register.

Bicarbonate use

Bicarbonate loading is a process whereby a performer ingests bicarbonate prior to a competition. An athlete can increase plasma bicarbonate levels that provide additional **buffering capacity**, thus allowing higher concentrations of lactate in the blood. Theoretically, this could delay the onset of fatigue in all-out anaerobic activity such as a 400 metre race. Bicarbonate loading can cause cramping, vomiting, bloating and diarrhoea.

Caffeine

- Caffeine **stimulates** the central nervous system thereby reducing reaction times.
- Caffeine acts as a **diuretic**, which can lead to dehydration and heat related conditions.
- Caffeine used to be illegal in large quantities, but the rules changed in 2002, when drinking large amounts of coffee became **legal** again!
- Caffeine is also used as a substance to promote **fat metabolism** and hence to reduce adipose tissue in the elite sportsperson.
- Consuming caffeine before prolonged exercise increases fat metabolism thus sparing precious glycogen reserves for later.
- Caffeine produces a state of **nervousness**, and can disrupt normal sleeping patterns therefore contributing to fatigue.
- Abrupt ceasing of caffeine intake can lead to severe headaches.

Water and electrolyte balance

Fluid intake has almost become an obsession with modern sportsmen and women. Modern athletes frequently use isotonic sports drinks, such as Isostar and Red Bull, just prior to competition to maintain rehydration and alertness respectively.

Exercise is thirsty work. Fluid loss during exercise depends on the intensity and duration of the exercise, temperature and humidity, body size and fitness levels. The **longer** and more **intense** the exercise period, for example in a long distance race, the more the need to drink before, during and after the event.

Bearing in mind that water comprises 60% of total body mass, it is important that **water balance** is maintained during exercise. **Water balance** depends on electrolyte balance and vice versa. For optimal performance, the body's water and electrolyte contents should remain relatively constant.

At rest, water loss occurs mainly via the **kidneys** (as urine) along with **excess electrolytes** - sodium and chloride.

Hydration

Water intake will depend on climate and body mass. The modern fashion of carrying water bottles for ready consumption reflects modern concerns about water balance.

During exercise urine production declines as electrolyte loss occurs primarily alongside water loss through sweating.
The need to replace body fluid is greater than the need to replace electrolytes, because sweat is very dilute (electrolyte concentration in sweat is much lower than in urine).

- Also, the loss of water raises the osmotic pressure in body fluids because the electrolytes become more concentrated in these body fluids.
- The thirst mechanism does not exactly match the body's hydration state, so more fluid should be consumed than thirst dictates.
- Only by replenishing water content can the electrolytes return to normal concentrations.

figure 4.4 – Paula Radcliffe will be taking in water throughout a marathon

In extreme exercise situations (for example during a marathon figure 4.4), 6-10% of body water content is lost, hence the need for water intake during exercise. This means that during 1 hour's exercise an average person could expect to lose around 1 litre of fluid, and even more in hot conditions. This could represent as much as 2 litres an hour in warm or humid conditions.

Dehydration and loss of performance

Excessive loss of fluid impairs performance as blood plasma volume decreases and body temperature rises. The graph in figure 4.5 shows how heart rate is affected by **fluid intake** during prolonged exercise. Heart rate rise without fluid intake is explained earlier, but the graph also shows how heart rate is kept constant - if suitable water is taken during the exercise.

figure 4.5 – fluid intake during exercise

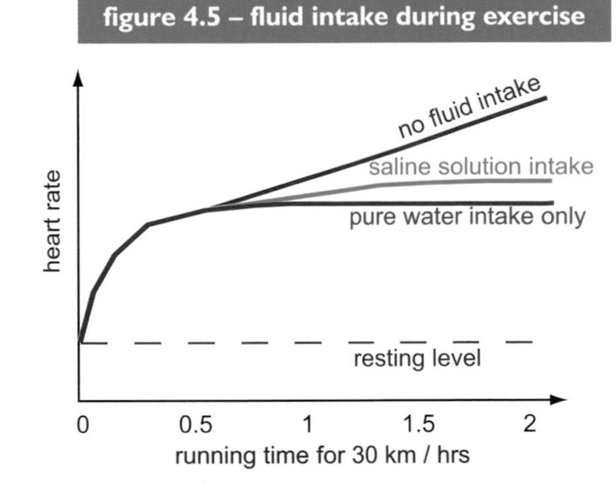

Look at page 44 below for some more details of how fluid intake affects the way in which the body controls its temperature before, during and after strenuous and prolonged exercise.

STUDENT NOTE

A balanced diet is discussed in the segment on page 21 of AS Revise PE for AQA, ISBN: 978 1 901424 56 0.

The athlete's diet

The primary dietary requirements for an athlete is to consume a **well-balanced**, nutritionally complete diet to meet the demands of the individual's training and competition programmes. This tailor-made diet will include the additional nutrient and fluid demands that will enable an athlete to train hard, recover between training sessions, and maintain an ideal body weight.

How much energy an athlete needs, and so how much an athlete needs to eat and drink, depends on the sum of the athlete's **basal metabolic rate** (BMR) and the energy required for physical activities. BMR represents the rate of energy that is used by basic bodily functions such as in resting and sleeping. These energy requirements will be primarily determined by training load (intensity, frequency and duration).

Examples of daily energy intake are illustrated in table 4.1 below.

Dietary requirements for exercise

Table 4.1 – **a comparison of daily energy intake for athletes**

activity	daily energy intake kJ – females	daily energy intake kJ – males
Tour de France		25000
triathlon		20000
rowing	12600	14700
swimming	8400	15500
hockey	9200	13400
soccer		14700
running	9200	13000
gymnastics	6000	
body building	5900	14500

STUDENT NOTE

Table 4.1 shows the variation in energy expended during competition and training (measured in kJ per day) in elite male and female endurance (figure 4.6), strength and team sport athletes. Except for high-energy intake of athletes at extremes of performance and training, the daily energy intake does not exceed 17000 kJ for men and 12500 kJ for women. Note that the difference between males and females can be accounted for by size difference. Values for energy intake per kg of body mass would be similar for most sports for either gender.

figure 4.6 – endurance cyclists consume huge amounts of energy

Within rather broad bands, a balanced diet from a regular food intake provides the nutrient requirements for active individuals. However, dietary requirements depend on the **intensity** and **duration** of the exercise period. This means developing a diet that is tailor-made to suit the needs of the individual, and many athletes find they need to supplement their meals with regular snacks between meals.

Case study of an elite athlete

So how does an elite athlete assess whether their diet meets the demands of their training and competition programmes? A qualified nutritionist normally undertakes a nutritional assessment of the athlete's current diet:

- The athlete will undertake a detailed dietary log containing all food eaten (including food portions) during a selected period of time.
- He or she will answer a questionnaire about food habits and training issues, such as symptoms of fatigue that may be due to poor nutrition.
- Analysis of training and competition demands.
- Body mass assessment to work out BMR.
- Body composition to assess ideal body weight (many female endurance athletes suffer from anorexia nervosa).

Additional assessments may include:

- Blood samples to test for iron deficiency anaemia. Female athletes are particularly vulnerable to low haematocrit levels.
- DEXA scan (DEXA stands for 'dual energy x-ray absorptiometry') to measure bone density. In general, the more dense the bone, the stronger it is, and the less likely it is to break. Dietary calcium is needed to maintain bone density levels.

Once a dietary assessment has been completed, a tailor-made diet can be created that meets the specific energy and dietary requirements of the athlete.

Summary of the nutritional recommendations for an elite female 800m athlete

Body fat and weight are fine – any slight increase in body weight must be muscle gain and not fat (her body fat was measured at 9%).

The food choices in table 4.2 below aim to keep body fat low. Low GI (glycaemic index, see page 23 of AS Revise PE for AQA, ISBN: 978 1 901424 56 0) carbohydrate intake should be considered, and a focus on protein-type foods supplemented by fresh vegetables and fruit. Notice also that snacks between the 3 main meals aim to top up the ever-depleting energy reserves and so aid recovery following training sessions.

Table 4.2 – **dietary suggestions for elite endurance runner**

	dietary suggestions for elite endurance runner
1	**breakfast** – include some protein (yoghurt/eggs) and carbohydrate (cereal/porridge and wholegrain toast)
2	**mid morning snack** – banana and water/cordial are fine
3	**lunch** is not enough - need cooked meal such as pasta or rice or potato dish with some form of meat/fish/salad + yoghurt and fresh fruit, in place of sandwiches
4	**afternoon snack** – suggest a protein shake
5	immediately after training go for a Yazzoo or Smoothie or protein shake
6	cooked **evening meal** with meat/fresh vegetables/yoghurt/fresh fruit/water
7	**light night-time snack** such as Carb Sense bar or porridge/muesli/water
8	more fluid should be consumed than thirst dictates
9	increase CHO intake 36 hours prior to competition date
10	need daily **supplements**: glucosamine and chondroitin for joints, 1 x multivitamin a day, 1 x 100mg of omega-3 fatty acid a day

Vegetarian athletes should give careful consideration to selecting plant foods that provide a good balance of the essential amino acids (such as beans, lentils, quorn and tofu), sufficient calories and adequate sources of vitamin A, riboflavin, vitamin B12 (dairy products), vitamin D, calcium, zinc and iron (dark green leafy vegetables).

When and what should you eat before an exercise period?

Pre-competition nutrition should consist of:

- Fluids for hydration.
- Light complex CHO such as pasta or wholemeal bread at least 3 hours before activity.
- Fruit (banana) containing complex CHO.
- Small amounts of glucose.

The effect is to provide the slow release of blood glucose and reduce hunger sensations.

figure 4.7 – the athlete's diet

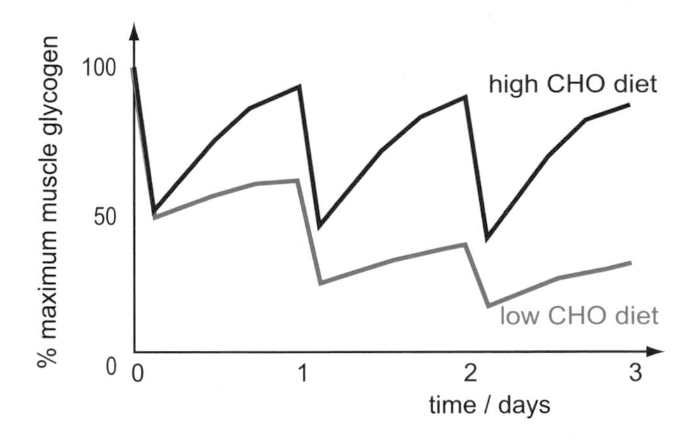

Post-competition or training nutrition

Should consist of:

- **Hypertonic** sports drink immediately after exercise has finished.
- This begins **replenishment of blood glucose** and **glycogen** stores.
- A **high CHO** meal within 15 minutes of exercise ending (or as soon as possible) continues glycogen replenishment.

Nutritional dietary manipulation during training

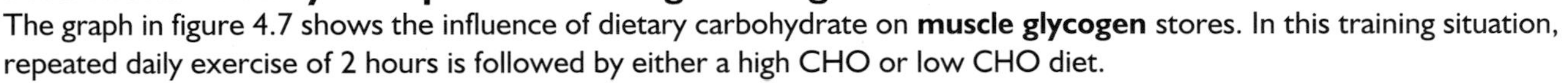

The graph in figure 4.7 shows the influence of dietary carbohydrate on **muscle glycogen** stores. In this training situation, repeated daily exercise of 2 hours is followed by either a high CHO or low CHO diet.

STUDENT NOTE

Refer to page 25 of AS Revise PE for AQA, ISBN: 978 1 901424 56 0, for notes on 'clinical methods used to assess levels of obesity'. You will need to cover BMI and measurement of body fat percentages as part of this A2 course.

Achieving optimal weight for activities

The following table 4.3 shows how the body fat content for people of various age groups depends on whether they are fit or not. The data takes us up to 40 years of age.

Table 4.3 – **example data of relative body fat values for untrained and trained males and females**

	relative body fat (%)			
	untrained		trained	
age group	**females**	**males**	**females**	**males**
15-19	20-24	13-16	12-20	7-13
20-29	22-25	15-20	10-18	6-12
30-39	24-30	18-26	12-20	8-14

STUDENT NOTE

The **average body fat** for **untrained females** is about 8% higher than untrained males. However, **trained females** are exceptionally lean and their relative body fat values are **well below** those values for untrained males. Therefore **females** can **reduce fat stores** well below what is considered normal for their age.

Untrained males and females have increased body fat when they get older, whereas trained people (both sexes) remain lean.

The achievement of optimal body weight will require manipulation of the **energy balance**. When energy input and output are balanced (**energy input = energy output**), an athlete's body mass will be stable, with no tendency to add to or subtract from stored adipose tissue.

Controlling excess body mass

The only method of controlling excess bodyweight is to shift the energy relationship so that energy output exceeds energy intake, known as a negative energy balance and expressed as **energy output > energy intake**.

Sports in which control of bodyweight is important include:

- Martial arts.
- Boxing,
- Weight lifting.
- Rowing.
- Any sport in which bodyweight categories determine the competitive regime.

Cause of excess bodyweight

The main cause of excess bodyweight is a positive energy balance, expressed as: **energy intake > energy output**, or more food than exercise.

Excess carbohydrate (CHO) is stored as glycogen. When glycogen stores are filled, CHO together with excess fat intake, is converted to fatty acids and glycerol, and then is stored as triglycerides or fat in adipose tissue, situated around major organs such as the heart and stomach, underneath the skin, and in skeletal muscle.

What is a good level of fat?

A minimum requirement which would allow full body functions, are a body fat percentage for men of between 2% and 3% and for women between 8% and 12%. Normally only healthy elite athletes attain these percentages (or more as in table 4.3).

Relative body fat is a major concern of sportspeople, and achieving a desired weight goal can lead to clinical eating disorders such as anorexia nervosa. This is caused by a person restricting food intake to levels well below energy expenditure.

It is important to have a diet that maintains appropriate weight and body composition to maximise physical performance.

Drugs as ergogenic aids and supplements

Figure 4.8 summarises the categories of illegal ergogenic aids used by sportspeople.

figure 4.8 – illegal ergogenic aids

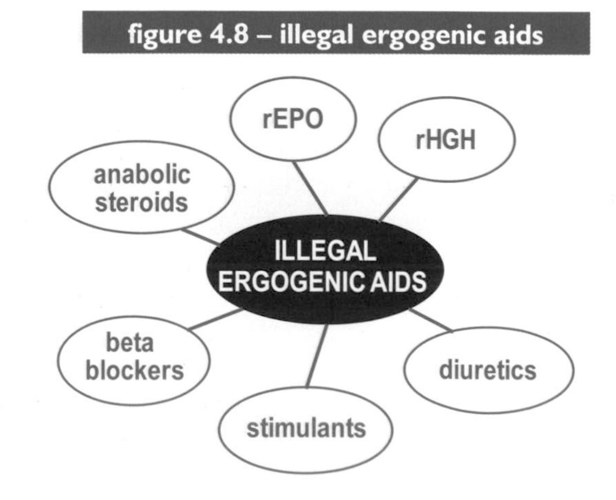

Table 4.4 outlines the details of the different doping substances used in sport.

Table 4.4 – **the categories of substances used in top level sport today**

type of substance	known ergogenic effects	known health risks
stimulants example: amphetamines	increase alertness, reduce fatigue, increase competitiveness and hostility	can drive competitor beyond safe boundaries can cause lasting tissue and organ damage as well as masking injury are addictive, known to cause death
rHGH recombinant human growth hormone cloned through genetic engineering	mimics body's naturally occurring hormone HGH produced by the pituitary gland which increases protein synthesis and lean muscle mass stimulates bone growth increases blood glucose levels enhances healing after musculo-skeletal injuries used by power athletes such as sprinters, weight lifters, American football players	muscle joint weaknesses acromegaly (giantism) causes bone thickening of hands, feet and jaws enlargement of internal organs causes glucose intolerance, diabetes, hypertension and heart disease
anabolic steroids related to naturally occurring hormone testosterone example: THG tetrahydrogestrinone stanazolol	increases synthesis of protein within cells increases fat free mass, strength and power for aggressive sports such as American football or wrestling reduces recovery time between sessions increases muscle strength and bulk, promotes aggressiveness	excessive aggressive behaviour outside the activity testicular atrophy in men masculinisation in women liver damage cardiovascular diseases causes acne causes pituitary failure
diuretics example: bumetanide	reduce weight quickly used by gymnast and combat sports where there are bodyweight categories reduce concentration of substances by diluting urine (hence increasing urine flow), also used as a masking agent to dilute concentration of illegal substances in urine	loss of water leads to dehydration and heat loss impairment loss of water-soluble vitamins leads to impaired performances
rEPO recombinant erythropoietin cloned through genetic engineering	mimics body's naturally occurring hormone EPO that stimulates red blood cell production to increase oxygen transport and therefore increase aerobic capacity, performance, and aids recovery in endurance based activities such as long distance cycling (Tour-de-France) and marathon running	major risk of thrombosis (blood clot) and heart failure due to increase in blood viscosity reduces resting heart rate to dangerously low level during sleep reduces production of naturally occurring hormone EPO
beta-blockers a class of hormonal drugs	blocks transmission of neural impulse from sensory nervous system to reduce heart rate and blood pressure this has a calming effect by steadying nerves and reducing tension used in target sports such as archery, golf, snooker	dangerously low heart rate could lead to heart failure

New drugs

New sophisticated drugs are being developed and used by unscrupulous scientists, athletes, agents, coaches and managers. The drug testers are desperately trying to develop ways of detecting these substances as soon as it becomes apparent that they are being taken.
The latest and most insidious attempt by the cheaters is to use **gene doping** to enhance performance. Gene doping is defined by the World Anti-Doping Agency (WADA) as '**the non-therapeutic use of cells, genes, genetic elements, or of the modulation of gene expression, having the capacity to improve athletic performance**'.

Example: Insulin-like growth factor 1 (IGF-1) is a protein that is important in promoting the growth of skeletal muscle. Injected into an athlete, a harmless virus, such as IGF-1, could carry a performance-enhancing gene and splice it into a muscle cell to increase muscle mass and achieve increased muscle hypertrophy.

Protein chemicals may be indistinguishable from their natural counterparts. In such cases, nothing unusual would enter the bloodstream so officials would detect nothing in a blood or urine test.

Practice questions

1) What is an ergogenic aid? Briefly provide a summary of the role that nutritional supplements play in improving performance. 8 marks

2) Give a brief outline and comment upon the following techniques, which may be employed in the belief that they will enhance sport performance.
   a) The use of recombinant human growth hormone (rHGH). 4 marks
   b) The use of creatine supplements. 4 marks
   c) Ingestion of drinks containing caffeine. 4 marks
   d) Highlight two potential health risks known to be associated with the use of each of these techniques. 6 marks

3) rEPO is an illegal drug taken by endurance athletes such as marathon runners and long distance cyclists.
   a) What is EPO? 2 marks
   b) How does rEPO benefit an endurance athlete? 3 marks
   c) What health dangers might there be in making use of rEPO to improve endurance performance? 2 marks

4) Under what circumstances might beta blockers be used as ergogenic aids? 3 marks

5) Certain sports people have been banned from sport for using illegal substances.
   a) What advantage does the use of anabolic steroids give to the performer? 2 marks
   b) What is a 'masking' agent and why is it significant? 3 marks

6) Discuss why sports people might wish to use banned substances. In your answer identify the hazards of taking such substances. 5 marks

7) The dietary requirements of a power athlete and an endurance-based athlete have similarities and differences. Discuss. 14 marks

8) How can an elite athlete assess whether their diet meets the demands of their training and competition programmes? 4 marks

9) a) When and what should an athlete eat before a competition? 3 marks
   b) Recommend when and what to eat post-competition. 3 marks

CHAPTER 5 – SPECIALISED TRAINING

figure 5.1 – specialised training methods

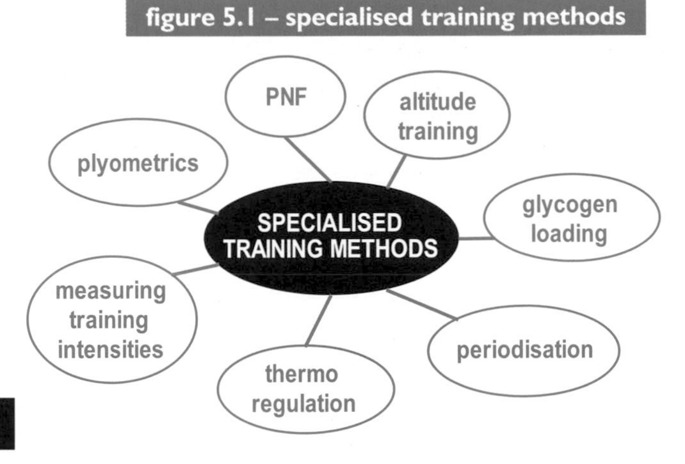

This chapter considers several specialised training methods used by elite sports performers as summarised in figure 5.1.

Plyometrics and power training

Power training involves performing exercises with maximum force and speed (**power** is a combination of **force and speed**). The neurological system will be activated at a rate sufficient to produce powerful movements by the muscles being exercised.

STUDENT NOTE

You have studied the principles of plyometric training at AS level, so to review this method of training with examples, refer to 'AS Revise PE for AQA' ISBN: 978 1 901424 56 0, pages 84-85.

- **Plyometrics**, also known as **stretch-shortening cycle** exercise, is a form of **resistance** training involving **eccentric-to-concentric** actions at 100% intensity, performed quickly so that the muscle stretches prior to the concentric contraction.
- Plyometrics uses the **stretch reflex** to facilitate the recruitment of motor units within the active muscle tissue.
- Muscles and tendons contain specialised **proprioceptors**, such as **muscle spindles** and **Golgi tendon organs** sensitive to stretch, tension and pressure.
- **Muscle spindles** respond to any stretch of a muscle, and through the reflex response they initiate a stronger muscle action to counteract this stretch. This response inhibits the overstretching of muscle fibres.
- Stimulated **Golgi tendon organs** cause relaxation of muscle tissue.

- The **adaptations** produced by these types of training are almost exclusively **anaerobic**, with muscle elastic strength and hypertrophy as the primary aim.
- Plyometrics additionally involve neuro-muscular adaptations such as the **recruitment** of additional **fast twitch** motor units and improved co-ordination of fast twitch motor units as the eccentric effect is utilised.

- For the training to be **most effective**, the greatest force is applied when the **concentric phase** of a movement **coincides** with the **stretch reflex response** occurring at the limit of eccentric stretch.

STUDENT NOTE

Muscle soreness (DOMS) often occurs following plyometric training. This is because of associated damage to muscle tissue and cell membranes (micro tears) and inflammatory reactions within the muscles.

figure 5.2 – PNF

a

b

c

Proprioceptive Neuro-muscular Facilitation stretching

PNF is a progression on passive stretching, whereby after a stretch is held, the muscle is contracted **isometrically** for **between 6-10 seconds**. It then **relaxes** and is **contracted** again, usually going further the second time. This is known as the **CRAC** method (Contract-Relax-Antagonist-Contract).

The PNF method is best described in **three** stages:

Stage 1:
- The athlete and partner assume the position for the stretch (figure 5.2a), then the partner extends the body limb until the muscle is stretched and tension is felt.

Stage 2:
- The athlete then contracts the stretched muscle isometrically for 5-6 seconds and the partner must inhibit all movement (figure 5.2b).

Stage 3:
- The muscle group is relaxed, then immediately and cautiously pushed past its normal range of movement (figure 5.2c) for about 6 seconds.

Allow 30 seconds recovery before repeating the procedure 2-4 times.

PNF

The aim of **PNF** is to toughen up or **inhibit** proprioceptors such as the **Golgi tendon organs** (GTO) situated at the muscle/tendon junction. The GTO is **activated** by an increase in tendon tension. The GTO overrides the excitory signals from the muscle spindles, thus delaying the stretch reflex and allowing the muscle/tendon tissue to relax. This reflex mechanism prevents damage to both muscle and tendon and facilitates a long-term increase in the muscle stretch.

Altitude training

The effects of altitude on the respiratory system

The higher the altitude, the more that aerobic performance is affected by the lack of oxygen pressure in the air.

When you exercise at higher altitudes (see figure 5.3) you will have to work harder to achieve the same sea level performance, because your aerobic system will be taxed that much harder.

figure 5.3 – effects of altitude

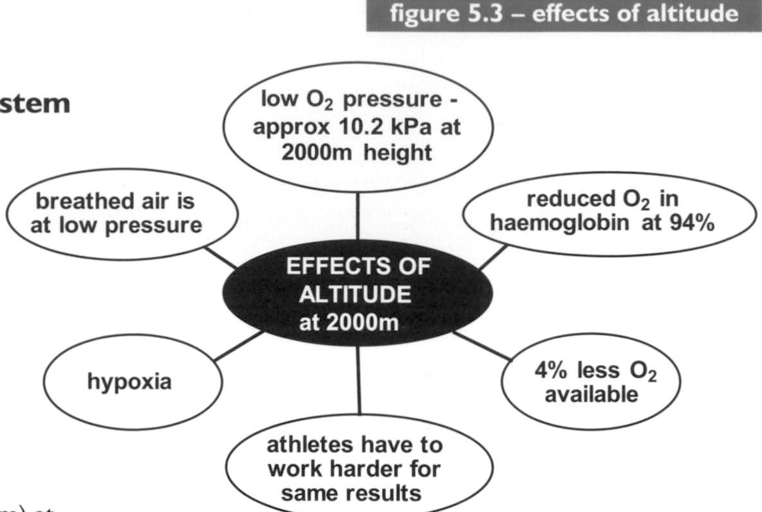

Adaptations to respiratory systems at altitude

During the first Global Games to be held at altitude (2240m) at the Mexico Olympic Games in 1968, African athletes who lived at altitude won all the track events at 1500m and over, with the World record holders (who were sea level dwellers) running a lot slower than their best.

- What happens is that residents at altitude are found to have between 12% and 50% more haemoglobin per unit of blood than sea level residents.
- Also, sea level residents who travel to altitude are found to **adapt** by producing more Hb at a rate of between 1% and 2% per week.
- This is done by **increased manufacture of red blood cells** (erythropoietin production).
- Also, there is a **reduction in plasma volume**, a slower long-term adaptation to living at altitude.
- The effect of these **two** factors is to increase the haemoglobin **concentration** in the blood flowing to active tissue, and hence the oxygen-carrying capacity of the blood.

This is why endurance athletes (long distance runners, cyclists or triathletes) nowadays try to spend a period of time before competitions living and training at altitude – before returning to sea level, where the extra oxygen carrying capacity of their blood would help improve the intensity and duration of aerobic activity.

figure 5.4 – altitude training

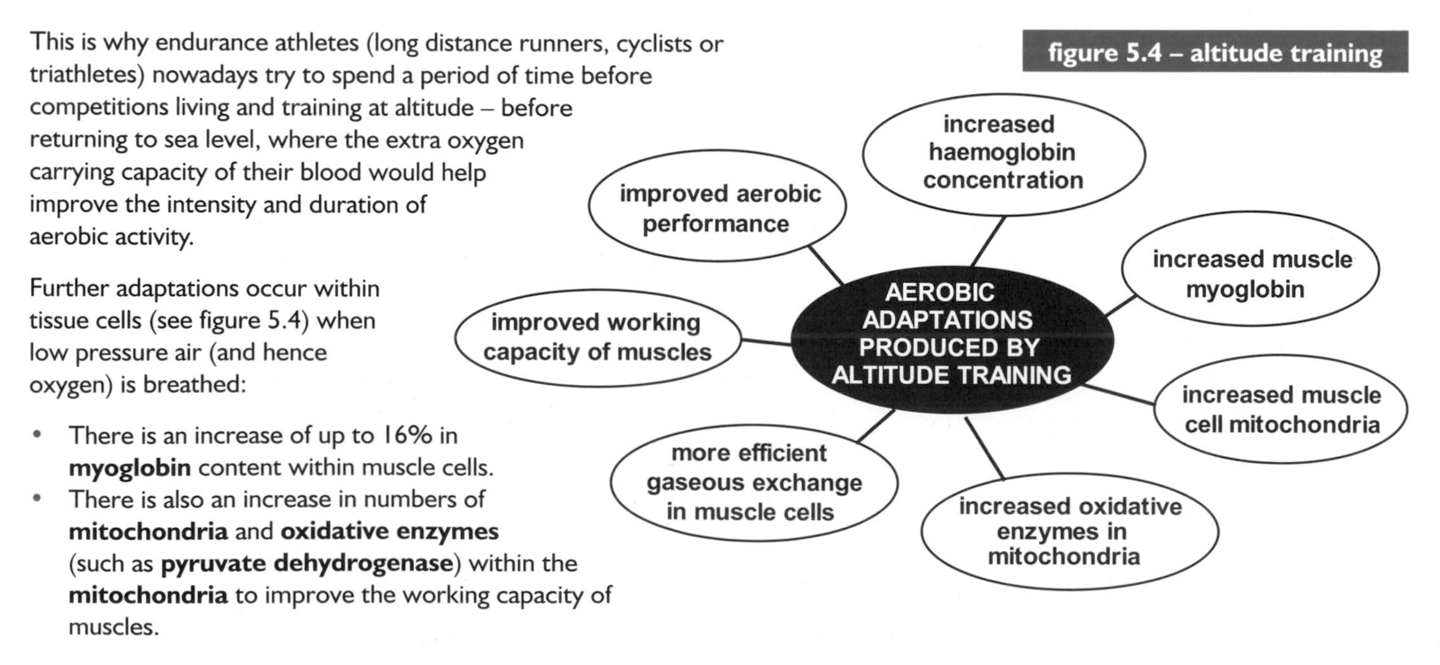

Further adaptations occur within tissue cells (see figure 5.4) when low pressure air (and hence oxygen) is breathed:

- There is an increase of up to 16% in **myoglobin** content within muscle cells.
- There is also an increase in numbers of **mitochondria** and **oxidative enzymes** (such as **pyruvate dehydrogenase**) within the **mitochondria** to improve the working capacity of muscles.
- This happens because the efficiency of gaseous exchange improves **within muscle cells** for the sea level dweller that spends some time at altitude.
- Hence he or she would improve **aerobic** athletic performance and oxygen recovery after exercise.

Altitude training

- Hence altitude training is a predominantly **endurance-based exercise programme** used by elite endurance athletes from a range of sports.
- Most elite athletes have a minimum of 2 training blocks or visits per year, one long training block of between 4-6 weeks during the preparation training phase, and then a shorter block of between 2-3 weeks just prior to a major competition. During a second visit the body adapts more quickly.
- **Short-term symptoms** to altitude exposure include headaches and dizziness and increased breathing and heart rates. The key is to adjust gradually (**acclimatise**) to higher altitude.
- Hence during the first week of altitude training an elite athlete would normally work at between 60-70% of sea level intensity thus avoiding very hard lactate sessions.
- During the second week, the training would increase to full intensity (within days 10-14) and continues until returning to sea level. This would include 'tapering' or reducing the workload during the final couple of days just prior to a major competition. Paula Radcliffe chooses to compete within 2 days of returning to sea level.
- The process of altitude training will stimulate production of more **haemoglobin** and bigger increases in **myoglobin, mitochondria** and **oxidative enzymes** than at sea level in the way outlined above and in figure 5.4.
- Hence on return to sea level the sportsperson would have **increased** $\dot{V}O_{2max}$ and tissue cell respiration, leading to enhanced aerobic performance.
- The optimum time to compete is within 2 to 14 days of return to sea-level. After this, the adaptations gradually return to sea-level norms over a period of weeks, depending on the time spent at altitude and the individual's basic physiological state.

Hypobaric (hypoxic) chambers or houses

This recent development uses dwelling places which use **low-oxygen environments** (hypobaric means low pressure) to simulate altitude training.

An athlete will live and sleep in a hypobaric house situated at sea level, and will train and exercise outside the chamber (at normal oxygen levels, and in his or her normal training environment). This has the effect of elevating EPO, red blood cell levels (hence haemoglobin), myoglobin, mitochondria and oxidative enzymes in a similar way to altitude training.

Hypobaric chambers are used by distance runners, triathletes and endurance cyclists.

A more recent development is the **hypoxic tent**. This is a less expensive system in which a tent is infused with low oxygen air (extra nitrogen infused) but at normal sea-level pressures. Hence a sportsperson can sleep in a tent and gain hypoxic adaptations while asleep (figure 5.5).

figure 5.5 – a hypoxic tent - sleep high, train low!

Glycogen loading, carboloading

Carboloading aims to raise muscle glycogen stores above their normal resting levels prior to endurance competitions with over 90 minutes continuous activity. This process is suitable for activities with low anaerobic and high aerobic components.

Figure 5.6 outlines the **depletion-repletion** model upon which carboloading is based. It is suitable for any activities lasting longer than 15-20 minutes. Note that a two-day high CHO diet beforehand provides the best CHO boost for an endurance event.

figure 5.6 – carboloading

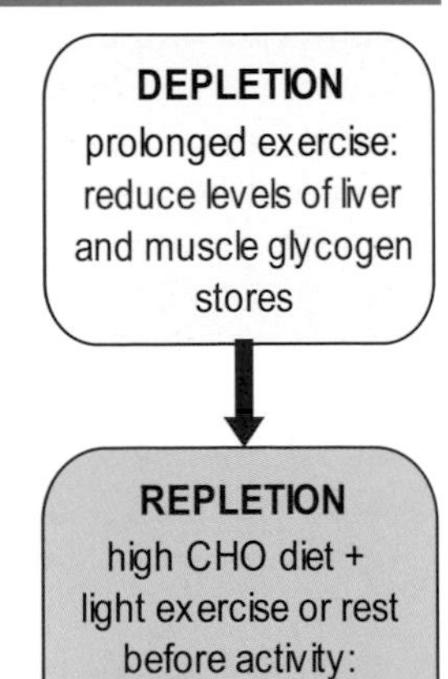

figure 5.7 – glycogen supercompensation

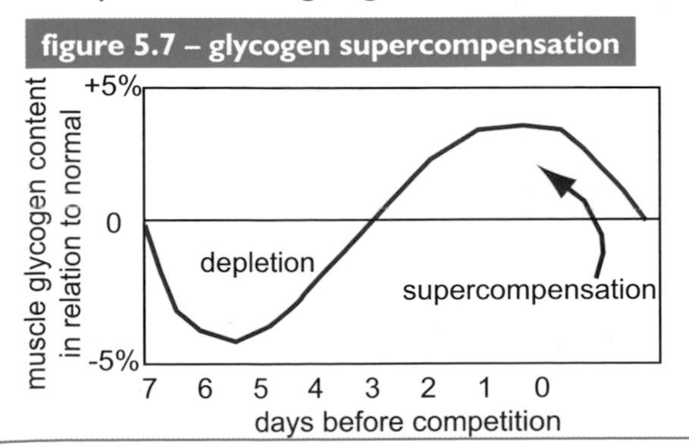

Carboloading - glycogen supercompensation

The graph in figure 5.7 shows how the muscle glycogen level returns to above normal values when the depletion-repletion process is undertaken as outlined in the previous paragraph. In effect the body reacts to a loss of glycogen by vigorously replacing it to a level above normal. This is a normal reaction to **biological stress**.

The importance of high glycogen content in muscle before a marathon race

The graph in figure 5.8 shows that a runner's time would increase by around 10 minutes in a 2 hour run if muscle glycogen started at 50% of its maximum possible. The effect of reduced muscle glycogen begins to be felt at the 1 hour mark. Hence the importance of glycogen loading to endurance sportspeople.

figure 5.8 – effect of glycogen store on endurance running times

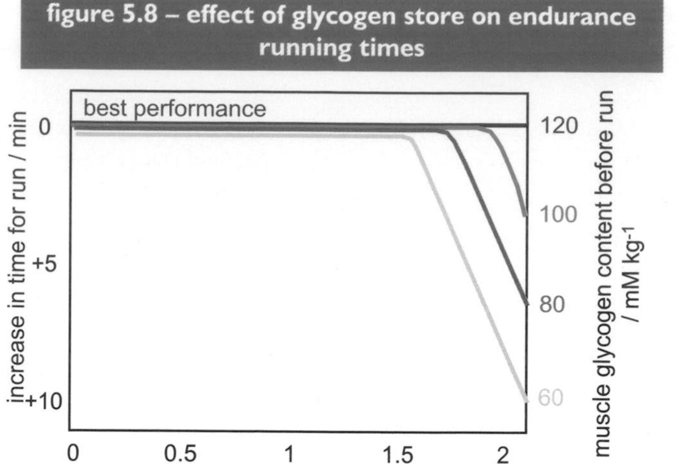

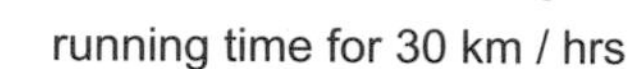

Periodisation

Periodisation is a method of training which varies training intensity cyclically, organised in periods and cycles of training. Such cycles of training take place long-term, over time spans of months and years.

Each period within a training plan will have a specific aim or objective within the overall training plan, for example:

- Period 1 may be aimed at basic conditioning.
- Period 2 may be aimed at strength development.
- Period 3 may be aimed at speed development.

figure 5.9 – a single periodised year

months	nov	dec	jan	feb	mar	apr	may	jun	jul	aug	sep	oct
phases	1				2			3	4	5		6
periods	preparation							competition				recovery/transition

The time intervals within this training method can be defined as follows:

- A **period** is a basic year subdivision between 1 and 6 months.
- A **macrocycle** is a phase lasting between 4 and 26 weeks.
- A **mesocycle** is a phase lasting 2 to 4 weeks which would be part of a macrocycle.
- A **microcycle** is a phase lasting 1 week or less, and is the basic repetitive cycle of activities.

- Sometimes **daily cycles** of up to 3 sessions may be required for elite performers.

Figure 5.9 shows how periods and cycles can be laid out for a whole year. Note that an elite athlete may need a four or five year periodised programme to peak for an Olympic Games.

Planning a periodised training programme

- You will need to utilise the principles of training, decide on general activities, and then decide on specific activities.
- You will need to break down activities into relevance to different energy systems and ensure that this fits the energy system profile for your sport.
- You will next decide on time allocations (**duration**), and decide on the volume of work in a session (**intensity**).

- See figure 5.10 for an example breakdown of training intensity over the days of a microcycle (in this case 7 days long, one week).
- Note that elite athletes who don't need to plan round the working week (most people would have to fit in with school, college or work), often use 5, 6 or 8 day micro cycles to fit in with the time needed to recover from intense training.

- Decide on how many times in the microcycle you would like to train (**frequency**).
- Set out sets and repetitions within an activity (**repetition**).
- Ensure that **warm-up** and **cool-down** are included.
- Make notes on **progression** for future microcycles.
- Ensure that appropriate rest and **rest relief** is indicated.

figure 5.10 – variation in training intensity during a microcycle

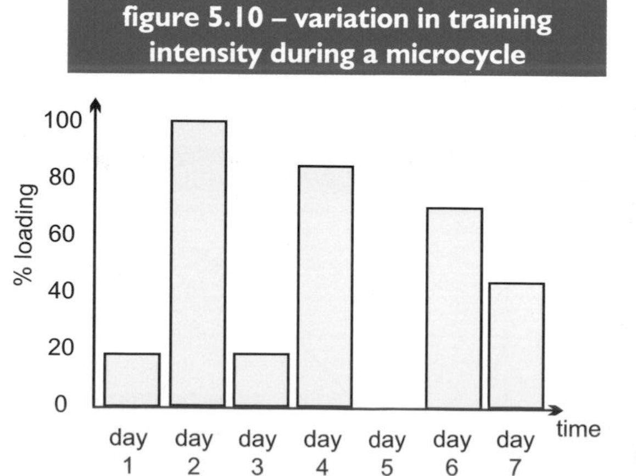

Planning mesocycles

- You need to establish your **maximum training intensity** using fitness tests - this is your initial **100%** training intensity.
- Then decide on a **starting point** below this (for example, 80%).
- Then plan a **progressive intensity** mesocycle taking you up to 100% in say 4 weeks (figure 5.11).
- Next plan the subsequent 4-week **cycle** taking you up to 110%.
- With subsequent 4-week cycles taking you up to your planned goal for the year.

figure 5.11 – training intensity by mesocycle

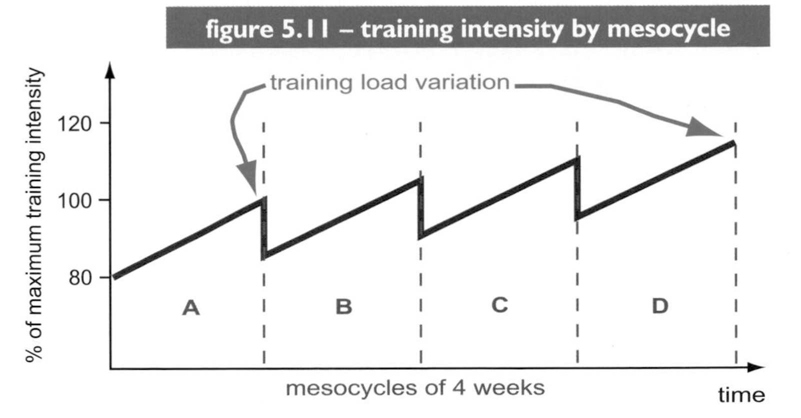

Alternative methods of periodisation

- The example in figure 5.9 previously is a single periodised year (just one competitive period). The same sort of arrangements can be made for two competitive periods - called a **double periodised year**.

- Figure 5.12 shows the possible layout for a **double periodised** year, the blue vertical line shows the end of the first competitive period.
- At this point the second half of the year (period) begins and the process of structure towards the second competitive period starts. Research has shown that this sort of programme can initiate greater progress in various indicators of fitness (strength, speed, endurance).

figure 5.12 – a double periodised year

months	nov	dec	jan	feb	mar	apr	may	jun	jul	aug	sep	oct
phases	1	2		3	4	5		6		7	8	9
periods	preparation			trans	comp	preparation				trans	comp	recovery

trans = transition comp = competition

Tapering and peaking

- The periodisation method of training enables the coach to vary training intensity and quantity, so that a performer can **peak** for a major games such as the Olympics.
- This peaking usually involves **tapering**, which means that training intensity gradually reduces over a period of up to 14 days beforehand, which enables the athlete to be fresh and full of energy for the big event.

Peaking is partly psychological. How a performer feels about him or herself, and how confidence is flowing, are often as important as the stage of fitness or strength.

Thermoregulation

Thermoregulation is the ability to maintain body temperature within certain boundaries, even when the surrounding temperature is very different. The acceptable range is between 36.1 and 37.8°C.

The **thermoregulatory centre** is situated in the hypothalamus - in the brain. Changes in body temperature such as caused by exercise, are sensed by central and peripheral receptors, and body temperature is maintained by balancing heat input and heat loss. Figure 5.13 and table 5.1 list the heat energy transfer methods from the human body.

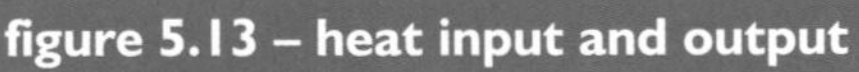
figure 5.13 – heat input and output

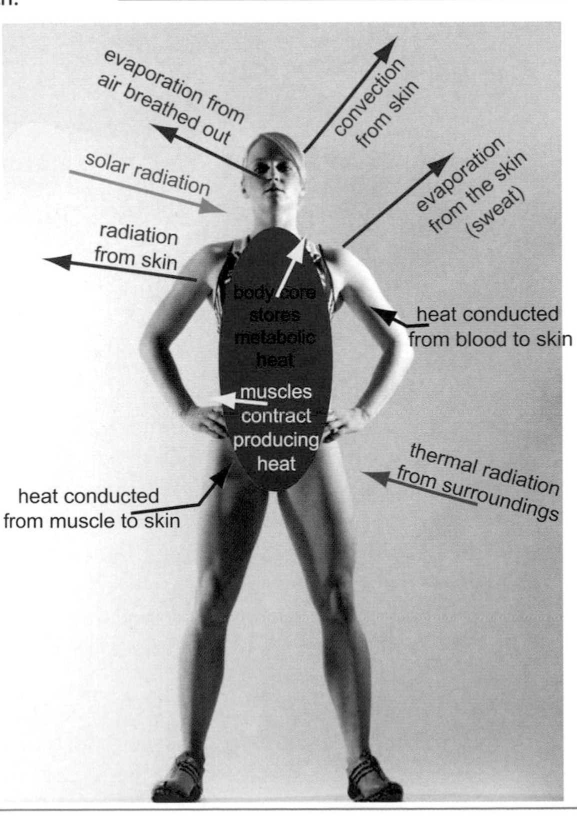

Table 5.1 – **heat energy transfer methods**

heat input	heat output
metabolic heat	radiation
exercise	conduction
shivering	convection
solar radiation	evaporation

The proportions of different methods of heat energy transfer are different between at rest and during exercise, and are set out in table 5.2.

Table 5.2 – **proportions of the different methods of heat energy transfer from the body**

mechanism of heat loss	% of total at rest	% of total during exercise
conduction & convection	20	15
radiation	60	5
evaporation	20	80

figure 5.14 – summary of main thermoregulatory mechanisms

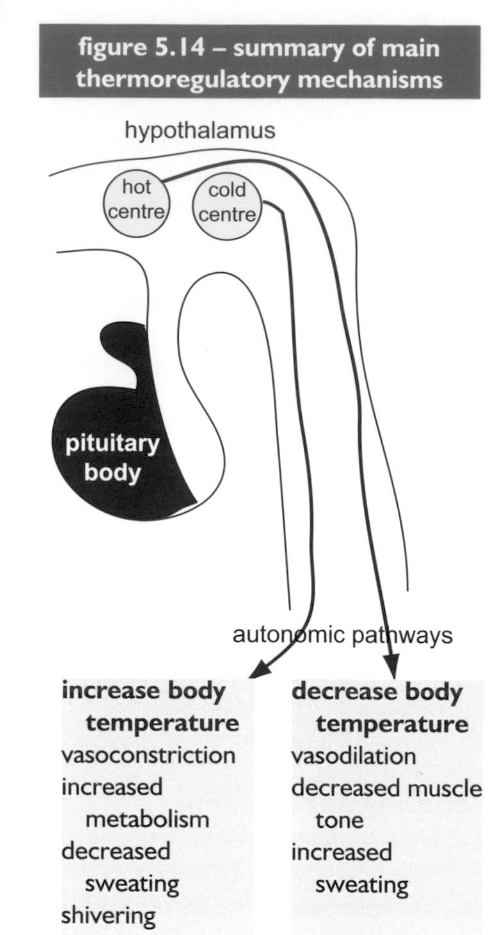

- Activity of the sweat glands is controlled by **autonomic nerves** which in turn are controlled by the thermoregulatory centre (figure 5.14).
- Increased **skeletal muscle activity** increases the core temperature by increasing **metabolic heat** production.
- Increased **sweat gland activity** decreases the core temperature by increasing **evaporative heat loss** (as in table 5.2).
- **Smooth muscle** in the **skin arterioles** can cause these vessels to **vasodilate** to direct blood to the skin for heat transfer out of the body, or **vasoconstrict** to retain heat energy deep within the body.

- The **amount of heat generated** during tissue respiration depends mainly on the volume (therefore the **mass**) of the body.
- Because most of the heat is lost through the skin, the **surface area of the skin** determines the amount of heat lost.
- Hence the effectiveness of the mechanisms of body temperature control depend on the **surface area to mass ratio** of the body.
- Small people (children, gymnasts, distance runners, jockeys) therefore will lose temperature much more quickly than large people (weight lifters, sumo wrestlers, throwers, rugby players).

Exercising in hot conditions

- Under **hot conditions** the surrounding temperature can exceed both skin and core temperature. This makes evaporation the predominant method of heat loss compared with conduction, convection and radiation.
- **Skin cooling** occurs when sweat evaporates, so exercising in hot dry climates feels more comfortable than in cooler but more humid tropical conditions.
- This is because in **humid conditions** the presence of high water vapour pressure in the surrounding air suppresses evaporation even though large quantities of sweat bead on the skin.
- The practice of **removing sweat** with a towel before sweat evaporates will hinder evaporative cooling, since lack of moisture on the skin will mean that no evaporative cooling can take place.
- Hence a physically active person is vulnerable to the dangerous state of **dehydration** and **increased core temperature** (**hyperthermia**).

Adequate fluid intake before, during and after exercise is important. Fluid is needed to preserve plasma volume, maintain circulation and reduce the effects of the cardiovascular drift (see page 40 of 'AS Revise PE for AQA', ISBN: 978 1 901424 56 0).

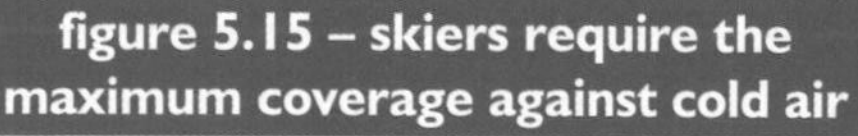
figure 5.15 – skiers require the maximum coverage against cold air

Exercising in cold conditions

- Heat production by **shivering** (which is the very rapid alternate contraction and relaxation of the skeletal muscles) and physical activity, is the mechanism the body uses to offset heat flux to a cold environment.
- Withdrawal of blood from **peripheral body parts**, such as hands and feet, help to preserve core temperature, hence the skin will pale when exposed to a low temperature environment.
- **Increased water loss** occurs from the respiratory passages, and kidneys excrete more water as urine to reduce the total fluid volume (plasma volume) held centrally.
- Also if **thick clothing** is worn in these conditions, sweating can increase - which would again cause fluid loss and possible dehydration.
- Hence **fluid** will need to be **replaced** in cold conditions.

Wind chill

- **Wind** increases evaporative cooling of exposed body parts, and in cold conditions this is known as the **wind-chill factor** (temperature felt on exposed skin is lower than the air temperature).
- **Wet skin** exposed to the wind will cool even faster.
- Hence a sportsperson training in **cold windy conditions** should wear appropriate kit to reduce this effect and minimise the risk of **hypothermia**.
- Examples of this are a hat to reduce heat loss through the head, a Gore-tex training jacket to enable moisture to escape from the body while keeping out moisture from the environment, and suitable thermal gloves.

- Many of Britain's elite athletes have access to **indoor training** facilities and also go **warm-weather training** to escape the usual British cold, wet, winter weather conditions.

Training and competing in extreme climates requires time for an athlete to acclimatise or to get used to the prevailing conditions. In the case of heat acclimatisation, within 3 days there is an increase in plasma volume, thus supporting stroke volume and cardiac output, combined with the increased ability to sweat.

In the case of adaptation to cold conditions, the physiological effects are less pronounced than in hot conditions. Most of the effect is called **habituation**, in which people just get used to the conditions. A sportsperson will also have an increase in metabolic rate (producing more heat energy within the body), and the skin tends to become more **insulating** (after an extended period) which means that they will tend to develop thicker layers of subcutaneous fat. The effect of these cold-adaptations is to improve cold temperature tolerance.

Measuring training intensities

STUDENT NOTE

You have been introduced to the concept of working intensities at AS level: refer to 'AS Revise PE for AQA', ISBN: 978 1 901424 56 0, page 75. These are Karvonen's method and Borg's rating of Perceived Exertion. These two methods are not very accurate and in the case of Borg's scale can be subjective. Hence today's elite athletes tend to use more sophisticated methods of measuring training intensity as discussed below.

Lactate sampling

As work intensity increases lactic acid starts to accumulate above resting values. This section explains how taking samples of lactate levels from blood can determine how and when OBLA occurs, and a coach would then be able to relate this to training intensity (for example, the maximum sustainable speed at which an athlete can run).

The effects of continued high intensity exercise

As work intensity increases, **lactic acid** starts to accumulate **above resting values**, and this produces muscle **fatigue** and **pain**. The resultant **low pH** inhibits enzyme action and cross-bridge formation, and hence muscle action is inhibited, and of course physical performance deteriorates.

A **lactate sampler** is a small hand-held device that can be taken into the training environment, with which top athletes take pin prick blood samples and test for lactate concentration (immediate read-out from the device). This enables them to work out the maximum possible exercise intensity within which they must work to avoid OBLA.

figure 5.16 – OBLA for an athlete

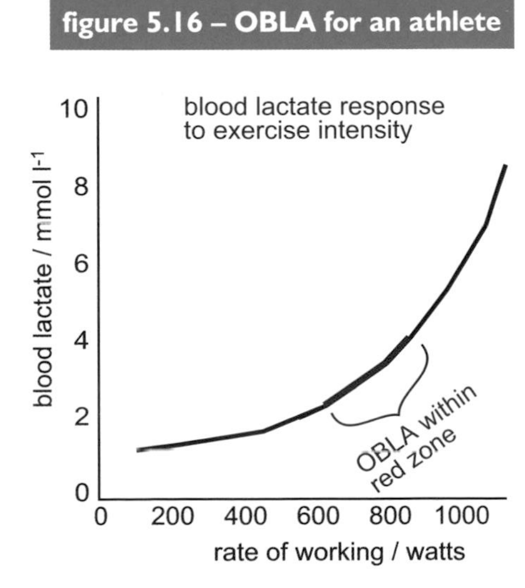

Figure 5.16 shows how **blood lactate rises** as exercise intensity increases, and approximately where OBLA causes difficulties for the performer. OBLA depends on the level of training and lies **between 2 and 4 mmol l^{-1}**. Figure 2.8 on page 22 above shows how OBLA begins at higher exercise intensities for trained athletes as opposed to untrained people.

OBLA governs the **lactic/aerobic threshold**, and since trained athletes begin OBLA at higher work intensities, they will have higher values of $\dot{V}O_{2max}$ than untrained people. This is the reason that athletes need to know whether OBLA has started or not. The lactate level will tell a coach to increase or reduce training intensity, so that OBLA can be pushed to higher $\dot{V}O_{2max}$.

Respiratory exchange ratio (RER)

RER is an indicator which is a way of estimating which fuel type (CHO, fat or protein) is being used within a given activity. It can be estimated by measuring oxygen taken in and carbon dioxide expired during the activity, using a portable or laboratory based gas analyser. Estimation of RER for a person can also tell you whether or not the sportsperson is operating anaerobically (without sufficient oxygen for aerobic effort) or not.

Energy released by a given volume of oxygen

- This energy depends on whether the fuel is carbohydrate, fat or protein.
- Different amounts of energy are released by combination with oxygen because of the different chemical formulae of CHO, fat or protein.
- Complete combination with oxygen will produce CO_2 and water.
- The amount of O_2 needed to completely oxidise a molecule of CHO, fat or protein is proportional to the amount of carbon in the fuel.

RER

RER is the ratio: $\frac{\text{volume of } CO_2 \text{ produced}}{\text{volume of } O_2 \text{ consumed}}$

For glucose: $6O_2 + C_6H_{12}O_6 \rightarrow 6CO_2 + 6H_2O$ + energy to resynthesise 38ATP

Therefore for **glucose**: $RER = \frac{6CO_2}{6O_2} = \mathbf{1.00}$

For fat: $23O_2 + C_{16}H_{32}O_2 \rightarrow 16CO_2 + 16H_2O$ + energy to resynthesise 129ATP

Therefore for **fat**: $RER = \frac{16CO_2}{23O_2} = \mathbf{0.70}$

For protein: $C_{72}H_{112}N_2O_{22}S + 77O_2 \rightarrow 63CO_2 + 38\,H_2O + SO_3 + 9CO(NH_2)_2$ (for example)

Therefore for protein: $RER = \frac{63CO_2}{77O_2} = \mathbf{0.82}$

Protein is rarely used as an energy source except in extreme conditions.

Measuring RER

RER is estimated for a sportsperson by measuring CO_2 output and O_2 input while exercising either on a treadmill or a cycle ergometer, or while out running with a portable device (see figure 5.17). During this process, the sportsperson breathes in and out of a tube connected to a gas analyser.

A value of RER near 1.0 means that the sportsperson is deriving most of his or her energy from CHO aerobically.

A value of RER over 1.0 means that less O_2 is being used than is required to produce the CO_2 from aerobic respiration which means that anaerobic respiration and lactate production are occurring.

So measurement of RER can tell a sportsperson whether he or she is reaching his or her aerobic limit or not, and whether the training intensity is too high for aerobic work. The average value for RER for a mixed diet and for mild aerobic exercise is 0.82, showing a mixed uptake of carbohydrate and fats.

figure 5.17 – measuring RER while in action

Practice questions

1) a) Plyometric training is a type of power training, which involves performing exercises with maximum power and speed.
Describe the main concepts of plyometric training, illustrating your answer with an example of an exercise. Identify the type of sports performer who would most benefit from this training method. 6 marks

b) Discuss the advantages and disadvantages of plyometric training. 4 marks

c) Why does muscle soreness (DOMS) often occur following a plyometric training session and how could muscle soreness be reduced? 4 marks

2) Explain the role of Golgi tendon organs during proprioceptive neuromuscular facilitation (PNF). 4 marks

3) a) Describe the conditions at altitude that could limit performance. 3 marks

b) An elite group of endurance athletes spend three weeks training at 2000 metres. What major physiological responses and adaptations would they expect during this period of acclimatisation? 10 marks

c) What is meant by the concept 'living high and training low'?
Identify two advantages of using this acclimatisation method. 6 marks

4) a) How can a balanced diet be manipulated to increase an athlete's glucose reserves prior to a marathon race? 6 marks

b) Carbohydrates are used as an energy source during both aerobic and anaerobic conditions. It is therefore beneficial that an elite athlete's stores of carbohydrate are at a maximum before competition day. Discuss the advantages and disadvantages of glycogen loading. 4 marks

5) Periodisation is a training concept that explains the variation in training volume and intensity over a specific period of time. Outline the basic structure of a single periodised year and illustrate how a coach is able to use this structure when planning a training programme for an athletics group. 14 marks

6) Discuss the role of the thermoregulatory centre in maintaining the core temperature of the body. 3 marks

7) a) What are the major avenues for loss of body heat energy?
Which of these four pathways is important for controlling body temperature at rest, and during exercise? 6 marks

b) What happens to the body temperature during exercise and why? 4 marks

8) How does the body regulate temperature when an elite athlete is training in a warm climate? 3 marks

9) What are the physiological effects of dehydration on an athlete and how does this affect exercise performance? 4 marks

10) List four environmental factors that limit the ability of an athlete to continue to exercise in hot conditions. 4 marks

11) Describe how an athlete is able to control his or her body temperature during a marathon race. 4 marks

12) Why is humidity an important factor when an athlete is performing in high temperatures? Why are wind and cloud cover important? 4 marks

13) Winter sports performers regularly compete in extreme cold conditions often held at altitude.

a) How does the human body physiologically respond to cold, hypobaric conditions? 6 marks

b) How can an athlete minimise excessive heat loss during cold exposure? 2 marks

c) What factors should be considered to provide maximum protection for sports performers exercising in a cold environment? 3 marks

14) Many elite swimmers use blood lactate sampling during training as a means of establishing their training load.

a) What do you understand by the term lactate threshold? 2 marks

b) How is lactate threshold related to $\dot{V}O_{2max}$? 2 marks

c) How might knowledge of blood lactate levels taken during a swimming session assist both coach and elite swimmer? 2 marks

15) a) Show how the data in the following equation can be used to calculate the respiratory exchange ratio (RER) and identify which fuel food is being used. Show your workings. $6O_2 + C_6H_{12}O_6 \rightarrow 6CO_2 + 6H_2O + \text{energy}$ 3 marks

b) How can this information be of value to an elite sports performer? 2 marks

CHAPTER 6 – SPORTS INJURIES

figure 6.1 – sports injuries

A **sports injury** is any kind of injury, pain or physical damage that occurs as a result of sport, exercise or physical activity.

Sports injuries are unfortunately inevitable, and are dependent on a performer's intensity of training, the preparation he or she makes to avoid injury, and the ways in which rest and recovery are planned into a training and competitive programme. Figure 6.1 outlines the factors influencing how injuries are caused and can be dealt with.

Sports injuries are:
- Most commonly associated with the musculo-skeletal system, which includes muscles, joints and their associated tissues such as ligaments and tendons.
- Commonly classified as **acute** or **chronic**.
- Mild, moderate or severe.
- Characterised by pain, swelling, tenderness, weakness and the inability to use or place weight on the injured area.

- **Acute** injuries refer to sports injuries that happen in a moment.
- **Chronic** injuries are characterised by a slow, sustained development of symptoms, that culminate in a painful inflammatory condition.

Extrinsic and intrinsic factors affecting sports injuries

Table 6.1 outlines the intrinsic and extrinsic factors which affect sport injury. Intrinsic factors are those within the performer, and extrinsic factors are those derived outside the performer.

Table 6.1 – **intrinsic and extrinsic factors in sport injuries**

intrinsic factors	extrinsic factors
gender	training volume, overtraining
age	sport technique
body mass and body composition	playing surfaces
muscle strengths and weaknesses, general fitness	equipment difficulties
joint flexibility (or lack of it)	use of inappropriate clothing
orthopaedic and skeletal features	use of inappropriate footwear
	environmental conditions

To avoid injury, a coach will need to plan training that takes into account the intrinsic factors, the age or sex of the performer for example. It will be important to improve strength and fitness so that the physical requirements of the sport will not cause injury, whether the athlete can jump high or run quickly without hurting her or himself for example. Prevention of injury by improving joint flexibility so that the body positions required by a sport can be achieved without strain, will also be important.

Causes of sports injuries

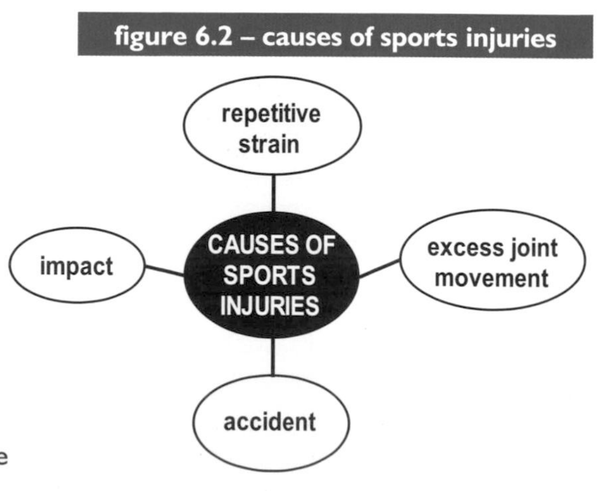

figure 6.2 – causes of sports injuries

Figure 6.2 lists the categories of causes of sports injury.

Impact

Impact between participants can occur in many sports as a matter of routine, for example:
- Soccer, rugby, Australian rules and American football.
- Ice hockey and field hockey.
- Basketball, netball and handball.
- Water polo.

Such impacts can cause injuries from haematomae and joint sprains, to long bone, pelvic or cranial breakage. An extension to this category is impact between the playing object (ball or puck) and a player in for example cricket, field or ice hockey, or golf.

Playing surfaces
Environmental factors such as weather and ground conditions are potential risk factors for injuries, including the hardness of the ground.

- For example, the four Grand Slam tennis tournaments are played on hard courts (Australian Open, US Open), clay (Roland Garros) and grass (Wimbledon). On clay surfaces lower friction leads to longer sliding movements (longer contact times) which can result in a higher incidence of upper thigh muscle strains/spasms.
- Modern advances in turf technology have gone a long way towards preventing knee and ankle injuries.
- The risk of traumatic injury in indoor sports in which pivoting movements occur, is higher when playing on artificial floors than on wooden floors. The higher shoe to surface friction on the former surface is likely to explain the higher injury risk.

Different surfaces may also influence the incidence of injuries as in-shoe-landing patterns differ depending on the surface used.

Equipment and rules
Equipment used in sport can itself cause injury, particularly if used incorrectly. Both equipment and rules of the game should be amended if they are in any way likely to contribute towards the causes of injury.

Repetitive strain
Repeated low level impacts can cause chronic injury if long-term prevention measures (such as rest or massage) are not taken. Such impacts affect the ankle, Achilles tendons, shins, and bones of the feet for impacts between feet and the ground. Also wrists and finger joints for impacts between fists and another person (in for example, boxing or karate).

Repetitive strain injuries can be caused by repeated use of any part of the muscular system without adequate rest and recovery. For example:
- Strains to gastrocnemius or soleus for sprinters or jumpers in any sport.
- Strains to wrist and finger joints for shot putters.
- Strains to trunk or back muscular system for pole-vaulters, gymnasts, sprinters and throwers in any sport.
- Strains to shoulder or elbow muscles and tendons for javelin throwers, baseball pitchers, cricket bowlers.

Sportspeople use strapping and taping of vulnerable joint/muscle areas to avoid this type of injury.

figure 6.3 – injury prevention

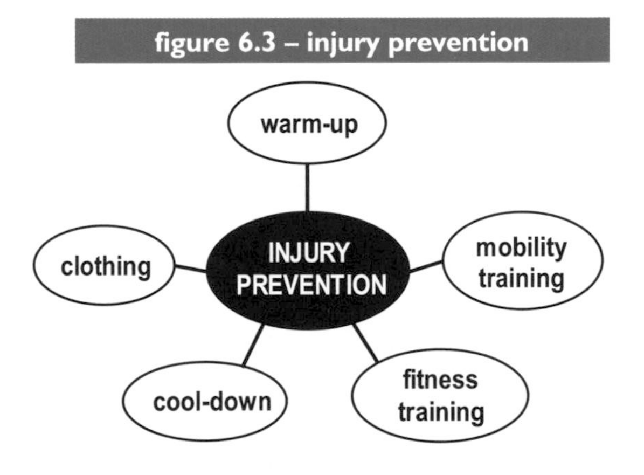

Excess movement joint strain
By this we mean single actions to various joints where the normal range of movement is exceeded. For example:
- Back or knee injuries caused by a single deep squat movement (one or both legs), as in a rugby scrum or a sprint start.
- Shoulder or elbow injuries caused by a grapple in wrestling.
- Neck or upper back injury caused by a collapsed rugby scrum.

Accident
This category of cause for injury covers almost everything else! For example:
- The tibia/fibula double break occurring during a rugby tackle.
- The femur break caused by an awkward landing after a jump in soccer.
- The biceps tendon rupture during a tackle in rugby.

figure 6.4 – specialist clothing for injury prevention

Injury prevention

Figure 6.3 summarises the main ways in which sports injuries are prevented.

Clothing
Many sports require specialist protective clothing (examples in figure 6.4), with well known examples from fencing, ice hockey, field hockey, cricket, baseball, American football, and equestrianism.

Protective clothing

Boxing and other martial arts require helmets (with or without face guards), padding, boxes, strapping, gloves, mouth guards and so on, depending on the rules of the sport, and the damage allowed to be inflicted within the rules of the sport.

Specialist clothing is also required for low and high temperatures to maintain body temperature within a safe range (see page 43 above). **Compression sportswear** is thought to reduce the risk of muscle injury and speed up muscle recovery after injury (see page 132 below).

Taping, strapping and bracing

- **Taping** has many roles such as to **support** and **compress** ligaments and capsules of unstable joints by limiting excessive or abnormal anatomical movement. Taping also enhances proprioceptive feedback from the limb or joint.
- **Strapping** is often used in training. For example, strapping a shot putter's hand or gymnast's wrists.
- There are a range of **brace** products that support and protect joints.

Footwear

Footwear are key items of an athlete's sports equipment. Anyone participating in sports that require a lot of jumping and running such as jogging, tennis, basketball and football are more susceptible to repetitive strain injury. It is important therefore to wear **proper fitting** footwear that is **activity-specific**, to avoid putting him or herself at risk of injury to the soft tissue, bones or joints of the lower limb.

figure 6.5 – snowboarding boots prevent injury

Proper footwear should have **flexible soles**, and provide the correct **arch support** and **counter cushioning** devices. This includes custom-fitted **orthotics** that can provide protection against foot impact injuries such as stress fractures and shin splints. Most elite athletes will have had orthotic assessment for shoe inserts, which correct foot posture from excessive pronation or supination.

Boots provide foot stability in many sports, since ankle breaks and sprains are very common sports injuries, particularly in basketball, skiing or snow boarding (figure 6.5).

Warm-up

Warm-up has a **physiological role in injury prevention,** and is a way of preparing the muscular system for exercise.

The fact of rise of temperature of the muscular system due to increased metabolic activity (heat energy is produced as a by-product of the tissue respiration process), helps muscle to be fully oxygen ready, and enzyme ready for action.

Warm-up is an essential principle of training which **prepares** the body for exercise effort.

Figure 6.6 summarises the issues within warm-up. Warm-up usually consists of a series of **low level aerobic exercises** which can be sport specific or general in nature (jogging, SAQ, cycle ergometer, stretching).

The **sport specific** element usually includes exercises of increasing intensity up to the moment of game or competition beginning.

The **aim** of this element is to get the sportsperson into the **rhythm** and flow of their forthcoming activity, practise skills and movements expected later, and build **confidence** before the event starts.

figure 6.6 – warm-up

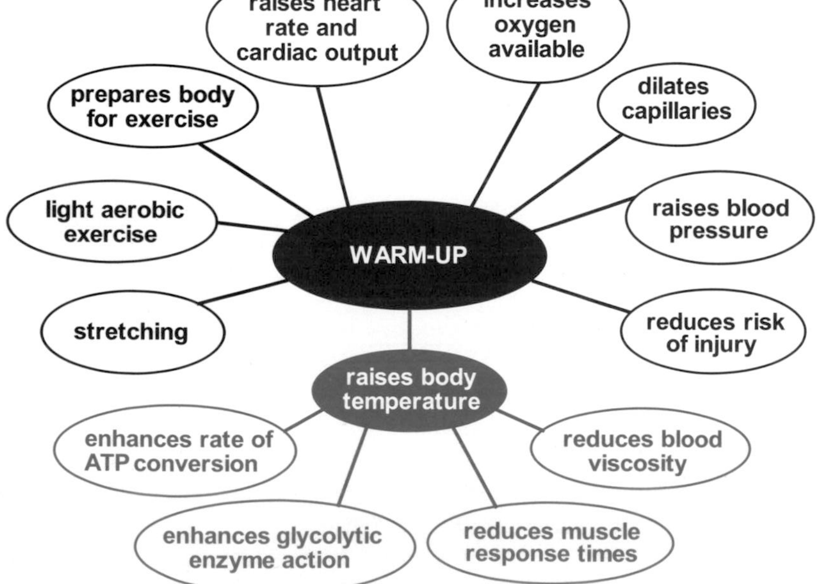

STUDENT NOTE

Refer to page 80 of AS Revise PE for AQA, ISBN: 978 1 901424 56 0, for notes on warm-up.

Stretching

Most sportspeople include some stretching in their warm-up routine, partly to prevent injury. Joints are enabled to move through a greater normal range without stress, and the sportsperson is able to use the joints without overstretching.

However, the inclusion of lengthy stretching in warm-up is controversial, since some research has shown no effect on joint mobility for stretching done during warm-up, and a risk of injury if violent static stretches are performed on cold muscle.

Stretching as part of a warm-up programme

Most people use rhythmic stretching movements as part of an effective warm-up programme.

Figure 6.7 outlines the different types of stretching, and page 81 of the book 'AS Revise PE for AQA' ISBN: 978 1 901424 56 0, sets this out in more detail.

figure 6.7 – flexibility / stretching

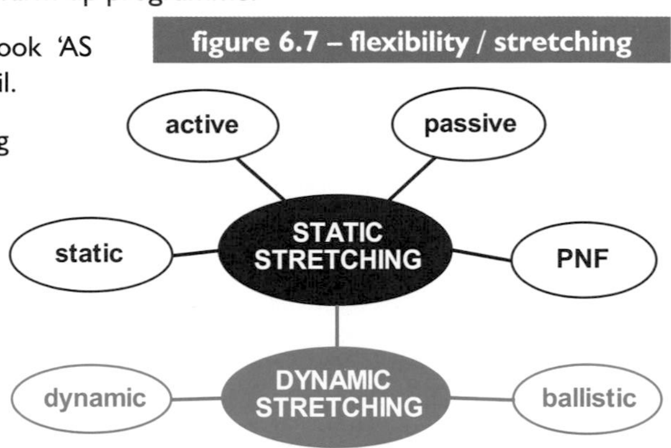

The reasons that stretching prevents injury are because limited stretching of soft tissues such as ligaments, tendons and muscle causes an increase in resting or residual length of these tissues. In skeletal muscle tissue, stretching (over an extended period of time) causes **inhibition of the stretch reflex** as muscle spindles lengthen. Since normally the stretch reflex limits flexibility, this inhibition would improve flexibility.

The muscle stretch reflex

The **muscle stretch reflex** is controlled by stretch receptors called **proprioceptors**, which provide sensory information about movement, orientation in space, and muscle stretch. These receptors are located in skeletal muscle, joint capsules and tendons.

Proprioceptors such as muscle spindles produce the stretch reflex (reflex contraction of a muscle) in response to a **rapid** longitudinal stretch of that muscle. This reflex causes the muscle fibres to contract, and is the basis of muscle tone. The biological purpose of this activity is to protect the muscle against tears, strains and pulls.

Training as injury prevention

The principles of training (see page 31 above) can be used to improve general and specific fitness. These principles are based on the fact that stress to the muscular system will force it to adapt to the stressor, by becoming stronger, fitter, and better able to withstand stress. Hence the muscular system will be more likely to withstand the excess forces applied in extra stressful situations which would normally cause injuries.

Conditioning the neuromuscular system

During training, the function of the nervous system is developed. The brain learns movements by developing motor programmes which tell the person what to do almost automatically when faced with a physical task, without having to relearn the mechanics of the task each time.

figure 6.8 – examples of specialist core activities

Conditioning using repetitive movements improves the feedback of proprioceptors (such as muscle spindles and Golgi tendon organs) to muscles, so that movements are more certain and less likely to have errors which might lead to injury. This is at a subconscious level, since a person would not have to think about a movement to perform it successfully.

This is why modern sports training includes balance and core activities (figure 6.8), so that the neuromuscular system which establishes posture and balance is better developed, and hence injury risk reduced.

Dangers of overtraining

Overtraining is explained as 'when the intensity of training and/or volume of training are increased to extreme levels, and there is a lack of recovery within or between training sessions leading to an associated decline in physiological function'.

This situation can lead to extreme muscle fatigue and loss of performance and a potential for injury, as focus and concentration fail.

Major symptoms of overtraining are:
- Change in appetite.
- Body-weight loss.
- Sleep disturbance.
- Irritability, restlessness, excitability, anxiousness.
- Loss of motivation, vigour or concentration.
- Depression.

A successful training programme will include **moderation**, in which note is taken of the sportsperson's state of physical health, and when signs of deteriorating performance are detected, training loads will be reduced and recovery times increased, until feelings of tiredness are reduced.

Dangers of overtraining for children

Training for children should be monitored for overtraining. Repetitive trauma to the physique should be carefully monitored for overtraining symptoms (joint and tendon pain for example).

Because of their size, children are more susceptible to high and low temperature induced injury or illness. This is because of the greater ratio of body-surface-area to mass for children. Body temperature will depend more closely (than for an adult) on temperature of the environment.

LTAD (long term athlete development) provides a valuable programme that prevents inappropriate training and poor coaching thus reducing childhood injuries. See page 108 below for details of this programme.

figure 6.9 – great care must be taken when coaching children

Diet and nutrition in injury prevention

To avoid fatigue and injury, the athlete and coach will need to ensure energy and mineral needs are met particularly in endurance activities (see page 33 above). This will usually involve a high CHO diet and sufficient fluid intake (since when dehydration reaches more than 2%, electrolyte balance can be disturbed and significant fatigue will occur).

Foods with high calcium content will reduce risk of stress fracture.

Rehabilitation after injury

Figure 6.10 summarises the issues surrounding rehabilitation after injury.

figure 6.10 – rehabilitation after injury

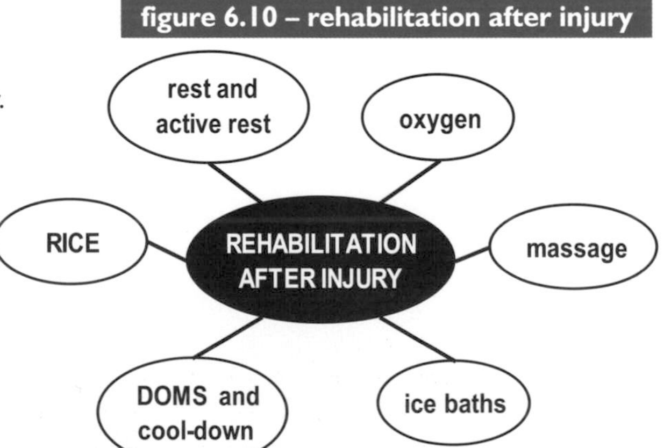

RICE

Rest of injured body part for recovery and healing for a period of about 72 hours before beginning rehab programme.

Ice uses the fact that local tissue inflammation and pain can be reduced by chilling the affected area (20 minutes maximum at any one time). This is because vasoconstriction reduces internal bleeding and hence the flow of fluids from damaged cells. The use of cold as treatment for injury is called **cryotherapy**.

Compression uses the fact that taping or strapping of a swollen joint or tissue area reduces the damage caused by the swelling itself, i.e. fluid leaking from an injury into the surrounding tissue.

Elevation uses the fact that if the injured part is raised above the heart, gravity can send fluid (within the swelling, or blood pooled within a body part after exercise) back toward the body core, thus reducing damage caused by the swelling itself.

Rest and active rest

- Modern rehab includes **rest** as essential recovery time after trauma. **Active rest** means that low level exercises are undertaken in order to improve the blood flow through affected areas without physical stress, and therefore to promote healing via blood carried nutrients, particularly oxygen.
- This also has the effect of preventing a muscle or other soft tissue from healing at a shorter length than it was before the injury. This is because post-trauma muscle length is unpredictable depending on joint flexibility and nutrition.
- Low level activity also has the effect of keeping muscle fit enough to exert force once an injury is healed.

Oxygen

Research has found that healing is promoted by increasing the oxygen partial pressure surrounding affected areas. The various techniques employed to promote this are:

- Oxygen tents.
- Sleeping in a greater than normal proportion of oxygen in breathed air.
- Hyperbaric (meaning high pressure) chambers, in which an injured athlete will spend periods of time in a zone in which the air pressure is above normal.
- Therefore forcing oxygen above normal pressure into the body. This is called **hyperbaric oxygen therapy** (**HBOT**).

HBOT greatly stimulates the growth of new blood vessels, thus improving blood flow to areas with arterial blockage that may have resulted from an impact injury. HBOT is also known to aid repair of stress fractures and breaks.

A further feature of this therapy is the treatment of infection, by boosting white blood cell activity around the damaged tissues, thereby controlling infection.

figure 6.11 – are ice baths fun?

Massage

Massage has a place in rehab from injury. During massage, joints and associated muscles can be passively moved to full range. Massage helps reduce DOMS symptoms. Care must be taken that excessive forces are not applied to traumatised tissue.

Ice

The use of cold therapy (**cryotherapy**) in acute sports injuries as well as in the rehabilitation of the injured athlete and injury prevention has become a generally accepted treatment method. Various cooling methods are used to apply cold to the injured area, for example, **ice packs**, ice towels, ice massage, frozen gel packs and **ice baths**. Its goal is to decrease cellular metabolism, decrease inflammation, pain and spasm, and promote vasoconstriction.

Ice baths (figure 6.11) use the fact that local tissue inflammation can be reduced by chilling the affected area. Athletes use total immersion ice baths or cryogenic chambers to implement this therapy.

figure 6.12 – aquajogging

Research has shown that the impact of an injury is substantially reduced by this therapy, and the sooner after the injury occurs, the more effective the therapy.

Precautions should be taken because prolonged application at very low temperatures could have detrimental effects.

Water-based training

Water-based activities such as aquajogging (figure 6.12), have proven a very good form of rehabilitation. This is because of its low impact on the muscles and the use of water resistance as an effective way of applying force to the lower limbs. This combination avoids muscle soreness, stress fractures and aching joints and enables an injured athlete to maintain fitness during a rehabilitation programme.

DOMS or Delayed Onset Muscle Soreness

Delayed onset muscle soreness is felt as tenderness and pain within a muscle belly, between 8 and 48 hours after intense training. It has two causes:

- **Excess lactic acid** delivered and retained in muscle following intense anaerobic exercise, primarily during eccentric muscle activity.
- **Micro-tears** and the resulting inflammation in muscle tissue occurring as part of the normal intense training process.

If intense exercise is repeated using muscles already affected by DOMS, there is a strong risk of muscle trauma.

DOMS can be reduced by having greater recovery between repetitions or sets or sessions, and by using therapies such as massage or ice.

Training programmes should include a progressive build up of exercise loading, and moderate concentric exercise to protect against muscle soreness.

Cool-down

Cool-down is the major way of reducing DOMS, and should be a part of every sportsperson's training.

The aim of a cool-down (figure 6.13) is to gradually return the body to its former resting state. This is achieved by performing low intensity exercise such as jogging and stretching. Static stretches during cool-down can increase flexibility of joints.

figure 6.13 – cool-down

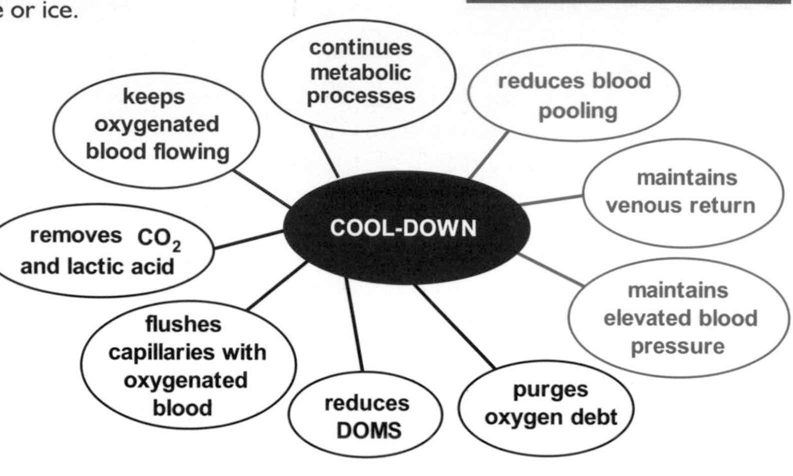

STUDENT NOTE

Refer to page 81 of AS Revise PE for AQA, ISBN: 978 1 901424 56 0, for notes on cool-down.

Practice questions

1) Sports injuries can be broadly classified as either acute or chronic injuries. Explain what is meant by these two classifications, using examples where appropriate. 4 marks

2) Playing kit and equipment are major factors that an athlete needs to consider in injury prevention. Identify the key factors that affect the selection of their use. 4 marks

3) Describe the RICE approach to the initial treatment of injuries. 4 marks

4) a) What is meant by the term over-training? 2 marks

   b) How can over-training lead to injuries? 2 marks

5) Discuss the principles and guidelines for injury prevention. 5 marks

6) Why should stretching be part of an injury preventative training programme? 2 marks

7) a) How does core stability assist in injury prevention? 3 marks

   b) Identify and describe a stabilisation exercise that would be suitable within a rehabilitation programme. 3 marks

8) Hyperbaric oxygen chambers and ice baths are aids to rehabilitation for elite performers. Briefly describe how each of these therapies assist in this process. 6 marks

9) What is meant by the term DOMS? How is it caused and how can its effect be reduced? 7 marks

CHAPTER 7 – LINEAR MOTION AND NEWTON'S LAWS

Vectors and scalars

figure 7.1 – direction of a vector

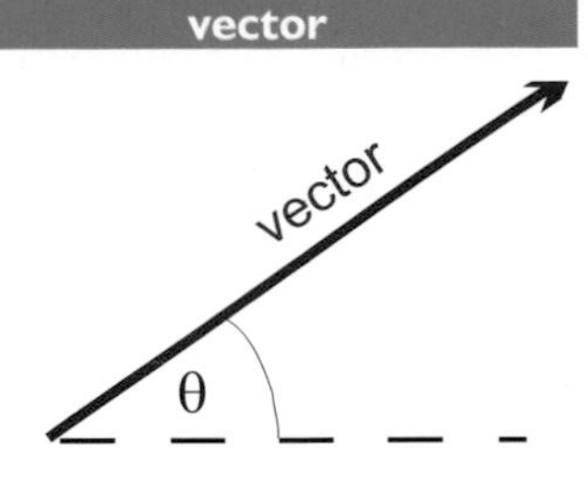

The ideas behind **vectors** and **scalars** are used extensively in maths and physics. A **vector** is a quantity which has **size** (called magnitude) and **direction**. By quantity we mean something like weight, displacement, velocity, acceleration, force, and momentum, all of which are vectors, and therefore have to have a direction connected to them as well as value or size. For example, a force could be 100 newtons downward (the downward specifies the direction), an acceleration could be 10 metres per second squared forwards (the forwards specifies the direction).

Usually in maths, the direction is specified by the angle to the x-axis in a graph of an arrow drawn on the graph, with the value represented by the length of the arrow (figure 7.1).

figure 7.2 – vectors cancel out

A **scalar** is a quantity which has size or value only. Quantities like mass, speed, energy, power, and length have a value only. For example, a person could have a mass of 60 kg, or an amount of 1000 joules of energy are used up when performing an exercise. No directional angle is required when talking about these quantities.

The point of this is that when more than one vector has to be taken into account, then they must be added together taking note of the direction of each vector. In figure 7.2 for example, two forces of 500 newtons are acting, the green force acts upwards, and the red force acts downwards. Because they are acting in opposite directions, they add up to nil, in other words they exactly cancel out to give zero net force.

- In figure 7.3, the vertical forces acting on the sprinter are the weight (W = force due to gravity) acting downwards, and the ground reaction force (R) acting upwards. These two forces are identical in value but opposite in direction and therefore cancel out exactly to give zero net force vertically.
- The horizontal forces are the friction force (F) acting forwards, and the **air resistance** or drag (A) acting backwards. These two forces are equal in value but opposite in direction, and hence cancel out to give zero net force acting horizontally.
- Hence relatively large forces can act, but they can cancel out because of their direction. Note that zero net force does not mean that the sprinter is stationary, see Newton's first law of motion (page 57 below).

figure 7.3 – forces cancel out

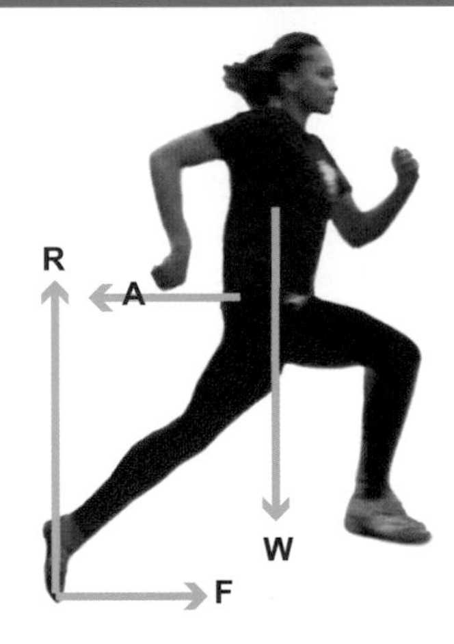

Weight and mass

These two ideas are often confused. **Mass** is a scalar and represents the total quantity of matter in an object. **Weight** is the force due to gravity on a mass (with a direction towards the centre of the Earth) and can be calculated from the fact that the gravitational field strength at the Earth's surface is approximately 10 newtons for each kilogramme of mass. Hence if the mass of the sprinter in figure 7.3 is 50 kg, then her weight would be 50 x 10 = 500 newtons towards the centre of the Earth.

STUDENT NOTE

If this sprinter were to obtain astronaut status and visit the moon (where the gravitational field strength is 1.67 newtons per kilogramme), then her mass would still be 50 kg, but her weight would be 50 x 1.67 = 83.5 newtons towards the centre of the moon.

Distance and displacement

Distance is a scalar - usually measured in metres, **displacement** is a distance (also measured in metres) as the crow flies from start to finish of a movement. **Displacement** therefore has a value and a direction and is a **vector**.

For example, the total distance run in a 10k race will be 10,000 metres - and this is the measure which the runner will be interested in. But the displacement will be zero, since the start and finish of a 10k race are usually in the same place. Start and finish of a marathon race are often not in the same place, so the displacement between start and finish will have a value in metres and a direction. But again, runners will be interested in the distance ran, not the displacement between start and finish.

Speed and velocity

Speed = **distance moved / time taken** or **v = s / t** unit ms^{-1}

= **scalar** (no direction)

= distance moved in 1 second

Velocity = speed in a given **direction**

= **vector**

figure 7.4 – distance time graph

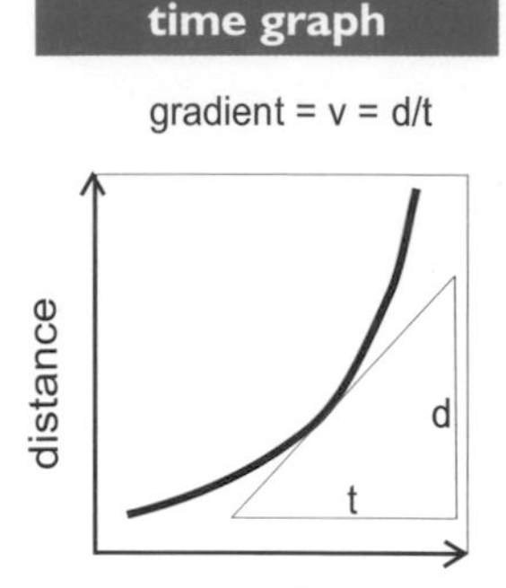

The vector property of velocity is important because not only does it add up or cancel out a bit like the force example in figure 7.3, but it can change direction without changing value. Examples of this are a swerving rugby player, or the head of a hammer which moves in a circular path, both of whose velocity changes in direction. This means that the player or the hammer head is accelerating which means that from Newton's second law (see page 57 below) a force is required.

If you plot a graph of distance against time for a 100m sprinter, then the gradient of the graph will be a measure of speed (figure 7.4).

Acceleration

Acceleration = **change of velocity / time taken to change** a = v - u / t unit ms^{-2}

- **Acceleration** will be in the same direction as net force, and therefore acceleration is a vector (has direction).
- In the case of the swerving rugby player, the direction of acceleration is along the radius of the path of the player. This is a **radial acceleration**.
- **Deceleration** is **negative acceleration** (slowing down).

figure 7.5 – velocity time graph

velocity

time

The 100 metre sprinter

A graph of velocity against time for a 100m sprinter will look as in figure 7.5. An upward slope (positive gradient) means an increase in speed hence acceleration, and a downward slope means a negative acceleration or deceleration. The gradient of the graph at any point is the acceleration, with the area under the graph being the distance moved.

- At the **start of the race** (figure 7.6a), there is a steep upwards slope which means a large acceleration. This corresponds with a large forward net force applied at the start when friction is a large forward force acting on the foot of the runner. From figure 7.6a you will see that the vertical forces cancel out, and the friction force forward is much larger than the air resistance drag force backward. This produces a large net (resultant) force forward (marked in black on figure 7.6a). This force provides forward acceleration (from Newton's second law, see page 57 opposite).
- During the **middle of the run** (figure 7.6b), the velocity time graph is almost level, which means that acceleration is almost zero, therefore forces cancel out.
- At the **end of the run** (figure 7.6c), the velocity time graph has a small negative slope, which means that the sprinter decelerates, and that therefore there is a net force backwards (shown in black).

figure 7.6 – start, middle and end of a sprint

See page 58 below for the application of the concepts of momentum and impulse to the sprinter.

Newton's laws of motion

Newton's first law

Newton's first law of motion describes what happens when **zero net force** acts, which means that all forces acting must cancel out. In figure 7.6b, the forces (green arrows) **cancel out**. The vertical forces are the same size (arrows are the same length) but in opposite directions. The horizontal forces are also of the same size and in opposite directions, hence all forces cancel out.

When there is zero net force acting on an object:

- The object is **stationary**.
- **Or** the object moves at **constant velocity**.

Hence when any object moves at constant velocity, all forces must cancel out, the net force must be zero.

This law is also known as the law of **inertia**. The concept of inertia is that a massive object will remain at rest and will require a force to shift it, and once moving, will require a force to change its motion (accelerate or decelerate it).

Newton's second law

Newton's second law of motion describes what happens when a **net force acts** on a body. **A net force** produces **acceleration** or **deceleration** of the body or changes the direction of the body (swerving). In the motion of a sprinter the acceleration is produced by the net force applied, which must be forwards if the sprinter is accelerating forwards. When the sprinter **decelerates**, there is a net **force backwards**. In figure 7.6c, the vertical arrows (representing vertical forces) are the same length but in opposite directions, and hence cancel out. The horizontal forces are both acting backwards, therefore there is a net force acting backwards on her. This means that she is **decelerating** (horizontally!).

- Newton's second law also says that the bigger the **net** force, the greater the **acceleration** of the person.
- Hence a **stronger** sprinter should be able to **accelerate** out of the blocks quicker.
- However, the more mass an object has, the less the acceleration for a given force.
- Hence a heavier (more massive) sprinter will accelerate less than a lighter sprinter.

This is expressed mathematically as: $F = m \times a$ (force = mass x acceleration)

As discussed above, slowing down (**deceleration**) is also caused by force – so a bike hitting a barrier encounters a large force, large deceleration slows the bike very quickly – possibly wrecking it and hurting the rider. However, if the cyclist had applied the brakes moderately, he or she would have encountered less deceleration, taking longer to stop, but would do so safely.

Newton's third law

Newton's third law of motion describes what happens when **two bodies** (or objects) exert forces on one another. Action and reaction are equal and opposite and always occur in pairs.

figure 7.7 – a swimmer pushes away the water

Action acts on one of the bodies, and the **reaction** to this action acts on the other body. At a sprint start, the athlete **pushes back** on the blocks as hard as possible (this is the **'action'**), and the blocks **push forward** on the athlete (this push forward is the **'reaction'**) - and provides forward acceleration on the athlete. In figure 7.7, a swimmer pushes backwards on the water with hands and feet (this is the force in **black** – the **action**). At the same time, the water thrusts the swimmer forward (this is the force in **red** – the **reaction**).

figure 7.8 – forces at origin and insertion

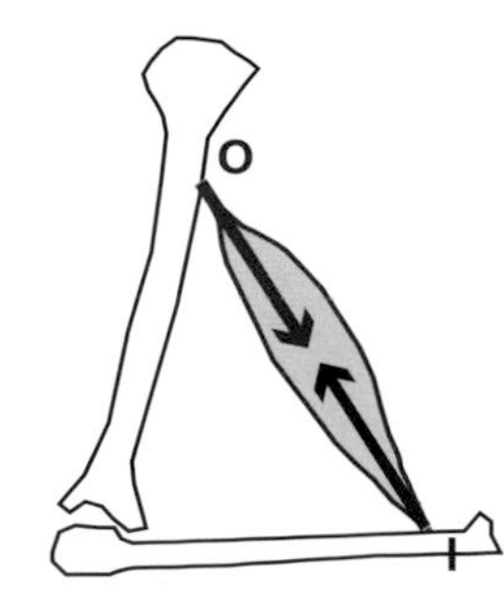

For **internal forces** within the body, for example in figure 7.8, the origin (**O**) and insertion (**I**) of a muscle pull in opposite directions to change the shape of the body. In this example, the **action** is the pull of the muscle (red arrow) on the origin of the muscle, and the **reaction** is the pull of the muscle (**black arrow**) at its opposite end, on the insertion. The effect is to change the shape of the person, by pulling the origin towards the insertion, and bending the limb in question.

Momentum

Momentum is a concept derived from Newton's second law which says: **force** = **rate of change of momentum**

(linear) **momentum** = **mass** x **velocity**

Note that linear means in a straight line, and that momentum includes both mass and velocity.

- Hence an object which has a lot of momentum requires a lot of force to stop it, which is a good argument for fast heavy rugby players or American footballers.
- Momentum is a vector (and therefore has direction).

Impulse

Impulse is another concept derived from Newton's second law. **force** = **rate of change of momentum**

$$= \frac{\text{change of momentum}}{\text{time taken to change}}$$

Hence force x time = total change of momentum

Impulse is defined as **force x time**, therefore **impulse** = **total change of momentum**

unit **newton second** (Ns)

This is useful when large forces are applied for short times. Examples of the use of impulse:

- A cricket fielder catching a hard cricket ball. The incoming cricket ball will change its momentum from some high value when travelling, to zero when caught. This fixes the impulse (force x time), so if you catch the ball in a short time, a large force will be exerted, and the ball will smack the hands and hurt! If, on the other hand you let the hands go with the ball, you would increase the time over which the momentum of the ball would change, and therefore reduce the force of impact. The hands would no longer hurt!
- A bat, racquet, stick, golf club striking a ball. If you use follow-through during a strike you would increase the time of contact with the ball, therefore increase the impulse, and increase the change of momentum of the ball. The ball would therefore leave the bat with greater velocity.
- A footballer kicking a ball. Again, follow-through will increase the time of contact and therefore increase the outgoing velocity of the ball.
- The turn in the discus throw. The turn increases the time over which force is applied, and therefore increases the impulse, and increases the final momentum of the discus. This therefore increases the speed of release and the distance thrown.

Impulse and force-time graphs

The formula: **impulse** = total change of momentum = force x time

can be used to calculate change of momentum if force and time the force is acting can be measured.

Using total change of momentum = force x time

Or total change of momentum = impulse

= **area under graph** of force against time

Once you have calculated the change of momentum, you can calculate the change of velocity (by dividing by the mass of the object experiencing the force).

Force-time graphs

The area under this graph is the **impulse**, and in the graph in figure 7.9 of the force between foot and ground during a foot strike when sprinting, the bigger the area under the graph, the bigger the impulse, and the greater the change of momentum of the runner (and hence the greater the acceleration and therefore the change of velocity).

figure 7.9 – area under a force-time graph

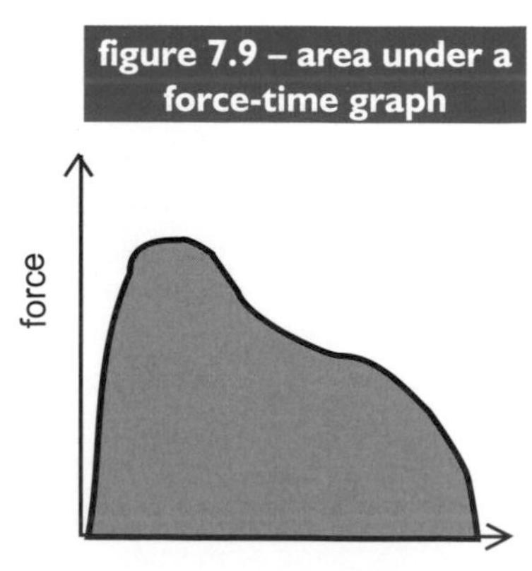

The sprinter

Figure 7.10 continues the theme started above of the 100 metre sprinter.

The graphs in figure 7.10 show the force-time graphs for the horizontal force acting on a single foot of a sprinter at four stages of a 100 metre sprint.

The sprinter

- **a** when the runner is in contact with starting blocks or immediately at the start.
- **b** when he or she is accelerating during the first 2–3 seconds of a run.
- **c** when the runner is running at approximately constant speed during the middle of a run.
- **d** during the slowing down at the end of a run.

- In figure 7.10a, the area under the **force–time curve** is above the horizontal axis (and hence **positive**), which means the force is acting **forwards** on the runner. The force lasts for a relatively long time, therefore the impulse is high and positive and would cause large forward acceleration and change of forward velocity of the runner.
- In figure 7.10b, some of the area of the graph is below the horizontal axis and therefore **negative** but the **overall impulse** is **positive**, meaning that the runner is still accelerating forwards but not now as much as in case (a).
- In figure 7.10c, the **positive** area above the horizontal axis is exactly **cancelled** by the **negative** area under the axis. This means that the **horizontal impulse is zero** so the sprinter would not be accelerating or decelerating and would be running at **constant speed**.
- In figure 7.10d, the **negative** area below the axis of the graph is **bigger** than the **positive** part and hence the **overall impulse is negative**. This means that the runner will be experiencing an overall **force** (averaged over the stride) **backwards** and hence would be **decelerating** or losing speed.

figure 7.10 – horizontal foot impulse during a sprint

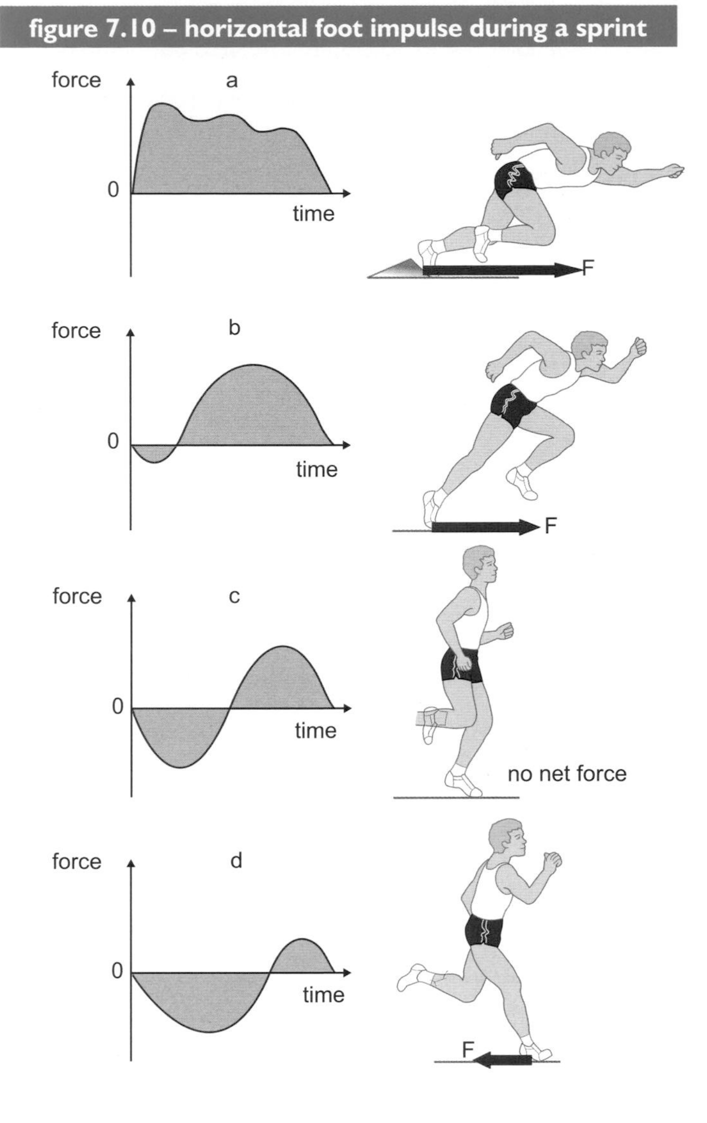

In Figures 7.10 b, c and d, the parts of the graphs which show a negative impulse (area below the horizontal axis of the graph) correspond to the situation where the foot placement is in front of the runner's centre of mass and so exerts a backwards force for a short time. This is immediately followed by the centre of mass moving forward over the contact foot which then applies a forward force on the runner and hence a positive impulse for the latter part of the foot contact.

Practice questions

1) Table 7.1 shows the speed of a 19 year-old male sprinter during a 200 m race.

Table 7.1 – **data for a 200 metres sprint**

speed/ms^{-1}	time/seconds
0.0	0
6.0	1
7.5	2
8.2	3
8.4	4
8.5	5
8.5	7
8.4	8
8.3	10
8.2	13
8.1	18
8.0	22

a) Plot a graph of speed against time during this race.
When does he reach maximum speed and what happens to his speed between 8 and 22 seconds? 7 marks

b) Use the graph to establish his speed at 0.5 seconds and 1.5 seconds and calculate the average acceleration between 0.5 and 1.5 seconds. 3 marks

c) Successful games players are often able to change their velocity rapidly in the game situation. Explain the biomechanics behind this ability using examples from a game of your choice. 6 marks

2) a) A sprinter uses her calf muscles to push on the blocks at the start of a run. Explain, using Newton's Laws, how this enables her to accelerate forwards out of the blocks. 3 marks

b) If the resultant forward force was 300 newtons and the runner's mass was 60 kg, what would be her acceleration? 2 marks

c) What would be the speed of the runner after 1.5 seconds, assuming that the acceleration is the same over that period of time? 2 marks

d) A squash player drives forward into a forehand stroke. Show how Newton's third law of motion explains his ability to do this. 3 marks

e) Explain why the turn in the discus throw produces greater horizontal range than the standing throw. 3 marks

3) a) What characterises a vector quantity? 2 marks

b) Figure 7.11 shows the forces acting on a runner at the start of a race. Use a vector diagram to show how you could work out the resultant force acting. 3 marks

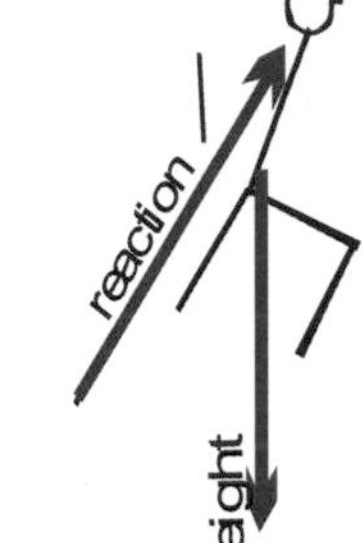

figure 7.11 – forces acting on a runner

c) Sketch a pin man drawing of a person standing still showing all the forces acting on him. 2 marks

d) Sketch a second diagram showing the vertical forces acting on a basketballer just before take-off while performing a jump shot. Represent the relative sizes of any forces you show by the length of the force arrows on your diagram. 2 marks

e) Use this second diagram and your understanding of Newton's laws of motion to explain why the basketballer is able to take off. If the vertical upward ground reaction force on him is 2000 N, and his weight is 800N, estimate the net upward force acting on him. 4 marks

4) The four man bobsleigh develops a large momentum during the first few seconds of its run.

a) Explain the meaning of the term momentum, and explain why the four man bobsleigh travelling at a speed of 28 ms^{-1} has a different momentum to a skier moving at the same speed. 2 marks

b) Explain using Newton's laws of motion how the bobsleigh acquires its large momentum during the first part of a run. 4 marks

5) The follow-through is an important aspect of a forehand ground stroke in tennis.

a) Sketch a graph of the force applied by the racquet (y axis) against time (x axis). Show the effect of a follow-through on your graph. 2 marks

b) Explain how the use of a follow-through would affect the motion of the ball. 4 marks

6) a) In a tennis match, the ball travels towards a player at 35 ms^{-1}. The ball has a mass of 80 g and the racket head has a mass of 0.6 kg. The racket head moves towards the ball at 10 ms^{-1}.
Calculate the momentum of the racket and the ball before contact. 3 marks

b) If the player stops the racket moving on contact with the ball, calculate the velocity of the ball after contact. 3 marks

c) The graphs in figure 7.12 show the forces acting on a runner's foot during a 100m sprint.

figure 7.12 – force acting on a sprinter's foot

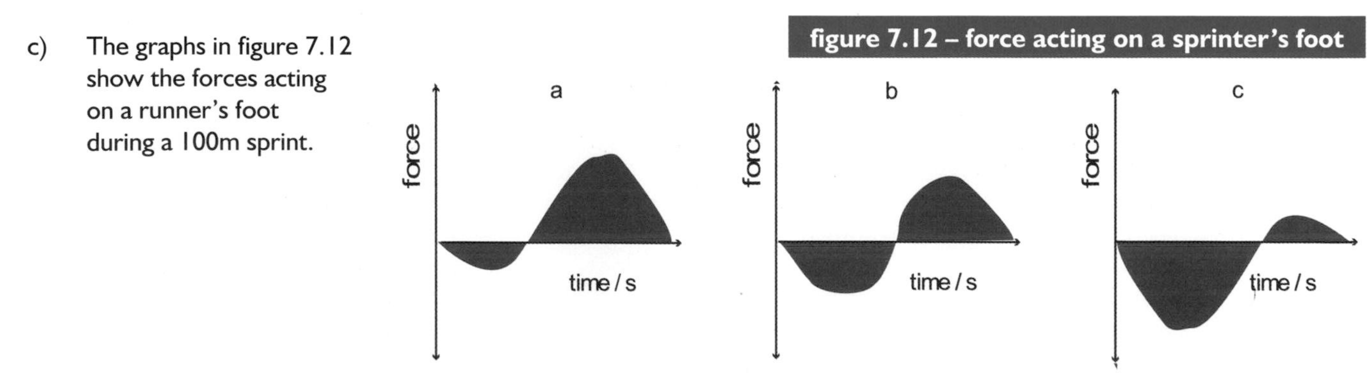

For each graph, describe the resultant impulse force and the motion that occurs. 6 marks

CHAPTER 8 – APPLICATION OF FORCE

Types of force

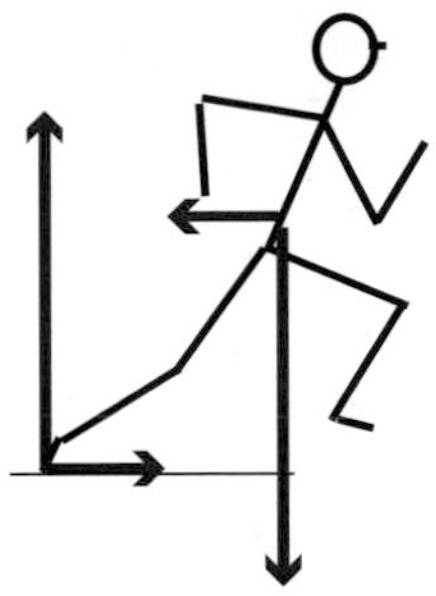

Force is push or pull. The unit of force is the **newton** (10 N is approx the weight of 1 kg). Force changes the state of motion of an object, and causes acceleration or deceleration or change of direction.

One newton of force is the force required to produce an acceleration of 1 ms^{-2} in a mass of 1 kg. This is related to the inertial property of mass, the more force applied, the more acceleration produced (see Newton's second law, page 57 above).

figure 8.1 – pin-man or free-body diagram

Force has **direction** and size (**value**), and is therefore a vector. When describing a force it is important to explain where the force acts (the point of action), as well as the direction.

figure 8.2 – examples of reaction forces

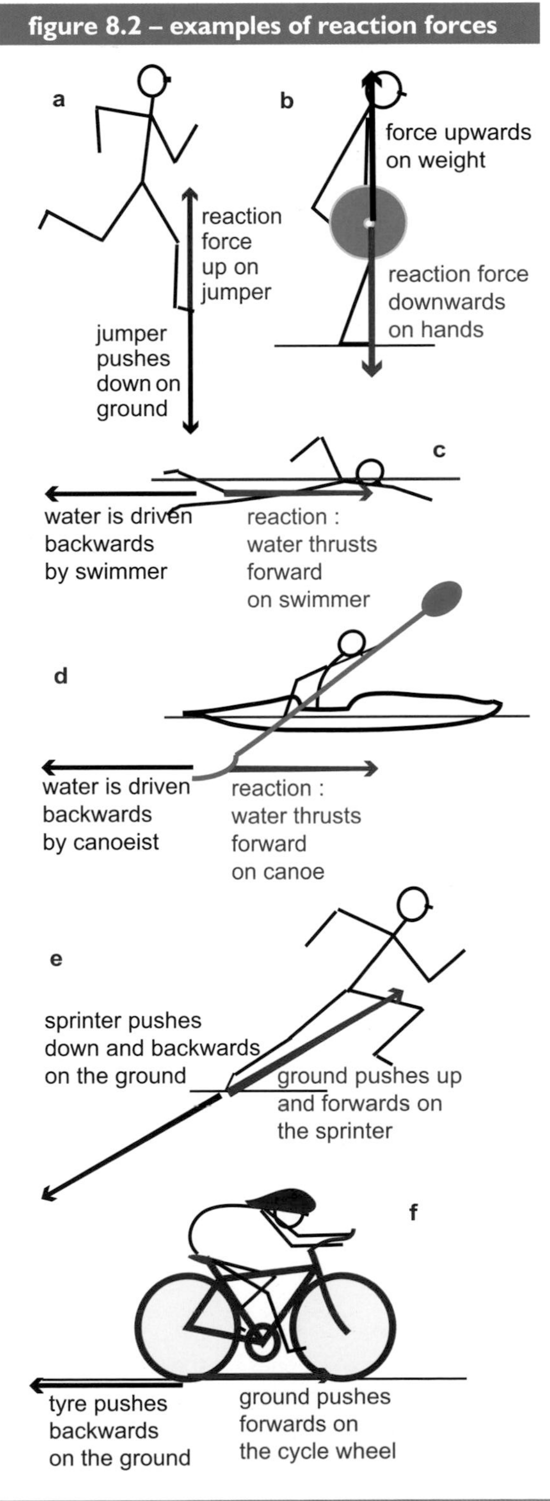

Pin men (free body) diagrams

It will be necessary when answering exam questions to use diagrams to represent the human body with forces acting on it. Free body diagrams are a way of doing this without any anatomical details.

In figure 8.1, a runner is represented by a pin man, with forces depicted by red arrows. The figure shows four forces acting, 2 forces acting up on the foot and down on the body, and 2 forces acting backwards on the body and forwards on the foot. Longer arrows mean greater force.

The **point of action** of a force is also important, remembering that drag forces will act over the whole body but are usually represented by a single arrow acting somewhere in the middle of the body, a friction force will act on the foot of the runner, and the weight will act on his or her centre of mass. Reaction forces act at the point of contact between two objects (on the foot of the runner in figure 8.1).

Reaction forces

Reaction forces are forces acting via Newton's third law as explained on page 57 above. When one object pushes on another, the first object experiences a force equal but opposite in direction to the second (figure 8.2):

- **a**, the jumper pushes down on the ground (black arrow), the ground pushes up on the jumper (red arrow).
- **b**, the weight lifter pulls up on the weight (black arrow), weight pulls down on lifter (red arrow).
- **c**, the swimmer pushes backwards on the water (black arrow), the water pushes forward on the swimmer (red arrow).
- **d**, canoeist pushes backwards on the water (black arrow), reaction force thrusts the canoe forward (red arrow).
- **e**, sprinter pushes back and down on the ground (black arrow), the ground pushes upwards and forwards on the sprinter (red arrow).
- **f**, in cycling, the tyre on the rear wheel pushes backward on the ground (black arrow), the ground pushes forward on the rear wheel (red arrow).

Weight

As discussed on page 55 above, **weight** is the force pulled downwards towards the centre of the Earth on any object by gravity. Weight will vary slightly over the surface of the Earth depending on the gravitational field strength.

Weight

The gravitational field strength changes slightly depending on the thickness of the Earth's crust, the longitude, the proximity of large mountains, and the height above sea level. Weight is approximately 10 newtons for each kilogramme of mass, and will act on the centre of mass of a body (the point which represents the averaged position of all the mass of a body), with examples shown in figure 8.3.

figure 8.3 – weight of various bodies

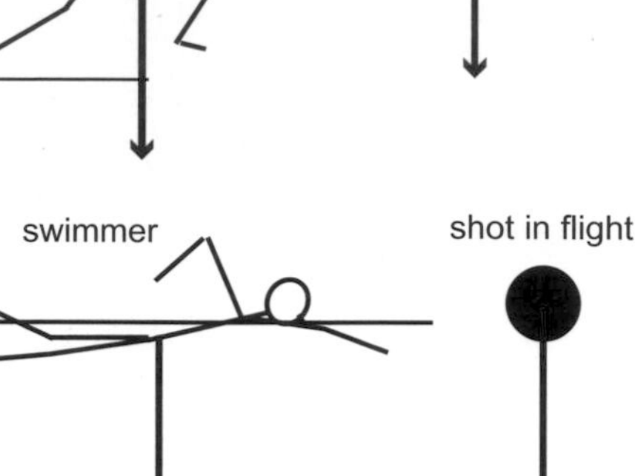

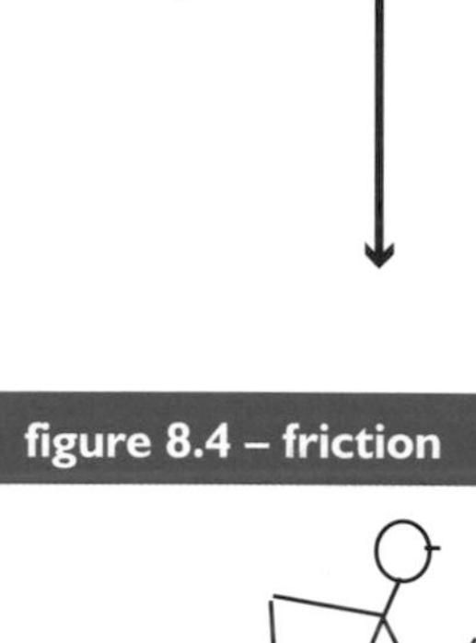

Weight is also the predominant force acting on an object projected into flight (see page 63 opposite).

Friction

Friction is a force which acts sideways between two surfaces which tend to slide past one another. This force enables sportspeople to accelerate, slow down, swerve, walk, and run.

The magnitude of friction depends on the grip of footwear on floor surface, and the nature of the surface itself (rough, smooth, slippy, greasy and so on), for example:

- Studs and spikes increase friction to enable better swerving and accelerating and decelerating in games or track situations. This applies to soft or wet surfaces.
- For dry hard surfaces, solid smooth rubber soles can give better friction as in discus or hammer shoes, rock climbing shoes, or tennis shoes for concrete surfaces.
- In snow and ice, long slender footwear (skates or skis) have low forward friction, but high sideways friction.

figure 8.4 – friction

friction acts forward on the foot of the accelerating sprinter

Note that friction acts forwards on the feet of the accelerating runner (see figure 8.4).

Friction depends on the force pressing the surfaces together, but not on the area of contact. For example:

- The inverted wings on racing cars increase the down force on wheels. This increases cornering friction between the wheels and the ground.
- When riding a mountain bike up a steep hill, you should sit back over the rear wheel to increase downward force on the rear wheel, so that there is more friction between the rear wheel and the ground.
- Friction also enables swerving by games players in rugby, soccer, hockey, and tennis. The friction force then acts sideways to the direction of motion, and changes the direction of motion.

Rolling or sliding friction

- **Rolling friction** is the term which describes the force between surfaces which do not move relative to one another, like a wheel rolling over a surface, or a foot driving and pushing without slipping. The friction can be anything from zero up to a maximum just before slipping occurs. As soon as slipping occurs, the friction force falls, and would not be enough to keep a sportsperson upright (so he or she slips over!).

- **Sliding friction** occurs when the two surfaces are moving relative to one another, and is always less then the maximum rolling friction. This is why ABS (advanced braking systems) will reduce braking force on wheels if sensors detect the beginning of sliding.

Fluid friction

Fluid friction (or **drag**) is a term applying to objects moving through fluids (gases or liquids). The force acts in the opposite direction to the direction of motion.

Fluid friction force depends on the shape and size of the moving object, the speed of the moving object, and the streamlining effect (summarised in figure 8.5).

figure 8.5 – factors affecting fluid friction

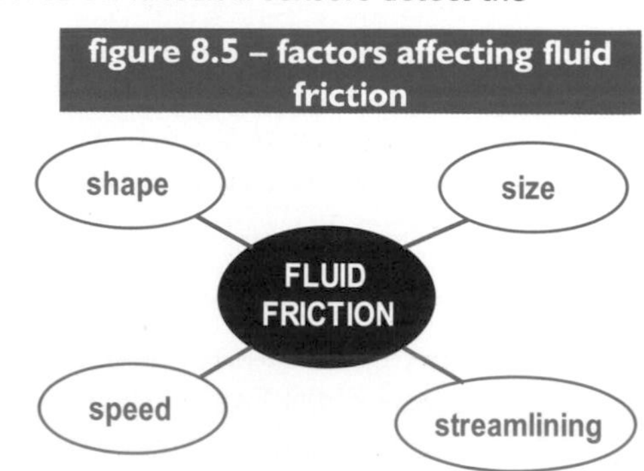

Drag

In order to minimise drag, the following developments affect sport:
- The body position and shape for a swimmer.
- The shape of helmets for cyclists.
- The use of lycra clothing.
- The shape of sports vehicles (cars or bikes).

Low values of fluid friction

This discussion concerns **low values of drag** compared with other forces. Examples are:
- Any sprinter or game player for whom air resistance is usually much less than friction effects and weight. Therefore streamlining is seen as less important.
- A shot or hammer in flight, in which air resistance would be much less than the weight, and therefore the angle of release should be around 45°.

High values of fluid friction

High values of drag will occur for any sportsperson or vehicle moving through water, and hence fluid friction is the critical factor governing swimming speed.
- Body shape or cross section, and clothing (surface material to assist laminar flow, see below), are adjusted to minimise fluid friction.

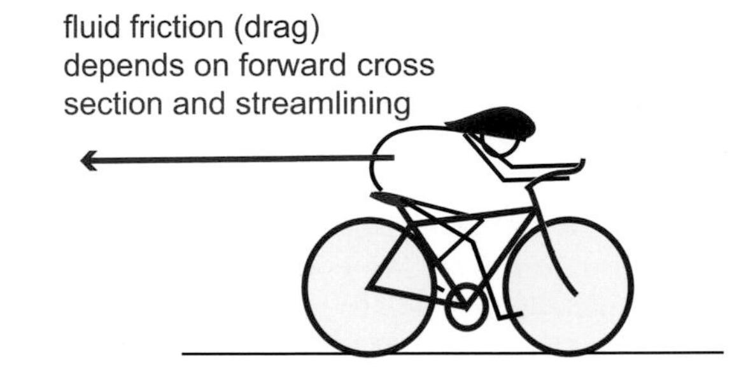

figure 8.6 – a cyclist needs good streamlining

A cyclist (figure 8.6) travels much faster than a runner and therefore has high fluid friction:
- He or she crouches low to reduce forward cross section.
- The helmet is designed to minimise turbulent flow.
- Clothing and wheel profiles are designed to assist streamlining.

Cross sectional area is the area of the moving object as viewed from the front. The smaller the better to reduce drag, hence cyclists crouch down, and keep elbows in!

Laminar flow and drag

Fluid friction (or drag) depends on **laminar** flow, the smooth flowing of air or water past an object. Laminar means flowing in layers, and streamlining assists laminar flow. Figure 8.7 shows images of a streamlined helmet, and a non-streamlined helmet. The point of the streamlined shape is that the air moves past it in layers whereas in the case of the non streamlined helmet, vortices are formed where the fluid does not flow smoothly. When this happens bits of fluid are flung randomly sideways which causes drag. The drag is caused by bits of fluid being dragged along with the moving object (the cycle helmet).

figure 8.7 – laminar flow and vortex flow

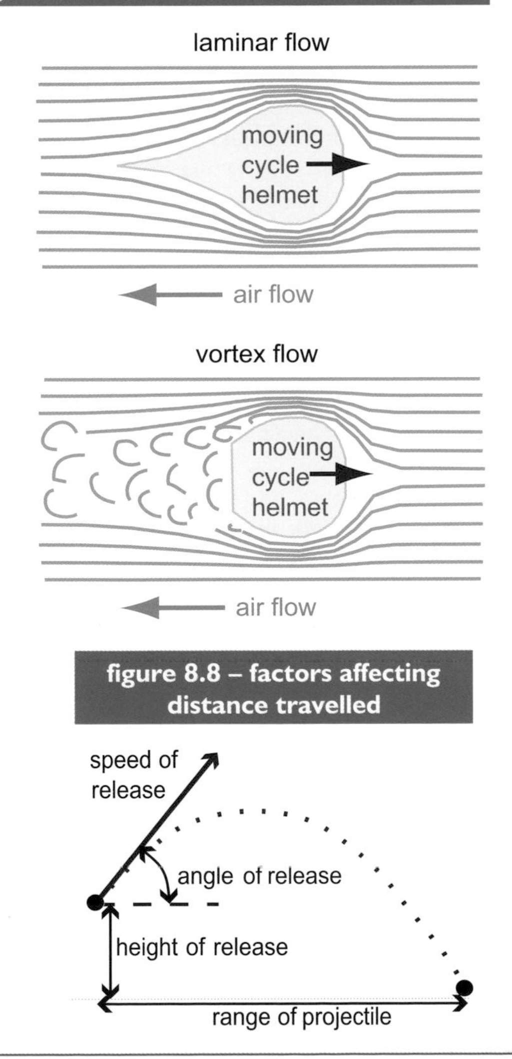

figure 8.8 – factors affecting distance travelled

Projectiles

This segment looks at the motion of objects in flight, such as human bodies (during the flight phase of a jump), throwing implements (shot, discus, javelin or hammer), and soccer, rugby, cricket, tennis or golf balls.

The flight is governed by the forces acting, the weight, air resistance, Magnus effect, aerodynamic lift, and the direction of motion. If weight were the only force acting, the flight path would be parabolic in shape, and some flight paths are similar to this (shot or hammer, the human body in jumps or tumbles or dives, where weight is the predominant force acting).

Distance travelled by a projectile

Figure 8.8 summarises the factors which influence the distance travelled, the angle of release, the speed of release, and the height of release.

Components of velocity during flight

Near the start of the flight:

- There is a large upward vertical component v_v.
- But a fixed horizontal component v_h.

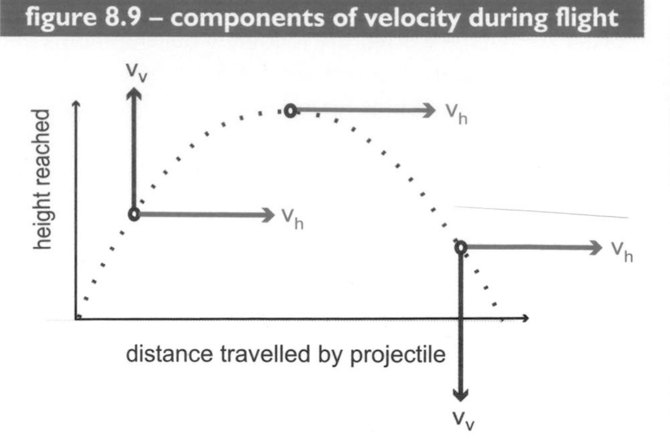

figure 8.9 – components of velocity during flight

At the middle of the flight:

- There is zero upward vertical component, since the object moves entirely horizontally at this point.
- There is still a fixed horizontal component v_h, which is the same as at the start.

Near the end of the flight:

- There is a large downward vertical component v_v, which is almost the same as the horizontal component since the object is travelling at approx 45° to the horizontal downwards.
- There is still a fixed horizontal component v_h, which is the same as at the start.

The relative size of forces during flight

The faster the projectile travels the greater will be the air resistance.
Aerodynamic lift applies to thrown objects with a wing shape profile (such as a javelin, discus, rugby ball, American football, and a frisbee).
The **Magnus effect** applies to spinning balls, but is not covered in this syllabus.

If the shapes of the flight path differ from a parabola then some combination of these forces must be relatively large compared with the weight.

For example:
For a badminton shuttle **struck hard** (figure 8.10a), the air resistance is very large compared with the weight, because the shuttle is moving quickly. The resultant force will therefore be very close to the air resistance. This would make the shuttle slow down rapidly over the **first part of the flight**.
Later in the flight of the badminton shuttle (figure 8.10b), when the shuttle is moving much more slowly, the air resistance is much less and comparable with the weight. This pattern of the resultant force changing markedly during the flight predicts a markedly asymmetric path.

figure 8.10 – forces on a badminton shuttle

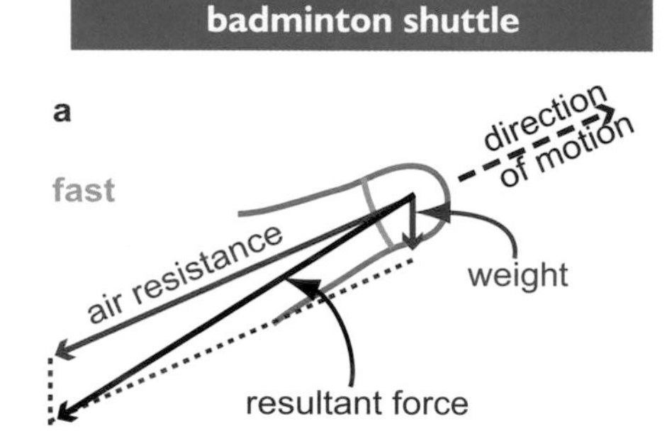

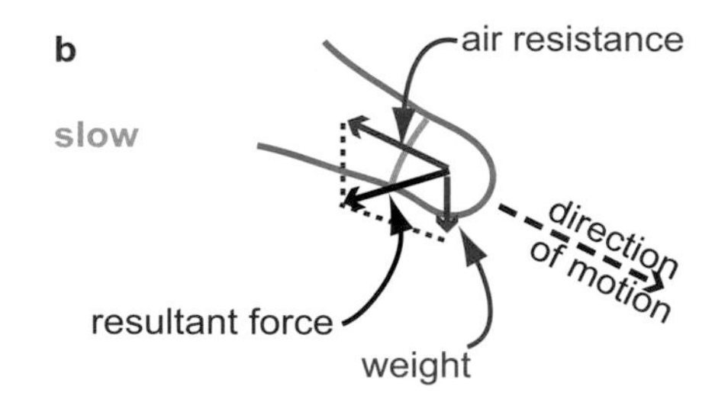

Lift forces

Lift forces are caused by bulk displacement of fluid and are similar to air resistance. They are caused by a wing shaped object moving through the air, like a discus or ski jumper.

As it moves forward and falls through the air, it pushes aside the air, creating a higher pressure underneath the object and a lower pressure over the top of the object. This creates a lift force which is similar to the force which enables a stone to skip over the surface of water.

Practice questions

1) Tennis players have to change direction quickly during a match to recover to the centre of the court. Figure 8.11 shows a tennis player just after hitting a forehand and then starting to recover to the centre of the court in the direction shown.

figure 8.11 – tennis player moves

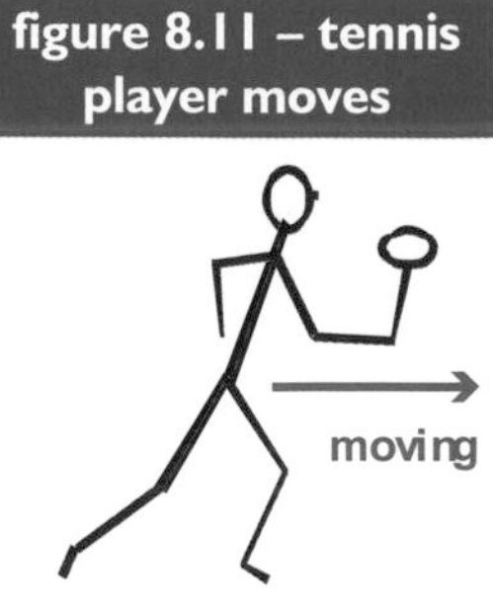

   a) Draw a pin diagram of the tennis player as he pushes off the court surface to recover to the centre of the court, showing all forces acting on the tennis player at this point. All forces must be clearly identified. 3 marks

   b) Explain the factors that affect the horizontal force at this point. Apply Newton's second law of motion to explain the effect of this force on the player. 4 marks

2) A sprinter uses her calf muscles to push on the blocks at the start of a run. Sketch a pin man diagram of the forces acting and use this to explain how this produces a forward force on her. 3 marks

3) Explain the nature of the reaction force which provides forwards impulsion for a cyclist. 4 marks

4) a) Using examples, explain how the shape of an object can alter its flight path. 4 marks

b) Explain the effect of air resistance on the flight of two badminton shuttles, one of which has been struck hard and the other gently. 10 marks

c) Briefly explain why the flight path of a shot in athletics is so different from the flight of a badminton shuttle. 4 marks

5) a) Identify three physical factors (not skill factors) which govern a swimmer's speed and explain how one of these occurs. 3 marks

b) Describe the factors which determine the amount of fluid friction acting on a swimmer. 4 marks

c) Explain how you would minimise turbulent flow (high drag) of the water past the swimmer's body. 2 marks

d) Give three examples, each from a different sporting context, to show how fluid friction affects the sportsperson. 3 marks

e) How would you attempt to reduce fluid friction? 3 marks

f) Look at figure 8.12 showing the vertical forces acting on a swimmer during a stroke. Explain why it is difficult for a swimmer to keep a horizontal floating position. 4 marks

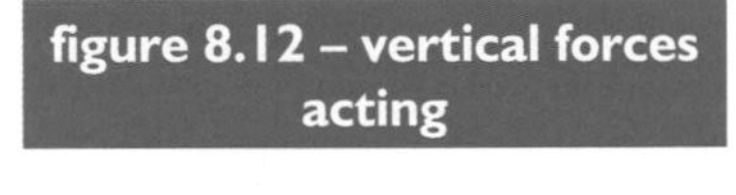

figure 8.12 – vertical forces acting

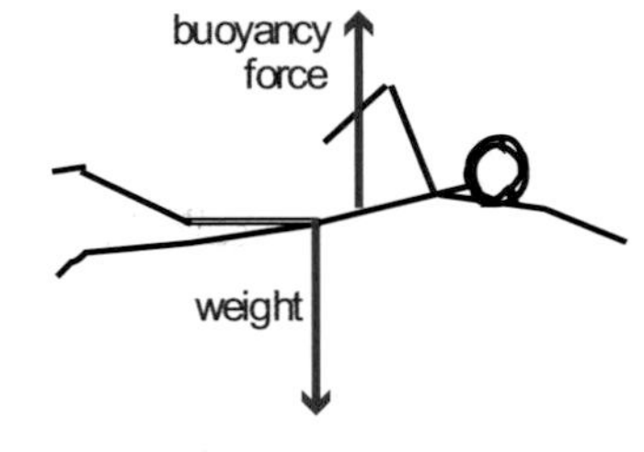

6) a) Fluid friction is a force which acts on a bobsleigh once it is moving. Identify the nature of the fluid friction in this case and explain how this might limit the maximum speed of the bob. 3 marks

b) Explain the term 'turbulent flow', and how the bobsleigh is used to minimise this factor. 3 marks

7) a) Sketch a diagram to show the flight path of a shot from the moment it leaves the putter's hand to the moment it lands. 2 marks

b) State and briefly explain three factors (excluding air effects) which should be used by the putter to optimise the distance thrown. 6 marks

c) Explain why the turn in a discus throw produces greater horizontal range than the standing throw. 3 marks

CHAPTER 9 – ANGULAR MOTION

figure 9.1 – moment of force

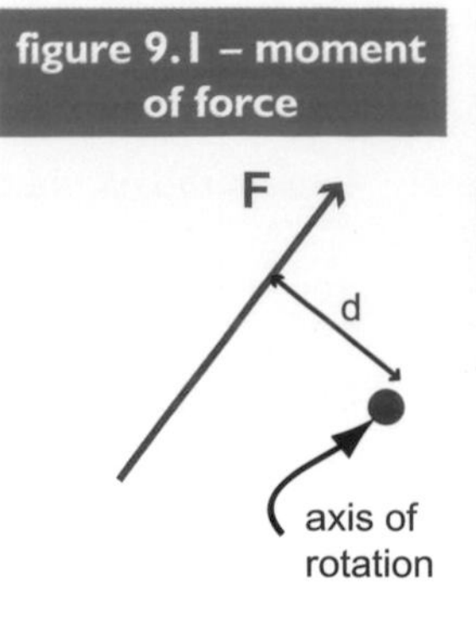

Moment of force

Moment of force, also called torque or couple, these are all terms which describe the turning effect produced by a force, when it acts eccentrically (to one side of) to an axis of rotation (see figure 9.1). The moment = F x d. Such a moment would cause rotation or turning about the axis of rotation.

Angle (angular displacement)

To be scientifically correct angle should not be measured in degrees, but in radians, see figure 9.2.

$$\text{Angle} = \frac{\text{arc length}}{\text{radius of arc}} = \frac{l}{r}$$

360 degrees = 2 x π radians = 6.28 radians.
180° = π radians = 3.14 radians.
90° = 1/2 π radians = 1.57 radians.
30° = 1/6 π radians = 0.52 radians.
and so on (see maths text book for more).

figure 9.2 – angle

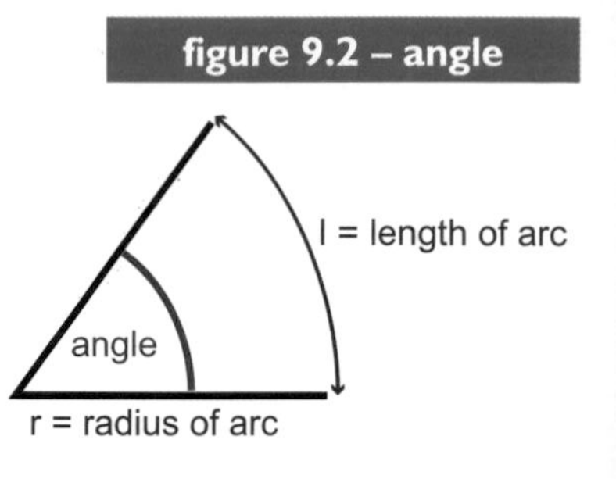

Angular velocity

Angular velocity = angle turned through per second

$$\omega = \frac{\text{angle turned through}}{\text{time taken}} = \frac{\theta}{t} \qquad (\theta = \text{symbol for angle})$$

ω = Greek letter omega. (ω = symbol for angular velocity)

This is **rate of spin**, most easily understood as revolutions per second (revs per sec). Revs per sec would have to be converted to the unit radians per second (radians s^{-1}) for calculations.

1 rev per second = 2 x π = 6.28 radians s^{-1}.

Rates of spin apply to:

- Tumbling gymnasts.
- Trampolinists (piked straight and tucked somersaults).
- Discus and hammer throwers.
- Spinning skaters.
- Skiers turning and twisting between slalom gates.

figure 9.3 – angular velocity

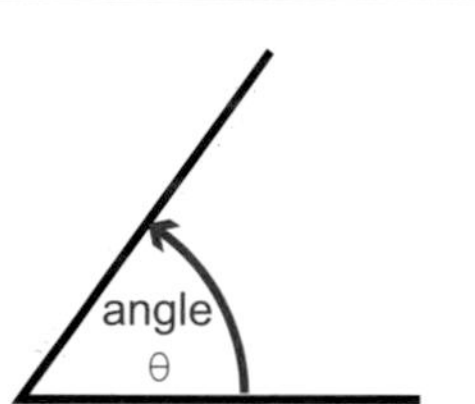

Moment of inertia (MI)

Moment of inertia is the equivalent of mass for rotating systems, it is rotational inertia. The mathematical formula is $MI = \Sigma mr^2$

Objects rotating with large MI require large moments of force (torque) to change their angular velocity, and objects with small MI require small moments of force (torque) to change their angular velocity or ω.

The formula above means that moment of inertia depends on the spread of mass away from the axis of spin, so as the body shape changes, the moment of inertia of the shape changes. The more spread out the mass, the bigger the MI.

The unit of MI is kilogramme metre squared kgm^2.

- Bodies with **arms held out wide** have large MI, the further the mass is away from the axis of rotation increases the MI dramatically.
- Sportspeople use this to control all spinning or turning movements.
- Pikes and tucks are good examples of use of MI, both reduce MI.

figure 9.4 – moments of inertia of different shapes

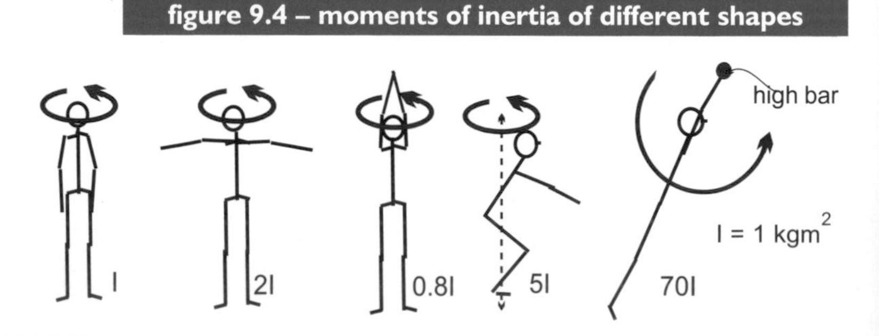

Values of moment of inertia

In figure 9.4, I is the MI for the left most pin man and has a value of about 1.0 kgm^2 for an average male person. From this diagram you can see how control of the arms will make a big difference to the value of MI, and that a tuck or pike can also change MI dramatically.

The sprinter's leg

This is an example of how a sportsperson uses moment of inertia to control his or her movement.

- From figure 9.5 you can see that when the leg is straight, the leg has high MI about the hip as axis. This therefore requires a large force or torque in the hip flexor muscles to swing the leg.
- On the other hand when fully bent, the leg has low MI, which therefore requires a low force or torque in the hip flexor muscles to swing the leg.
- Hence a sprinter tends to bring the leg through as bent as possible (with the heel as close to the backside as possible), and he or she will find that it is easier and faster the more bent the leg.

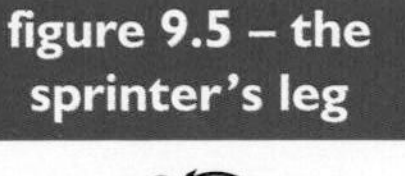

figure 9.5 – the sprinter's leg

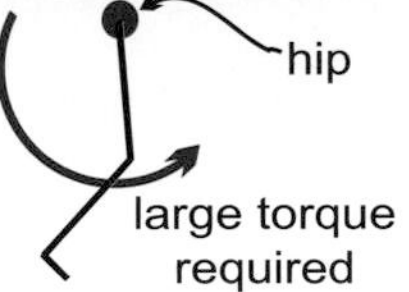

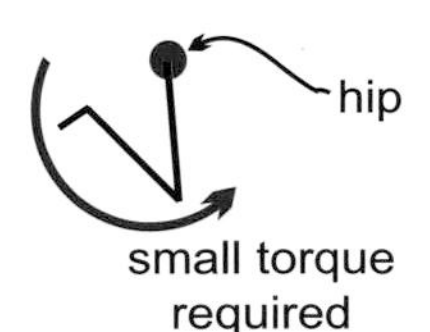

Angular momentum (H)

Angular momentum is a quantity used to describe what happens when bodies spin and turn, it is defined as:

angular momentum = **moment of inertia** x **angular velocity**
= **rotational inertia** x **rate of spin**

$$H = I \times \omega$$

Conservation of angular momentum

The **law of conservation of angular momentum** is a law of the universe which says that angular momentum of a spinning body remains the same (provided no external forces act).

- This means that a body which is spinning, twisting or tumbling will keep its value of H once the movement has started.
- Therefore if moment of inertia (I) changes by changing body shape, then angular velocity (ω) must also change to keep angular momentum (H) the same.
- So, if MI (I) **increases** (body spread out more) then ω must **decrease** (rate of spin gets less).
- And conversely, if MI (I) **decreases** (body tucked in more) then ω must **increase** (rate of spin gets bigger).
- Strictly, this is only exactly true if the body has no contact with its surroundings, as for example a high diver doing piked or tucked somersaults in the air, but it is almost true for the spinning skater!

figure 9.6 – a spinning skater

Sporting examples of conservation of momentum

- **The spinning skater**. If the arms are wide, the MI is large and the skater spins slowly. If the arms are narrow, MI is small and the skater will spin more quickly (figure 9.6).
- **The tumbling gymnast**. With the body position open, the MI is large and the gymnast (or diver or trampolinist) will spin slowly. When he or she creates a tucked body position, the MI is small and he or she will spin more quickly.
- **The dancer doing a spin jump**. The movement is initiated with arms held wide which would therefore have the highest possible MI. Immediately he or she has taken off, the angular momentum is conserved, and so by tucking the arms across the chest, this will create the lowest possible MI. This then means that he or she will acquire the highest possible rate of spin, so that more spins can be completed before landing.
- **The slalom skier**. The slalom skier crouches on approach to the gate and therefore will have a large turning MI. As he or she passes the gate, he or she stands straight up (reducing MI). This enables the person to turn rapidly past the gate, then he or she crouches again (figure 9.7 - increasing MI) to resume a slow turn between the gates.

figure 9.7 – a slalom skier

Practice questions

1) Define the term angular velocity. 2 marks

2) a) A diver can make a number of different shapes in the air (see table 9.1 for examples of these). Explain the meaning of moment of inertia (MI) in this context. 4 marks

b) During a dive a diver goes through the shapes shown in table 9.1.
Explain how the rate of spinning (angular velocity) would change through the dive. 5 marks

Table 9.1 - **data for shapes of diver during flight**

phase of dive	shape of diver	time during flight	MI of shape kgm^2
1	Z	0.0 - 0.5s	18
2	Y	0.5 - 0.7s	9
3	X	0.7 - 1.0s	3
4	Z	1.0 - 1.1s	18
entry	axis of rotation = ●	1.1s	

c) Sketch a graph of this rate of spinning against time. Your sketch need only be approximate. 4 marks

d) State the relationship between angular momentum, moment of inertia and angular velocity. 2 marks

e) Name the law of conservation which accounts for these variations in rate of spin. 1 mark

f) Explain and sketch the arc described by the diver as he or she falls. 3 marks

3) a) Describe in detail the body shape and movement within your chosen sporting situation where rates of spin are affected by body shape. 6 marks

b) How would you stop the spinning in this situation? 2 marks

c) Figure 9.8 shows a sportsperson's leg in two different positions. The values quoted are the moment of inertia of the leg as it rotates about the hip joint (shown as a red dot on each diagram). Explain the implications of these data for the efficiency of running style in a sprinter and long distance runner. 7 marks

figure 9.8 – shape of leg

hip
0.5 kgm^2

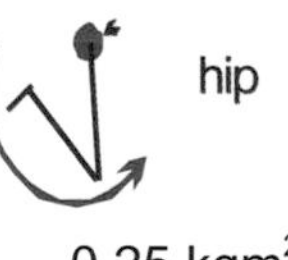

figure 9.9 – shapes of a gymnast

7 8 9

4) a) Figure 9.9 shows a gymnast undertaking a forward somersault following a run up. Sketch three traces on a single graph to represent any changes in angular momentum, moment of inertia and angular velocity for the period of activity between positions 2 and 9. 3 marks

b) Explain the shapes of the traces on the sketch graph that you have drawn. 6 marks

c) Table 9.2 sets out measurements of angular velocities (rates of spin) of the gymnast at successive frames from the start of the somersault.
Estimate from this table the ratio of angular velocities at times X and Y. 1 mark

d) If the moment of inertia of the gymnast is 8 kgm^2 at time **X**, estimate the moment of inertia at time **Y**, using data from the table in the chart. 2 marks

Table 9.2 - **data for angular velocity of gymnast**

	frame	angular velocity / degrees s^{-1}
	1	650
X	2	750
	3	850
	4	1100
	5	1400
Y	6	1500
	7	1000
	8	850
	9	650

SECTION B: PSYCHOLOGICAL ASPECTS THAT OPTIMISE PERFORMANCE

CHAPTER 10 – ASPECTS OF PERSONALITY

Personality is the term which describes the **unique** characteristics of an individual which makes him or her act as they do. Knowledge about personality is important to ensure **optimum** sporting performance.

Figure 10.1 outlines the main ideas various theorists have used to explain and describe personality and its features.

figure 10.1 – features of personality

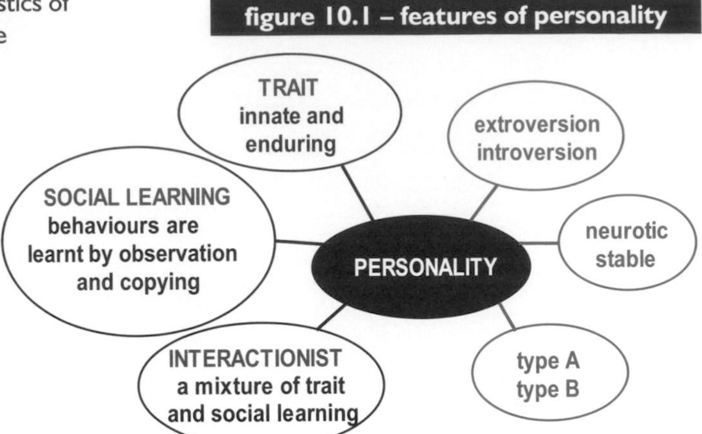

Theories of personality

Trait theories

Trait theories use the idea that a person has always had a feature of his or her personality, and always will have. Such features will be **general** (covering all situations), **underlying** (inside of and part of the person), **enduring** (long lasting), and include **predispositions** (inclinations or motives formed earlier). Such predispositions will tell you how a person will behave when faced with certain situations. For example, the prospect of failure such as losing an important sporting match or competition.

Most trait theories use labels for features of behaviour, and you should remember that such labels (attached to a person) would be intended to last for ever. Some labels for aspects of personality are:

- **Extroversion** (including liveliness, sociability, impulsiveness, activity, excitability).
- **Introversion** (including isolation, independence, shyness, quiet).
- **Stability** (including unchanging behaviour patterns).
- **Neuroticism** (including the fact that behaviour may change unpredictably).

- A **stable extrovert** would be talkative, outgoing, easy going, carefree, and showing leader qualities.
- A **neurotic extrovert** would be restless, aggressive, excitable, and changeable.
- A **neurotic introvert** would be anxious, sober, rigid, or pessimistic.
- A **stable introvert** would be careful, thoughtful, controlled, reliable, and even-tempered.

Which set of characteristics would enable you to predict who would become the next British Olympic champions (figure 10.2)?

figure 10.2 – which features of Chris Hoy's personality have led to him becoming a multiple Olympic champion?

Social learning theories

Social learning theory explains behaviour in terms of the reaction to specific situations. The main point of social learning theory is that we learn to deal with situations by **observing others** or by observing the results of our own behaviour on others and by **modelling** our own behaviour on what we have seen. Athletes learn **behaviour** by watching others. This is in addition to the idea of being able to learn skills by watching then copying others (this is the social learning theory of skill development).

Bandura says that behaviour is determined by the situation. In other words there is social comparison, and a person will behave the same way as the peer group. Social approval or disapproval determines our responses since such behaviour is reinforced or penalised by **the peer group**.

Vicarious conditioning is the learning of emotional responses through observational learning. For example, learning to become angry after a valid referee decision has gone against him or her by watching other players do the same.

Hollander's structure of personality

Figure 10.3 outlines the structure of personality as proposed by Hollander.

figure 10.3 – Hollander's structure of personality

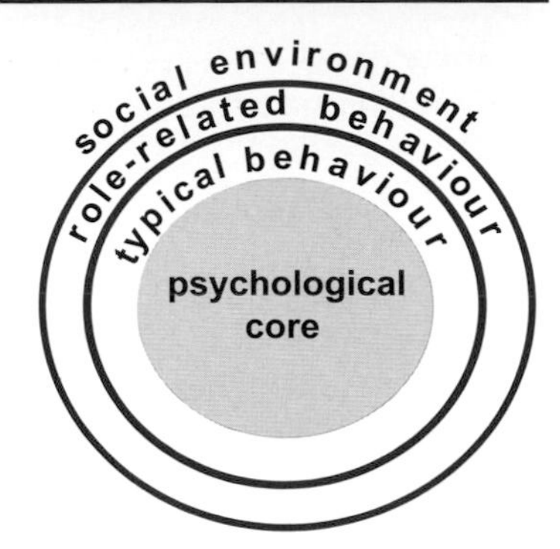

In this model:

- The **psychological core** (the inner core of beliefs) describes the beliefs and values that remain more or less permanent. For example, a sportsman's belief that fair play underlies his attitude on the field of play.
- **Typical behaviour** describes the way in which an individual responds in certain situations, for example, to stop fighting at the bell during a boxing bout.
- **Role-related behaviour** describes the fact that in other situations we may behave differently, for example, striking our opponents after the bell when annoyed or frustrated. This is the most changeable aspect of personality.
- **Social environment** describes how the behaviour and expectations of others affect our role. For example, a player argues with the referee because others have done so and he or she has got away with it before.

This is an example of an **interactionist** theory.

Interactionist theories

figure 10.4 – the interactionist model of personality

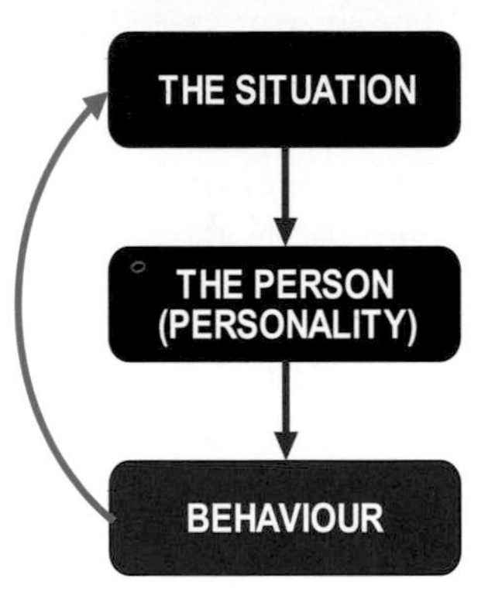

Interactionist theories (figure 10.4) are those which assert that a combination of trait and a person's situation or environment builds up a person's personality, and that traits determine behaviour but can be modified by situations. **Lewin** was the theorist who stated that behaviour is a function of both the person (personality P) and the environment (E), and put this in the mathematical form: **B = f(P,E)**

Example of the interactionist theory approach

A young field event athlete shows promise, but worries about competing in important competitions and underperforms in these situations. Her coach works with her on anxiety management strategies and in her next competition she achieves a personal best.

The innate (**trait**) factors of the athlete's personality cannot be changed by a coach, so the coach must therefore get her to view her **anxiety** (which could be a trait which emerges whenever undue stress is placed on her) in terms of the specific situation of the next competition. The anxiety could be channelled into positive images of her technical model, rejecting poor efforts as due to external factors (for example, the weather or the wind), and building on positive images of successful technical elements achieved. The athlete can then build success by focusing on factors other than her own anxiety.

This enables her to adjust her behaviour according to internal factors such as rhythm and fluency, and this strategy should enable the athlete to remove the stress from the situation and hence reduce anxiety - even if she competes poorly.

Types A and B personalities

Table 10.1 – **differences between personality types A and B**

type A characterised by:	type B characterised by:
impatience	relaxed and patient
works at a rapid pace	allows time for tasks to be completed
higher levels of stress	low personal stress
strong desire to succeed	less competitive
easily aroused and shows anxiety in stressful situations	calm and unflappable in most situations
lacking in tolerance	tolerance of others' mistakes
has a need to be in control	delegates easily
makes decisions quickly without much preparation or thought	prepared to wait and assess all options when decisions need to be made

Personality testing or measuring

There are 3 ways of testing or measuring personality:

- **Interviews**.
- **Questionnaires**.
- **Observation**.

STUDENT NOTE

Validity and reliability are key issues for discussion when testing or measuring personality. Refer to page 79 of 'AS Revise PE for AQA' ISBN: 978 1 901424 56 0 for a review of these concepts.

Interviews

Interviews are before or after the event, are not directly related to performance, are usually open ended and flexible and therefore difficult to quantify accurately. Transient feelings or attitudes may be expressed by the performer (attitudes felt in the heat of the moment but which on reflection the performer might realise were not his or her true feelings). Also, the performer may be influenced by the interviewer in what he or she says.

Questionnaires

Questionnaires are implemented either before or after the event, and are therefore not directly related to performance. Usually, they are rigidly and systematically set out, which means that the formal nature of the paperwork may influence the answers given. As with interviews, transient feelings or attitudes may be expressed which don't reflect a person's normal views or feelings. However, the results are usually able to be calculated accurately, so that accurate comparisons can be made with previous or future assessments. Also, the outcomes would not be influenced by another person (co-actor, coach or parent for example). Many such questionnaires can be used to assess **specific** traits which may be relevant to the sporting situation.

Observations

Observations are made during an actual event, and are therefore directly related to performance. These are usually made to a tick-list of what might be expected in a sports performance, with the opportunity to make notes 'outside the box'. Unfortunately, observational data is difficult to quantify accurately (difficult to give an accurate figure), since a person's behaviour varies according to the competitive nature of an event, and may also be influenced by the observer's views and attitudes.

The profile of mood states (POMS)

This sports-specific questionnaire asks questions which determine the mood of a sports performer and attempts to relate this to the quality of performance. Results are plotted on a chart similar to figure 10.5. Moods are an important aspect of personality which may influence sports performance. The moods assessed by this test are:

- Tension.
- Depression.
- Anger.
- Vigour.
- Fatigue.
- Confusion.

From figure 10.5 you can see that elite sportspeople show low tension, depression and confusion, and they also show high vigour.
Unsuccessful sportspeople show high tension, depression, fatigue and confusion, and lower vigour than the elite athlete.

figure 10.5 – profiles of mood states for good and poor performers

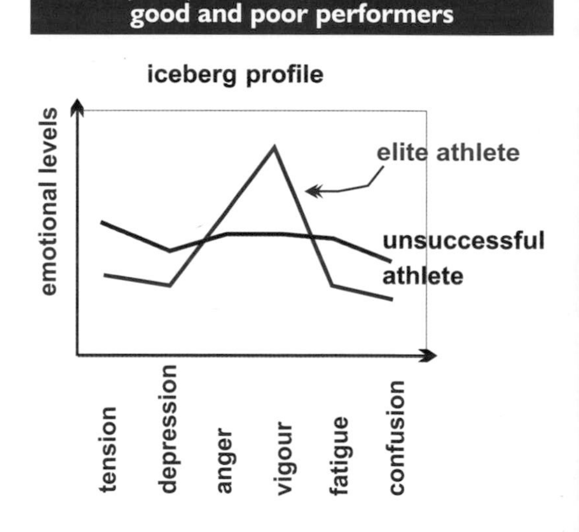

Evaluation of self-report tests

The difficulties with any sort of psychological test are its **validity**, does the test actually measure what it sets out to test, and its **reliability**, does the test measure the same thing every time it is used?

Problems with the tests are:

- Lack of accuracy (**reliability**).
- Participant **honesty**.
- The desire to create a **favourable impression** and therefore give answers which the questioner wants, not what the subject feels.
- Lack of **objectivity** (lack of an accurate means of quantifying data).
- Neurotics tend to **emphasise** certain traits over others.
- **Ambiguous** questions which might confuse the performer or the person making the assessment.
- Interview and observation techniques are usually on a one-to-one basis and hence very **time consuming**.

The answers to questions or observations can be influenced by the personality of the tester, the time of day or month, the previous experience of a test by a subject, and a participant's mood swings. The most important factor, however, is the fact that personality is too complex to be viewed in response to yes or no answers.

In spite of these statements, personality testing is used as part of the UK's sport talent identification programme, since it is accepted that there is a relationship between personality type and sport performance.

Motivation

A **motive** is seen as a cause of behaviour which **energises**, **directs** and **sustains** the behaviour. It can be explained as a **drive** to **strive** to meet the needs of the situation in which a person finds him or herself. The strength of such a drive (or motive) depends on the **person** and the **situation**. Different people will have different types and strengths of motives (drives) to meet the needs of the situation. In a sporting context, the term **motivation** implies the driving and striving to **succeed**, to **win**, to **improve performance**, and to **pursue goals** (having set them in the first place).

figure 10.6 – motivation

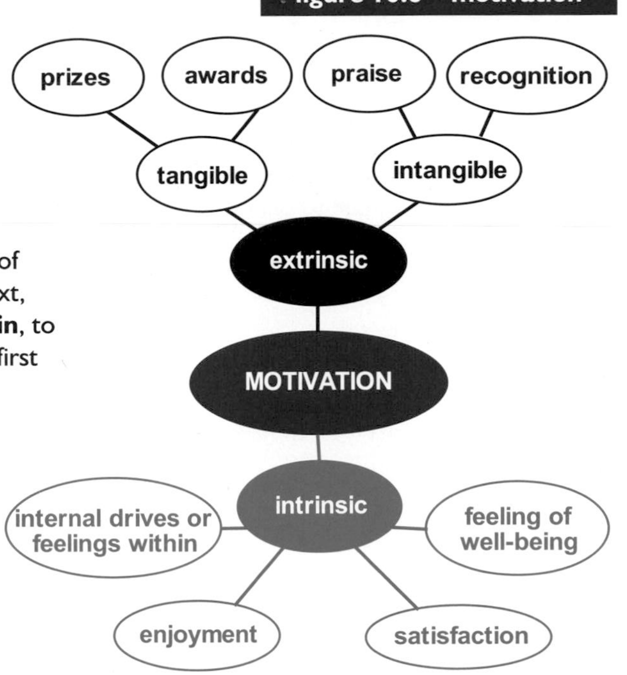

Intrinsic motivation

Intrinsic motivation (figure 10.6) is the term which describes the **internal** drives or feelings that make us do things.

These feelings come from **within** the performer and involve **enjoyment** of the performance, **satisfaction** of performing, **pride** and the feeling of **well-being** from a job well done.

Extrinsic motivation

Extrinsic motivation (figure 10.6) describes the feelings coming from rewards **externally** derived (from outside the performer).

These rewards could be **tangible** such as prizes, money, or awards. For example, a gymnastics badge, or wanting to win at basketball because a trophy may be won, or an Olympic medal. Or rewards could be **intangible**, such as approval, praise or recognition from others. For example, attaining a World record initiates praise by the media, initiates national recognition, and reinforces the glory of the situation. Raising social status is a further intangible reward which would reinforce extrinsic motivation.

Arousal

Arousal is a term which describes the level of **inner drives** and which forces the sportsperson to **strive to achieve**. It needs to be **under control** and at the **right level** depending on the task. This striving is linked with the concept of motivation.

Drive reduction theory

This theory (see figure 10.7) explains why it is sometimes necessary to **vary or renew** the need to learn.

The theory says that the **need to learn** to solve a problem, to learn a skill, or to achieve mastery inspires **motivation**, the **drive** to succeed at the task. This leads to the performer **achieving** the desired outcome (action) which in turn leads to a **reduction in drive** (motivation) to achieve the **same outcome** (since it has already been achieved). This is known as **inhibition**.

The theory explains why people give up sport when it becomes routine, and why changes in for example training venue, training partner, coach or manager, can renew motivation to succeed and continue with a high level of commitment of time and effort.

figure 10.7 – drive reduction

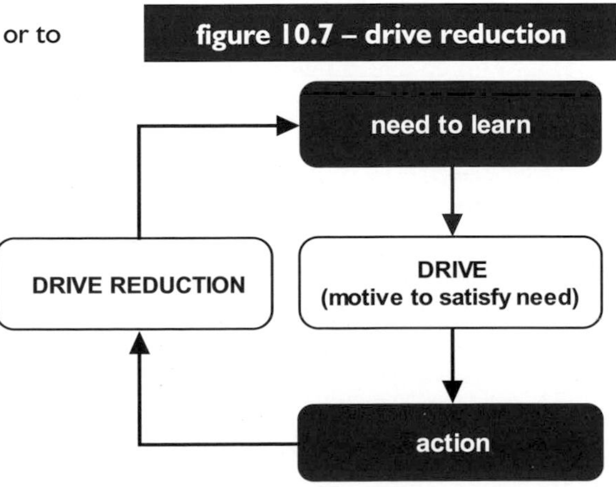

Motivational strategies

These ideas should aim at avoiding or **reducing drive reduction** (reduce **inhibition** of motivation) by changing the **importance** of a task (raise its **status**), or **matching** the task to the performer's needs ('you need to do this to be able to progress towards the Olympic Gold').

Developing and enhancing motivation

Motivation is a combination of personal characteristics and situational aspects.

Motivation is **highest** when:

- The performer is keen to **participate**.
- The performer is keen to **learn**.
- The performer is keen to **perform**.
- The performer is keen to **perform effectively**.
- The motivational **climate** is right.
- The training programme is **interesting** and **varied**.

figure 10.8 – personality aspects of achievement motivation

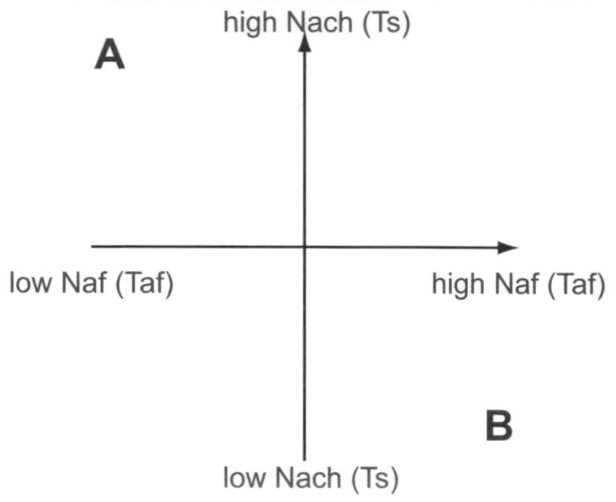

high Nach (Ts)
low Naf (Taf)
high Naf (Taf)
low Nach (Ts)
A
B

Enhancing motivation

Motivation is **reduced** by:

- **Routine**.
- **Competition between motives**.

People:

- Have **multiple** motives.
- **Share** motives.
- Have **unique** motivational profiles.
- Need **variation** in **training** and competition.
- Need **variation** in **intensity** and competitiveness.
- Need **structured coaching** and teaching environments.

Motives change over time, and teachers and coaches are important motivators.

Achievement motivation

Achievement motivation is the drive to achieve success for its own sake, and is related to competitiveness, persistence, and striving for perfection.

Achievement motivation is influenced by:

- **Personality** factors, which are:
  - The need to achieve (Nach).
  - The need to avoid failure (Naf).
- **Situational** factors, which are:
  - Probability of success.
  - Incentive value of success.

figure 10.9 – high Nach?

Personality components of achievement motivation

- **The need to achieve (Nach) or tendency to approach success (Ts)** personality type likes a challenge, likes feedback, is not afraid of failure and has high task persistence.
- **The need to avoid failure (Naf) or tendency to avoid failure (Taf)** personality type avoids challenges, does not take risks, often gives up, and does not want feedback.

The chart in figure 10.8 shows Nach against Naf. Most people participating in sport will occupy a small region of the chart, for example regions **A** and **B** as shown on the chart.

A = someone with a high need to achieve who will probably have a low need to avoid failure. Such a person will choose difficult or demanding tasks which are more risky, for example, the hard route up a rock face (figure 10.9).

B = someone with a high need to avoid failure who will probably have a low need to achieve, and who will choose tasks which are less risky and more easily achieved. For example, this person will take the easy route up the rock face.

Situational factors affecting achievement motivation

The chart in figure 10.10 shows probability of success against incentive value of success, and again most people will occupy a small region (examples here are marked **C** and **D**).

figure 10.10 – situational factors in achievement motivation

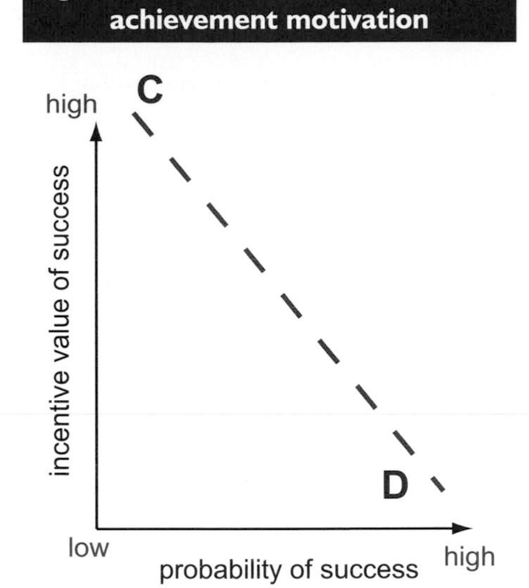

C = region of the chart where a task's **probability of success** is **low** (for example, competing against the World champion), and therefore the sportsperson has to strive very hard to win. The **incentive** to **achieve success** is **very high**, and the sportsperson will be highly chuffed if he or she wins.

D = region of the chart where **probability of success** is **high** (for example, competing in local club match), and the sportsperson therefore doesn't need to try as hard to win. Hence the **incentive to achieve** is **low**, because the person expects to win easily, and of course this is not so pleasing to the performer.

What should the coach do?

The prime need for a coach is to improve need and motive to achieve (Nach) in a sportsperson. This is the positive way to deal with motivational issues, and there are strategies he or she could use to **promote Nach**:

- Increase **positive reinforcement** hence increasing pride and satisfaction.
- Ensure that goals are **achievable**.
- Ensure that at least some situations **guarantee success**.
- And subsequently gradually **increase task difficulty** in line with progress.
- Ensure that tasks are **challenging**.
- Ensure that the **probability of success is good**.
- Ensure that the **incentive value of the success is high** (is the race worth winning?).

The coach should also **reduce tendency and motive to avoid failure** (Naf), and this can be done by:

- **Reducing punishment** hence lowering the chance of performer worrying about failure.
- **Focusing negative feedback** on effort rather than ability.
- This avoids the performer tending to believe that causes of failure are internal (due to lack of ability for example).
- And reduces the risk of learned helplessness (see page 93 below).
- **Avoiding** situations where defeat or **failure is inevitable** (such as performing against a much superior opponent).
- If this is not possible **alter the criteria for success** (you will have succeeded if you only lose by 2 goals).

Practice questions

1) a) What do we mean by the term personality? Why is it important for sports psychologists to know about personality? 3 marks

b) Eysenck identified two dimensions of personality as in figure 10.11. Describe the trait approach to personality. What do the traits extroversion and stability mean? 4 marks

figure 10.11 – dimensions of personality

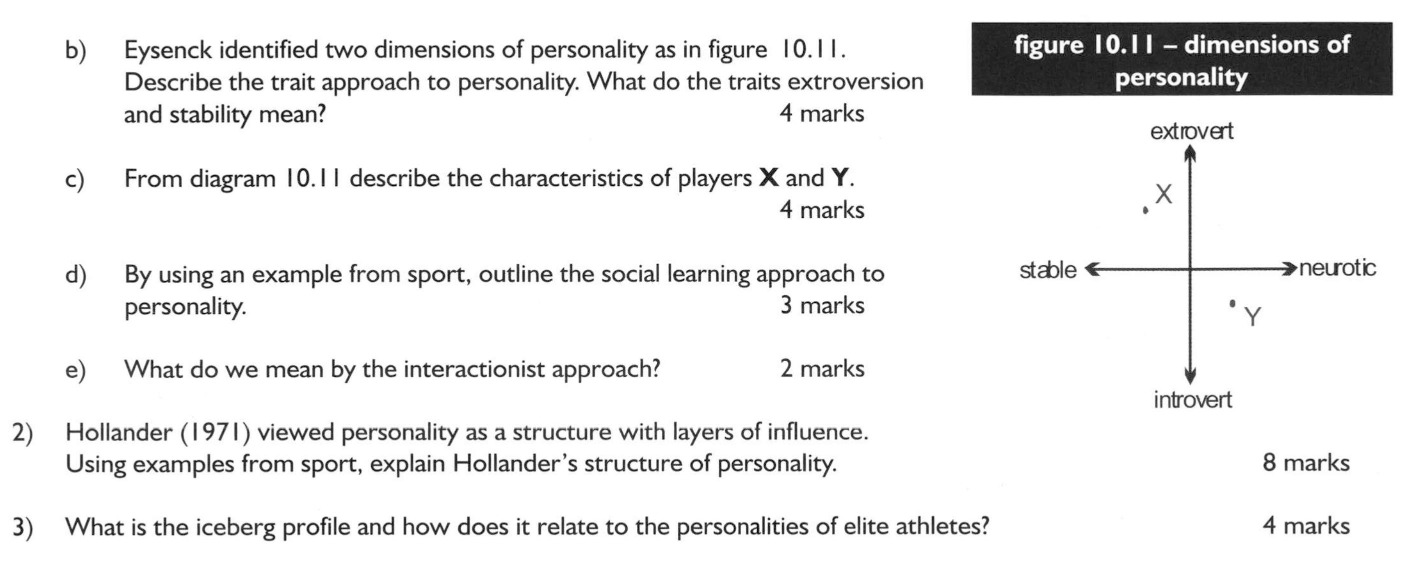

c) From diagram 10.11 describe the characteristics of players **X** and **Y**. 4 marks

d) By using an example from sport, outline the social learning approach to personality. 3 marks

e) What do we mean by the interactionist approach? 2 marks

2) Hollander (1971) viewed personality as a structure with layers of influence. Using examples from sport, explain Hollander's structure of personality. 8 marks

3) What is the iceberg profile and how does it relate to the personalities of elite athletes? 4 marks

4) A rowing coach wants to improve the performance of his squad. In doing so he would want to consider psychological and physiological factors. The coach wants to identify the personality types of the squad members.

a) What are the limitations of using personality tests? 2 marks

b) Some rowers behave differently between competition and training. Explain this pattern of behaviour, in terms of interactionist theory of personality. 2 marks

c) What do you understand by the term motivation? Explain the different types. 3 marks

d) How could a coach use the different types of motivation with a group of beginners? 2 marks

5) a) Describe the characteristics of the positive motive: 'the need to achieve'. 4 marks

b) Describe an example from sport of someone who has a high motive to avoid failure. 3 marks

c) Identify factors which could affect the use of motives to achieve and to avoid failure in sporting situations. 3 marks

6) How would you promote the need to achieve motive, rather than the need to avoid failure motive? 8 marks

CHAPTER 11 – AROUSAL AND ANXIETY

Arousal

Arousal is a state of **mental** and **physical preparedness for action**. It is the level of inner drives which forces the sportsperson to **strive to achieve**. It needs to be under control and at the right level depending on the task. Arousal has **somatic** and **cognitive** consequences as outlined above, is similar to the human response to danger, and is **closely linked** to anxiety.

The **reticular activating system** is a system within the brain which causes arousal:
- **Extroverts** have **lower** levels of **intrinsic arousal** than introverts, hence extroverts seek situations of **high arousal**.
- **Introverts** seek low arousal situations.

Theories linking arousal and performance

Drive theory

This theory (figure 11.1) describes the simple situation where the **higher** the **arousal** level, the **higher** the achievement or **performance** level.

figure 11.1 – drive theory

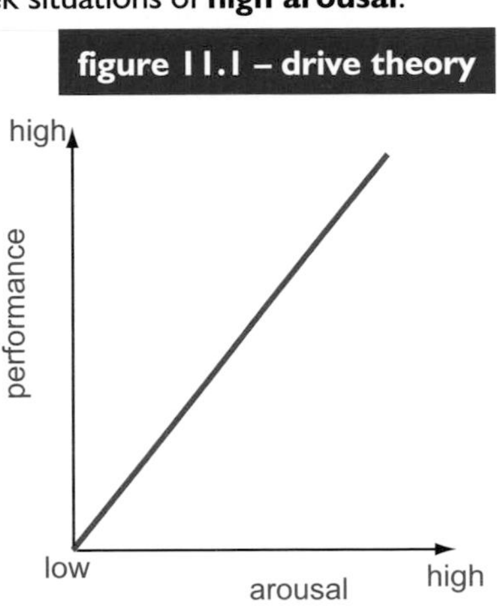

- Drive theory applies to **gross skills** like weight lifting and sprinting.
- The theory also states that the more arousal, the more likely that a **well-learned** skill (a **dominant response**) will be reproduced.
- This means that older, more deep-seated skills will tend to be produced when a person is very aroused rather than newer, less well-learnt skills practised more recently.

- The implication of this is that a **highly aroused performer** will need to focus very hard and direct his or her attention very strongly towards a **desired response**, particularly if this response includes recently learned elements.
- Otherwise the state of arousal will cause the person to regress to an older, less desirable but dominant response.

figure 11.2 – inverted U theory

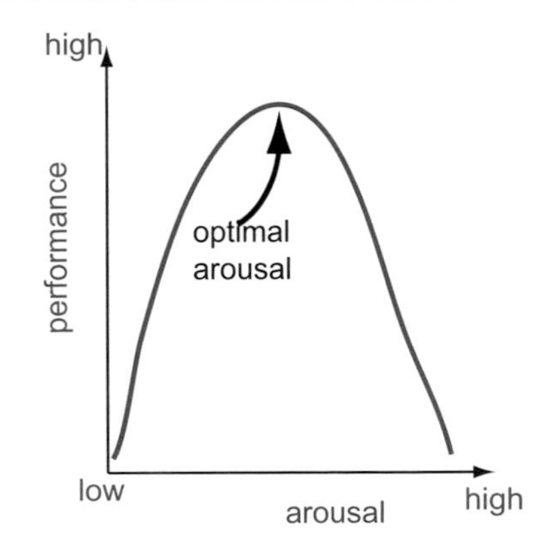

Inverted U theory

In **inverted U theory** (figure 11.2 - attributed to Yerkes and Dodson) there is an **optimum arousal** level. As arousal increases, performance increases up to a certain point. If aroused more than this, the performance will **go down**.

Optimum arousal depends on:
- **Type of activity**, for example, **gross** skills (like weight lifting) require **high arousal**, whereas **fine** skills (like snooker) require **low arousal**.
- The **skill level of the performer**, the more skilful the performer the **higher** the optimum arousal level could be.
- The **personality of the performer**, in which the more **extrovert** the performer, the **higher** the arousal likely to have to be attained by the performer to produce **optimum** performance.

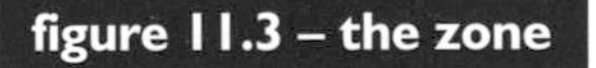
figure 11.3 – the zone

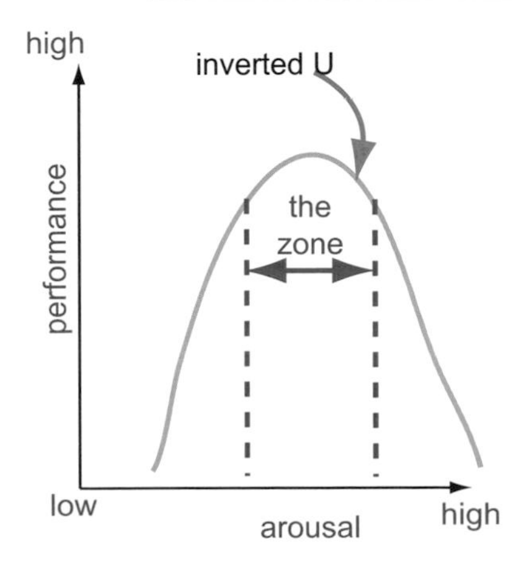

Zone of optimum functioning

Hanin worked out that the optimum level of arousal is not always at mid point of the inverted U, and that best performance will vary between sportspeople. For example, some athletes will peak at low arousal, and other athletes will peak at medium or high arousal.

Also, an athlete's best performance will be in a **zone** (not just a point of optimum performance - figure 11.3), and different athletes will have **different zones of arousal** for optimum performances depending on **personality**, **skill** or **task** and degree of **habit**.

Habit is defined as the strength and **permanence** of a correctly learned skill.

Peak flow theory

Csikzentmihalyi derived a theory which asserts that flow is an optimal experience which is intrinsically rewarding. Figure 11.4 shows the relationship between the task demands and the skill level of the performer, and you will see that there is a zone in which these two factors combine to produce an effective performance.

figure 11.4 – peak flow

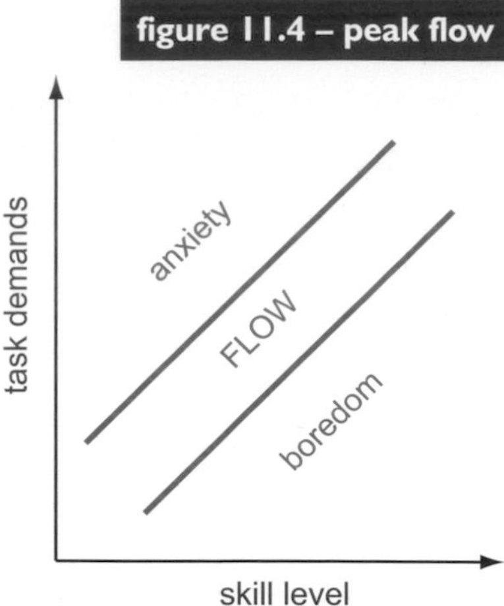

Flow is a period of peak performance, when the performer feels totally involved without effort, and without having to concentrate. If skill level exceeds task demands (task is too easy), the performer is bored, and if task demands exceed skill level (task is too hard), the performer becomes anxious.

Peak flow occurs when:

- The demands of the task match the skill level of the performer.
- Actions of a performer become automatic.
- Concentration is total without effort.
- The performer feels in control without effort.
- The performer loses self-consciousness.
- Time appears to speed up.
- Or time appears to slow down.
- The performer feels exhilarated by the activity.

Peak flow is achieved when:

- The performer has a positive mental attitude.
- The performer controls his or her anxiety.
- The performer maintains concentration and confidence (maintains focus).
- Peak fitness is maintained.

figure 11.5 – Usain Bolt with peak flow?

Perhaps Usain Bolt (figure 11.5) was both **in the Zone** and had **peak flow** when setting his multiple World records at the Beijing Olympics 2008, and the Berlin World championships 2009.

Catastrophe theory

Catastrophe theory (see figure 11.6) is a variation of inverted U theory in which performance **increases** as arousal **increases**, but if **arousal** gets **too high** a **complete** loss of performance occurs (the catastrophe).

The performance line on the graph plummets rapidly towards disaster. This almost always happens when the performer **tries too hard**, for example:

- The golfer who tries too hard and completely misses the fairway from his drive at the 18th hole when in a winning position.
- The gymnast who completely messes up her previously well-executed routine.

figure 11.6 – catastrophe theory

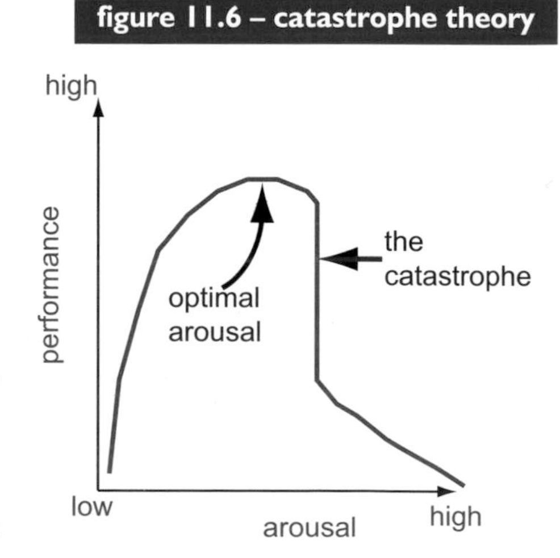

Anxiety affects arousal, and these theories can also apply to how anxiety affects performance.

Effects of arousal on technique

- The **point of optimum arousal** is of crucial importance to the learning and stability of a sportsperson's technique.
- Technique is the sequence of actions which enables a performer to successfully perform the skill of his or her event.
- Trying too hard (overarousal) can cause a performer to change his or her technique in an uncontrolled way - with a resultant loss of performance.
- This can be made worse by the anxiety which would accompany a major event - such as a major at tennis or an open at golf.

Choking and overarousal

High arousal can cause a performer to have negative thoughts. **Negative thoughts of failure** or lack of success can creep in if a performer is **over-aroused**. These thoughts can affect the performer's confidence and create an almost complete inability to perform skills properly. This is **choking** and is an aspect of inverted U theory.

Examples are:

- The snooker player who misses an easy shot when in the final frame of an important match.
- The golfer who misses the fairway from the tee when in the lead in a competition.
- This particularly applies to sports where there is a fine skill.
- Choking can be controlled by **cognitive management techniques** (see page 81 below).

Anxiety

Anxiety can be explained as an emotional state similar to fear, associated with:

- **Physiological** (**somatic**) arousal - connected with raised heart rate, raised breathing rate, sweating and so on.
- **Psychological** (**cognitive**) arousal - worry and negative feelings about the situation, feelings of nervousness, feelings of **apprehension**.

Anxiety is closely linked to arousal, since an anxious person is more likely to become aroused than a calm person. Hence the various theories linking arousal with performance (drive, inverted U, catastrophe) can also apply to link anxiety with performance.

It can have **behavioural** consequences - in which a person will experience:

- **Tension**.
- **Agitation**.
- **Restlessness**.

Trait anxiety - A-trait (Speilberger)

Trait anxiety is an inbuilt (**trait**) **part of the personality** which gives a person:

- A tendency to be **fearful** of unfamiliar situations.
- A tendency to perceive competitive situations as **threatening**.
- A tendency to respond to competitive situations with **apprehension** and **tension**.

State anxiety - A-state

State anxiety is an emotional response to a **particular situation**, characterised by feelings of nervousness and apprehension which is often **temporary** - as you might expect if the anxiety is related to a certain situation which of course will change as daily activities change.

Measuring anxiety

There are three methods of measuring anxiety, namely by **observation**, by **questionnaire** and using **physiological** measures. The observation and questionnaire methods have the same advantages and drawbacks associated with personality testing outlined on page 72 above.

There are several standard **questionnaires** which attempt to measure anxiety, these are:

- Martens' Sport Competitive Anxiety Test (**SCAT**).
- Martens' Competitive State Anxiety Inventory (**CSAI**).
- Speilberger's State, Trait Anxiety Inventory (**STAI**).
- Smith's Sport Anxiety Scale (**SAS**).

Each of these tests (**questionnaires**) are relatively lengthy and require interpretation for successful use.

Physiological measurements

Physiological measuring equipment are heart rate monitoring devices and skin conductivity devices (these devices measure sweating). The **disadvantages** are that the use of, and results produced by such devices, are affected by the exercise intensity being undertaken (as opposed to the anxiety of the performer). Also, since the performer has to be 'wired up' (figure 11.7) to make the measurements, there may be difficulties associated with the equipment being used in certain games or situations (in contact sports for example).

figure 11.7 – measuring anxiety?

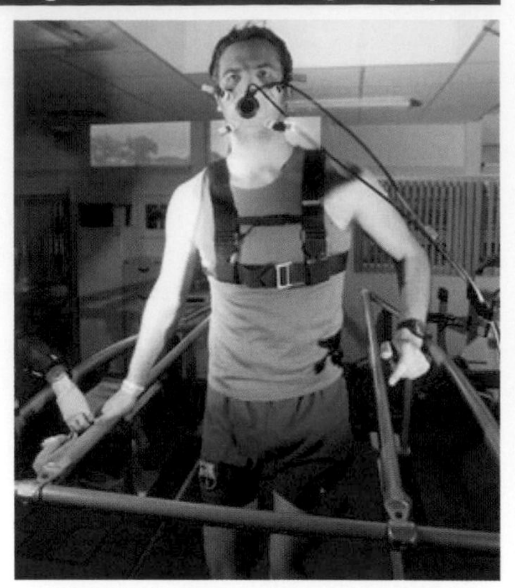

Physiological measures have the following major **advantages**.

- They can be made during, before or after the event, and are directly related to performance.
- Also they can be systematically and scientifically recorded (either by charting, or by numerical data).
- This would enable a person to quantify accurately the measures being made.
- Most of these measures can be used to assess **stress** or **anxiety**.

Stress

Stress and **anxiety** are closely linked, with stress being a major cause of health issues in our society. Figure 11.8 outlines the main factors associated with stress and stressors.

figure 11.8 – stress and stressors

Stress is a response of the body to any demands made on it. The symptoms of stress (figure 11.8) are **physiological**, **psychological** or **behavioural** (see table 11.1 below for details).

Stressors

Stressors are the cause of stress and are:

- **Social** including the disapproval of parents or peers, the rejection by peers or parents, or isolation from normal social interactions.
- **Chemical** or **biochemical** in which harm is inflicted by ingestion of nasty substances.
- **Bacterial**, which would be an illness caused by micro-organisms.
- **Physical** in which a person would suffer injury, pain or exhaustion.
- **Climatic** in which extremes of weather are experienced, such as hot weather for endurance activities, or rain and cold on bare skin.
- **Psychological**, in which there is a mismatch between the perception of the demands of a task and the ability of a person to cope with these demands.

Symptoms of stress

Table 11.1 – **symptoms of stress**

physiological symptoms	psychological symptoms	behavioural symptoms
increased heart rate	worry	rapid talking
increased blood pressure	feeling overwhelmed	nail biting
increased sweating	inability to make decisions	pacing
increased breathing rate	inability to concentrate	scowling
decreased flow of blood to the skin	inability to direct attention appropriately	yawning
increased oxygen uptake	narrowing of attention	trembling
dry mouth	feeling out of control	raised voice pitch
		frequent urination

Control of stress and anxiety

Stress and anxiety management techniques become important for sports performers when performances fall, or failure is experienced.

Cognitive relaxation techniques

These techniques use the power of **thought** to redirect attention away from failure or perceived failure. A performer will take **control** of emotions and thought processes, will **eliminate negative feelings**, and will develop **self-confidence** (self-efficacy, see page 88 below).

figure 11.9 – mental practice or rehearsal

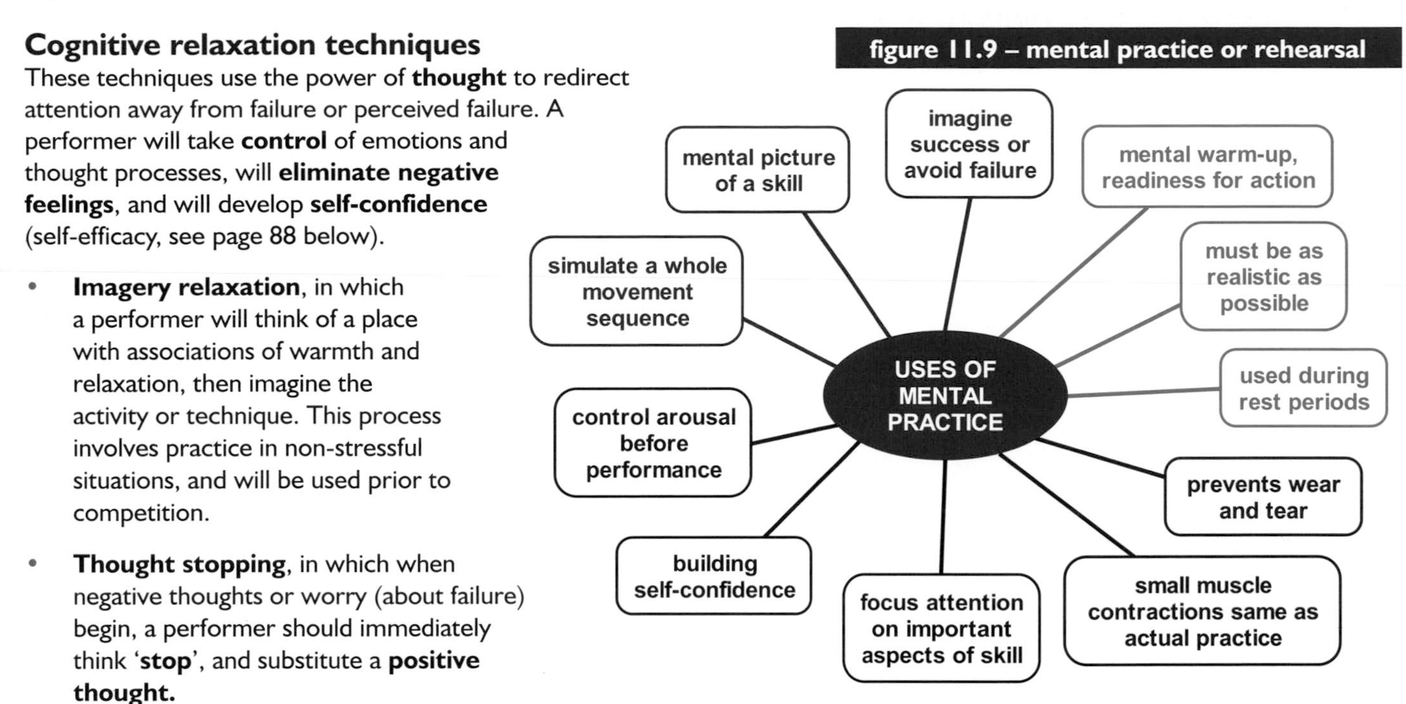

- **Imagery relaxation**, in which a performer will think of a place with associations of warmth and relaxation, then imagine the activity or technique. This process involves practice in non-stressful situations, and will be used prior to competition.
- **Thought stopping**, in which when negative thoughts or worry (about failure) begin, a performer should immediately think '**stop**', and substitute a **positive thought.**
- **Mental rehearsal** or practice (visualisation), in which the mental or cognitive rehearsal of a skill without actual physical movement is undertaken by a performer. The performer will consciously imagine a performance or rerun a past experience, and will continue with a preview of hoped-for success. This process helps concentration, and helps the performer to focus on strengths and weaknesses. This technique is used by most top level sportsmen, and is often prompted by video or talk from a coach. The point of this in stress or anxiety control is that it brings an activity away from the actual performance, and therefore away from any anxieties associated with the performance itself. Figure 11.9 outlines the main features of this process, which is explained in detail in 'AS Revise PE for AQA' ISBN 978 1 901424 56 0, page 95.
- **Concentration** is a state of mind in which attention is directed towards a specific aim or activity. Concentration and **attentional focus** (**control of attention** towards a task) are essential components of a sportsperson's armoury of mental techniques to assist performance.
- **Attentional control training** (ACT) is a personalised programme which targets a performer's specific concentration problems. It assesses the demands of the sport, the situation, and the personality of the performer.
- **Cue utilisation** describes a situation in which cues can be used by the sportsperson to direct attention, and to trigger appropriate arousal responses. This would enable attentional focus at a relevant moment. Sometimes, **narrowing of attentional focus** by an aroused player will cause lack of awareness of broader play issues.
- **Self-talk** is a procedure where a person will talk through the process of a competitive situation, talking positively and building self-confidence.

Somatic relaxation techniques

Somatic relaxation techniques control the physiological symptoms of stress and anxiety.

- **Progressive muscle relaxation**, sometimes called **self-directed muscle relaxation training**, enables a performer to focus on each of the major muscle groups in turn, then to allow breathing to become slow and easy. The athlete will visualise the tension flowing out of a muscle group until it is completely relaxed. Eventually a sportsperson will be able to combine muscle groups, and achieve total relaxation quickly.

Somatic relaxation techniques

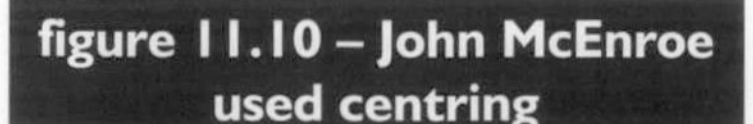
figure 11.10 – John McEnroe used centring

- **Centring** involves the control of physiological symptoms of stress by focusing on control of the diaphragm and deep breathing. The famous John McEnroe (famous for throwing tantrums on court 'you can't be serious', then going on to win Wimbledon titles), used centring to bring himself down from a major row with a court official to playing the perfect serve or shot - within 10 seconds!

- **Biofeedback** is the process of monitoring skin temperature (cold if stressed, warm if unstressed), and the galvanic skin response in which the electrical conductivity of skin increases when moist (tense muscle causes sweating). A further measurement is made by electromyography, in which electrodes are taped to specific muscles which can detect electrical activity and hence tension in muscle. The point is that these measures are perceived by the sportsperson during a performance, and he or she can then alter his or her behaviour to reduce the symptoms of stress or anxiety.

Goal setting as a motivational strategy

STUDENT NOTE

Goal setting has been covered in the AS programme, refer to page 109 of 'AS Revise PE for AQA' ISBN: 978 1 901424 56 0 for a review of these concepts.

The main function of goal setting (figure 11.11) is to increase **motivation**. The feeling of satisfaction gained from achieving a goal brings about this motivation. Goal setting can also be used as a means of **managing anxiety** or stress.

figure 11.11 – goal setting

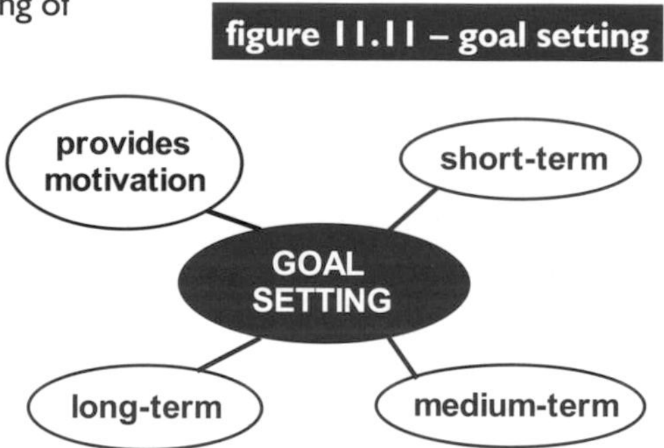

Goals can be **short**-term, **medium**-term or **long**-term. Short-term goals can be used as targets for single training sessions, or what can be expected after a period of training. Long-term goals may or may not be achieved, but are placed in the background of a performer's mind and can underpin everything he or she does. Kelly Holmes had the ambition (goal) of getting an Olympic gold, and she **eventually** did this – twice! This goal motivated Kelly to keep going through injury and disappointment, to keep her training through bad weather and good times.

Goals should be:

- **Easily** attained initially and therefore **realistic**.
- **Incremental**, a little bit at a time.
- **Challenging** but **achievable**.
- **Progressively** more difficult.
- **Training goals** should be planned around **overall goals**.

Goals are either:

- **Outcome oriented**:
  - Towards the end result of the sporting activity. For example to win a race.

- **Performance oriented**:
  - Judged against other performances. For example to beat his or her best time.

- **Process oriented**:
  - Obtain an improvement in techniques.

Practice questions

1) The catastrophe theory is used to explain a golfer's disastrous failure to win a match having been 3 strokes in the lead coming up to the last green. Explain this situation and why this theory might be useful in preventing a repetition.
4 marks

2) A number of PE students are attending trials at their chosen sport. Describe the Inverted U theory and explain how it might affect a student's performance at the trials. 5 marks

3) a) What is meant by the term stress? 2 marks

   b) Explain two psychological symptoms of stress. 2 marks

   c) Identify three main stressors in the context of sport. 3 marks

   d) What is the difference between state and trait anxiety? 2 marks

   e) What coping strategies should the anxious performer draw upon? 5 marks

4) a) Discuss the possible relationships between anxiety and performance in sporting activities. 7 marks

   b) High levels of arousal have often been linked with stress. Sketch a graph showing the relationship between the performance of a complex skill and level of arousal. 2 marks

   c) Add a second curve to your graph showing how the performance of a simple skill might be affected by arousal.
2 marks

5) Many elite athletes identify an emotional response called the peak flow experience that is associated with success. Describe what is meant by peak flow experience and give reasons why it might occur. 5 marks

6) With reference to sporting performance, explain how cognitive and somatic anxiety differ. 5 marks

CHAPTER 12 – ATTITUDES AND AGGRESSION

Attitudes

Attitudes are combinations of **beliefs** and **feelings** which lead us to think and behave **positively** or **negatively**.

Attitudes are combinations of beliefs and feelings about objects, people and situations (called attitude objects) which predispose us to behave in a certain way towards them. They are learned or organised through experience, and are evaluative (lead us to think and behave positively or negatively) about an attitude object. Attitudes tend to be deep seated and enduring, but can change or be changed.

Components of attitude, the triadic model

This model is outlined in figure 12.1, which lists the **cognitive**, **affective**, and **behavioural** components of attitude.

figure 12.1 – the triadic model of components of attitude

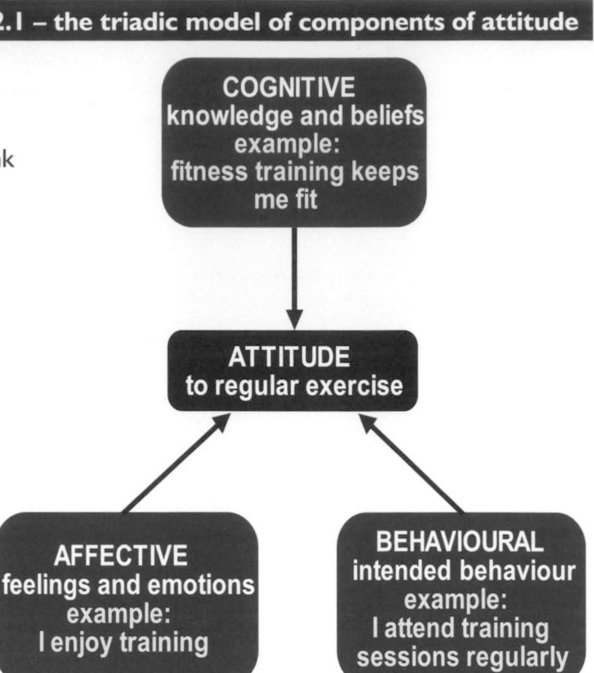

Influences on formation of attitudes

The major influences on the formation of attitudes are outlined in figure 12.2.

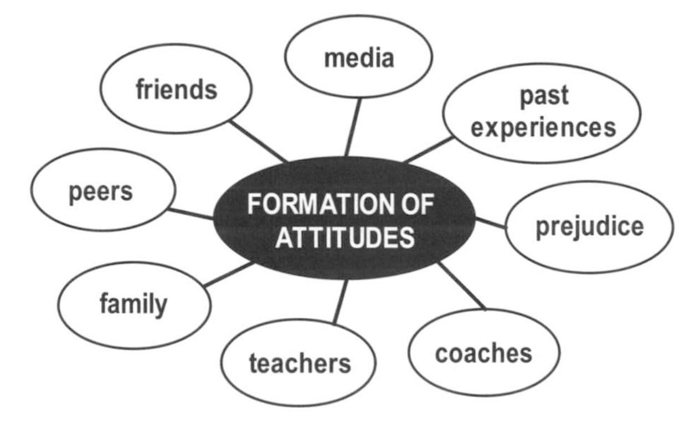

Additionally, **conditioning** (such as the use of rewards such as praise) will tend to strengthen attitudes, and **social learning** will have the same effect, in which people will learn by observing and imitating significant others.

Familiarity with an attitude object can change an attitude towards that object.

Prejudice

Prejudice is a prejudgement of a person, group, or situation, usually based on **inadequate** information, or inaccurate or biased information. This prejudice tends to reinforce **stereotypes**, for example, women are often excluded from male dominated sports clubs or events (historically golf, rugby and snooker clubs have been guilty of this).

Sport stereotypes

In the general population, people form attitudes which are negative stereotypes about certain groups participating in sport.
For example:

- Women in strength, endurance and contact sports, see figure 12.3.
- Participation of the disabled in physical activity.
- Older age groups' interest and ability at sport.
- Participation of particular ethnic groups in specific sports or positions within teams, for example:
  - The black quarterback in American football.
  - The white sprinter.
  - The black skier or swimmer.

figure 12.3 – participation in some sports has a negative stereotype with some members of the public

Changing attitudes

Sometimes, a coach or sport leader will want to change an attitude of a sports player or performer, particularly if this person displays aggression or negative feelings towards a colleague. There are two generally accepted ways of tackling this.

Attitude change by persuasive communication

In order for this method to be effective, the subject (the person whose attitude is hopefully to be changed) must pay attention, and must understand, accept and retain the message being given. The coach must be expert and be trustworthy, and the message must be clear, be unambiguous, be balanced between emotion and logic, and be balanced between pros and cons.

Attitude change by cognitive dissonance

Cognitive dissonance occurs when two completely different and contradictory facts affect the behaviour of a sportsperson. The most clear example of this is when a successful sports performer knows that to maintain his or her success, he or she must maximise the use of his or her lungs, and knows therefore that smoking is bad, yet continues to smoke because he or she likes the sensations produced.

In order to change the attitude of such a person (to smoking), he or she must be consistent between cognitive, affective, and behavioural components, and must realise that there is a conflict between the two behaviours (fitness and smoking). At this point, cognitive dissonance will occur and force the performer to change an attitude to smoking (or perhaps to participation in top level sport!).

figure 12.4 – good attitudes are important

Evaluation or measurement of attitudes

In order to assess whether or not attitudes need to be changed, it will be important to determine what the attitudes to certain situations or attitude objects actually are (figure 12.4). This can be done in one or more of three ways.

- By **observation**, which will be related to actual events as they are happening, will be difficult to quantify or measure, and will be open to interpretation by the observer.
- Using **questionnaires**, which are only as good as the questions asked. They are measurable using the Thurstone scale, the Likert scale, or Osgood's Semantic Differential Scale.
- Using **physiological tests**, in which indicators such as blood pressure, skin conductivity, or brain activity (ECG), can be interpreted to indicate whether a sportsperson is telling the truth about an attitude object. These tests are measurable, are independent of an observer, but take a long time to set up requiring special apparatus.

Aggression

- **Aggression** (figure 12.5) involves arousal and anger and intention to harm outside the rules.
- **Assertion** has no intent to harm and uses legitimate force within the rules, displays unusual effort, and may carry unusual energy. This is sometimes called **channelled aggression** (figure 12.6 - see overleaf).
- **Hostile aggression** has the intent to harm. The goal is to harm with arousal and anger involved.
- **Instrumental aggression** has the intent to harm with the goal to win. This is used as a tactic and is commonly named '**dirty play**'. There is no anger involved and is illegal in all sports except boxing (and other martial arts sports).

figure 12.5 – aggression - the details

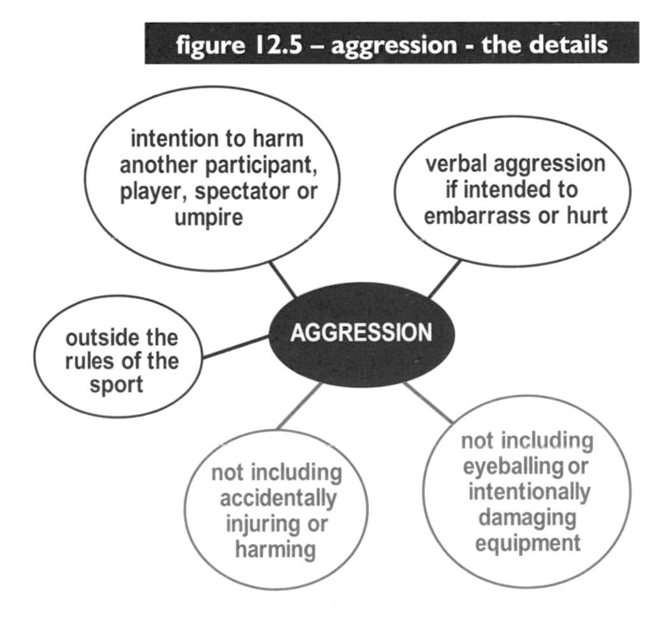

Causes of aggression

- **Physiological arousal** in which anger towards another person causes an increase in arousal. This is because the sportsperson is highly motivated.
- **Underdeveloped moral reasoning** in which players with low levels of moral reasoning are more likely to be aggressive.
- **Bracketed morality** in which there is a double standard of condoning aggressive behaviour in sport, but not in life in general. This way of dealing with aggressive behaviour may retard a player's moral development.

figure 12.6 – aggression or assertion?

Other causes of aggression

- High environmental temperature.
- Home or away.
- Embarrassment.
- Losing.
- Pain.
- Unfair officiating.
- Playing below capability.
- Large score difference.
- Low league standing.
- Later stage of play (near the end of a game).
- Reputation of opposition (get your retaliation in first).

figure 12.7 – theories of aggression

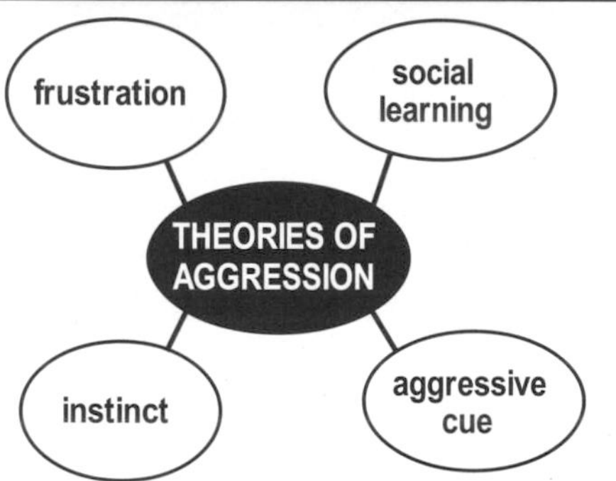

Theories of aggression

- **Instinct theory** (due to Lorentz, figure 12.7) suggests that aggression is innate and instinctive - caused by a 'survival of the species' response to situations as they arise. In this theory, sport releases built-up aggression, and the aggressive response is cathartic - it gets the aggression out of the system, and purges the person of aggressive intent.

- **Frustration aggression theory** (due to Dollard) states that aggression is caused by frustration as the sportsperson is being blocked in the achievement of a goal. This causes a drive towards the source of frustration.

- **Social learning theory** (due to Bandura) suggests that aggression is learned by observation of others' behaviour. Then imitation of this aggressive behaviour is reinforced by social acceptance of the behaviour.

- **Aggressive cue hypothesis** (due to Berkowitz) states that frustration causes anger and arousal which creates a readiness for aggression. The aggression itself can be initiated by an incident during the performance or game (the cue), so that the aggression is a learned response. For example, a player sees a colleague fouled then decides to join in.

figure 12.8 – responsibility for aggression

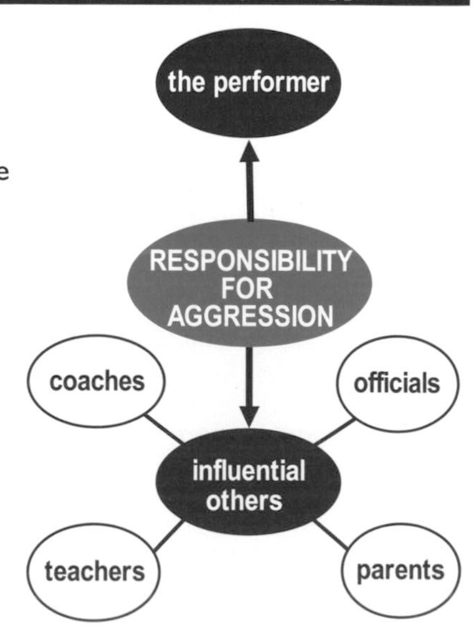

Deindividuation

The theory of deindividuation concerns the fact that people sometimes behave differently when by themselves, as compared with behaviour in a football crowd. The contrast between the behaviour of people with worthwhile jobs, in the workplace as compared with the terraces, has often been observed.

Responsibility for aggression

Responsibility for aggression lies within the factors listed in figure 12.8. Influential others can exert a moderating influence on the performer, but the performer must accept that aggression is the wrong thing to do, and modify behaviour accordingly. **Reinforcement** of good behaviour will be important to ensure behavioural change.

Strategies for control of aggressive behaviour

Governing Bodies

Governing Bodies are responsible for **player codes of conduct** which should involve coaches, players and officials. They will:

- Use strong officials where appropriate.
- Alter rules of games and implement punishment (remove league points, use sin bins and so on).
- Reward non-aggressive acts (for example, the FIFA fair play award).
- Encourage suitable use of language.
- Attempt to reduce media sensationalism in connection with aggression on or off the field of play.

A coach education programme is essential to reduce and control aggressive behaviour among players.

figure 12.9 – controlling aggression?

Coaches and players

- Coaches and players (figure 12.9) should promote ethical and sporting behaviour.
- They should control aggressive behaviour using stress management strategies and **relaxation techniques** among players.
- Coaches should initiate **self-control** strategies, and attempt to reduce levels of arousal in players.
- Both coaches and players should maintain a **healthy will-to-win** without winning being everything, and set **performance goals** rather than outcome goals.
- Coaches should **remove players** from the field if it is determined that he or she (but usually he!) is at risk of aggression.
- Their tactic would be to enable **channelling of aggression** towards a performance goal, and to use **peer pressure** to 'avoid letting the side down'.

Practice questions

1) a) What do we mean by the term attitude? — 1 mark

   b) We often refer to someone as having a positive attitude in sport. Using the triadic model describe the characteristics of a positive attitude. — 3 marks

   c) What factors influence our attitudes? — 4 marks

2) a) If you wished to change a young person's negative attitude to sport into a positive one, what strategies would you employ? Use psychological theory to back up your answer. — 4 marks

   b) What do we mean by the term prejudice and how does it manifest itself in sport? — 4 marks

3) Observing behaviour is one method of measuring attitudes. What are the advantages and disadvantages of such a method? — 4 marks

4) a) What do we mean by the term aggression in sports psychology? Give an example from a sport or game which would illustrate your answer. — 2 marks

   b) Using examples from sport, briefly describe the differences between aggression and assertion? — 2 marks

   c) Some team players display unwanted aggression. What are the possible causes of such aggression? — 4 marks

5) Explain in more detail what is meant by social learning when applied to aggression.
   How can aggressive tendencies be eliminated in a sports situation? — 14 marks

6) a) The aggressive cue hypothesis (Berkowitz 1969), is a theory which explains why aggression may be experienced by sports performers. Using an example from sport, describe the aggressive cue hypothesis. — 4 marks

   b) Using examples from sport, explain the frustration-aggression hypothesis. — 4 marks

7) Discuss how theories of aggression can be applied to sport. — 6 marks

CHAPTER 13 – CONFIDENCE

Confidence

Confidence is an element of mental preparation for sports performance, as outlined in figure 13.1. The explanation of how confidence affects us includes:

- It arouses **positive** emotions.
- It facilitates **concentration**.
- It enables **focus** on the important aspects of a task.

figure 13.1 – mental preparation for sports performance

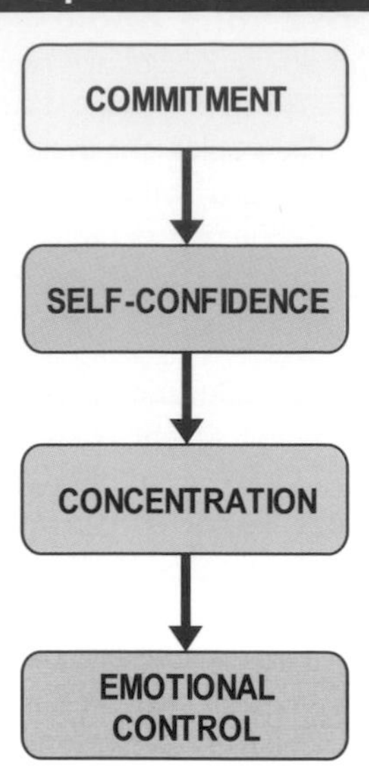

figure 13.2 – self-confidence and self-efficacy

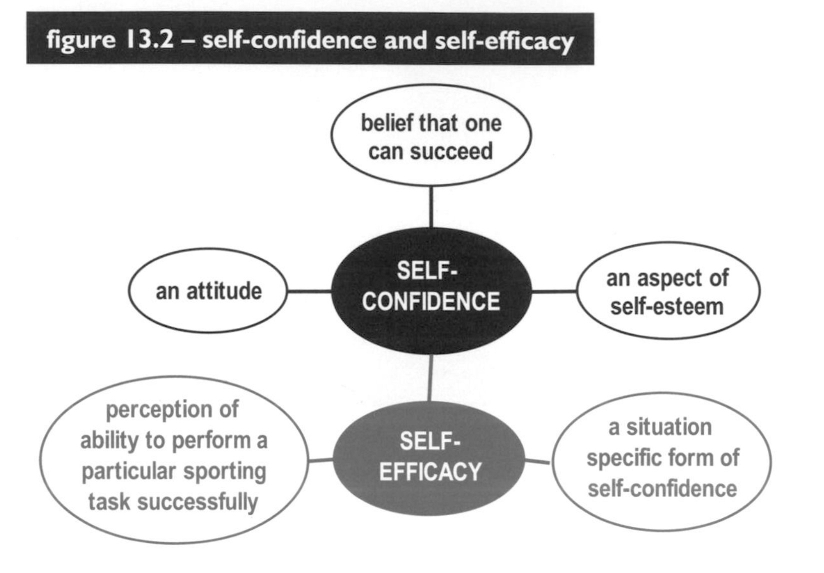

Self-confidence is a feature of a sportsperson's attitude to his or her sporting activity which boosts personal self-worth and self-belief as outlined in figure 13.2. This belief centres around the notion that he or she can win or perform well.

Self-efficacy is a situational form of self-confidence. It is specific to the sport or activity which a person is undertaking.

Confidence (figure 13.3) arouses positive emotions which allow the athlete to:

- Remain **calm** under pressure.
- Be **assertive** when required.
- **Concentrate** easily.
- **Focus** on the important aspects of a task.
- Set challenging but realistic **goals**.
- Increase **effort**.
- Devise effective game **strategies**.
- Keep psychological **momentum**.

figure 13.3 – self-confidence

A confident player plays to win even if it means **taking risks**, will take each point or play at a time, and **never gives up** even when defeat is imminent.

Self-efficacy

Bandura's self-efficacy model (figure 13.4) outlines **four** factors relevant to the self-efficacy of a sports performer.

- **Performance accomplishments**
  Performance accomplishments consist of **past experiences**, for example, a previously performed skill at dribbling a soccer ball. If this is successful, then this leads to greater self-efficacy at this particular task in the future.

- **Vicarious experiences**
  Vicarious experiences consist of what has **been observed in others** performing a similar skill (the sports performer experiences the same feelings of mastery and competence by watching another person perform a skill as if he or she has performed the skill himself or herself). For example, observing another player in your team dribbling a soccer ball. This is most effective if the model is of similar age or ability and is successful. This may lead to greater self-efficacy.

figure 13.4 – self-efficacy (Bandura)

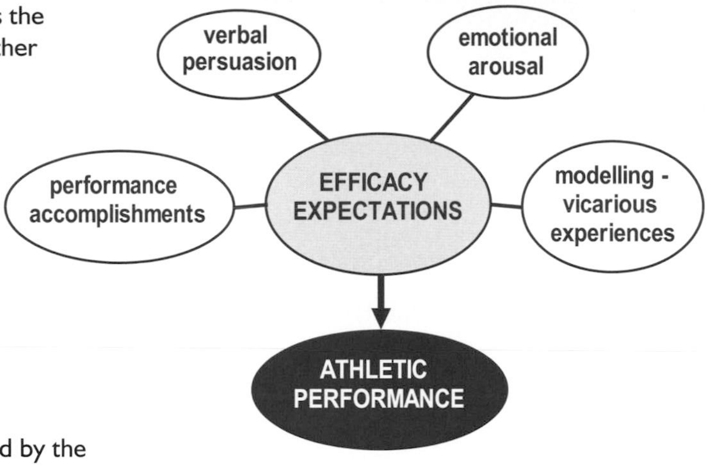

verbal persuasion
emotional arousal
performance accomplishments
EFFICACY EXPECTATIONS
modelling - vicarious experiences
ATHLETIC PERFORMANCE

- **Verbal persuasion**
  Verbal encouragement can lead to greater self-efficacy if the person giving encouragement is of **high status** compared with the performer.

- **Emotional arousal**
  If **arousal** is too high, then **state anxiety** (anxiety produced by the specific situation of an activity - otherwise known as **A-state**) can be too high. This could lead to low self-efficacy. Mental rehearsal or physical relaxation techniques could lead to greater confidence and a calmer approach - this also contributes to self-efficacy.

Social facilitation

figure 13.5 – effects of audience?

Social facilitation concerns how people other than the performer can influence his or her attitudes and behaviour.

The effect that the presence of spectators has on the way sportspeople play or perform can be positive (called **facilitation**), or negative (called **inhibition**). For example, a crowd (figure 13.5) encourages a team playing well (positive or facilitation), or the crowd jeers at a team not playing well (negative or inhibition).

Facilitation

Facilitation of a performance by an audience tends to lead to the fact that high arousal leads to improved performance by a highly skilled or extrovert performer. Gross or simple skills tend to be improved by audience effects. See the link between arousal and performance in drive theory (see page 77 above).

Inhibition

Where the presence of an audience **inhibits performance**, high arousal tends to lead to reduced performance by novices whose skills are not well-learned. This also applies to introvert performers. Fine and complex skills requiring great concentration will also tend to have performance levels reduced by negative audience effects.

Different types of audience

Passive others (social facilitation) are audience and co-actors, and **interactive others** are competitors.

figure 13.6 – ball-boys as co-actors

Co-actors

Co-actors are a passive form of audience involved in the same activity and at the same time as the performer, but not competing directly. For example:

- Officials, umpires or referees.
- Members of a player's own team.
- Ball-boys (figure 13.6) or helpers during a performance.

Factors affecting performance

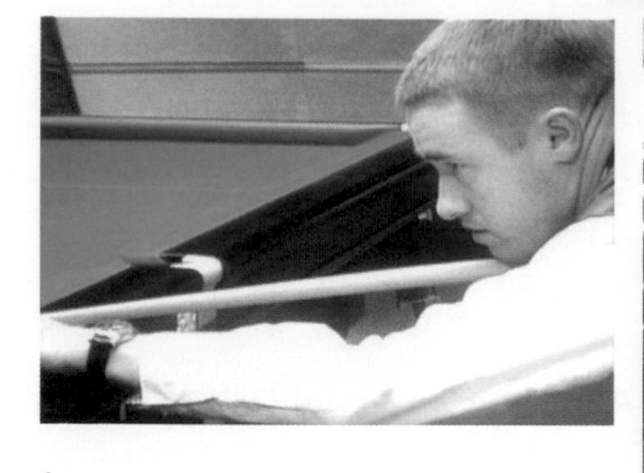

- **Size of audience** - larger crowds create more arousal.
- **Proximity of audience** - the closer the audience the greater the arousal.
- **Intentions of the audience** - can be positive or negative. If spectators are negative about a player (shouting or jeering) this may suppress arousal or increase arousal depending on the personality of the performer.

- **Skill level** or **difficulty** of the task - performance improves for a well-learned skill and decreases if the skill is not well-learned.
- **Personality** of the performer - extroverts perform better when aroused, but introverts can be over-aroused.
- **Type of task** (figure 13.7) - fine skills need lower levels of arousal whereas gross skills could be improved by increased arousal.

figure 13.7 – fine skills or gross skills

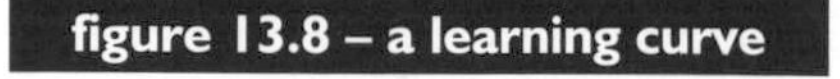

figure 13.8 – a learning curve

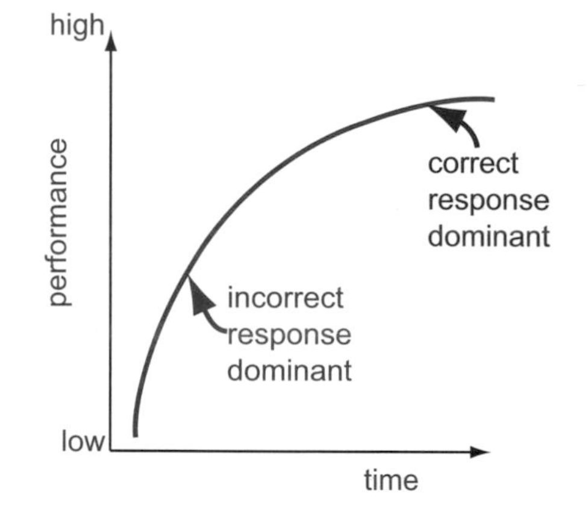

Zajonc's model

Zajonc's theory says that the mere **presence of others** creates **arousal**, which then affects performance negatively if a skill is poorly-learnt (early in the learning curve - figure 13.8).

In this case, arousal causes an incorrect response because the incorrect response is dominant.

On the other hand, if a skill is **well-learnt** (later in the learning curve), then **arousal** causes a **correct response** because the correct response is dominant.

Evaluation apprehension

This theory (due to Cottrell - figure 13.9) explains that an **audience is perceived as evaluating** (assessing the value or worth of) performance. This **causes anxiety** - which in turn causes arousal.

figure 13.9 – the process of evaluation apprehension

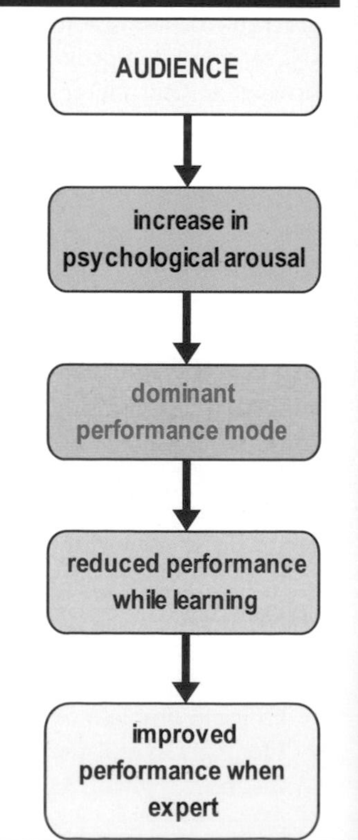

STUDENT NOTE

Look at inverted U theory for the connection between arousal and performance (see page 77 above).

The distraction effect

Baron's distraction-conflict theory says that **distraction** is an aspect of concentration (or **lack of concentration**). Attentional focus is very important for the effective sportsperson and if this is disrupted then he or she is distracted from his or her task. Audience and evaluation apprehension can act as a distraction. The sportsperson needs therefore to practise in distracting circumstances, and practise switching attentional focus when faced with potentially distracting circumstances.

Homefield advantage

Home or away effect on performance concerns the fact that more teams win at home than away.

A crowd may be judged as supportive or hostile (facilitation or inhibition), and high levels of anxiety caused by hostility may reduce performance.

The environment of their own stadium or playing situation is familiar to home teams, therefore home players are more comfortable. This limits anxiety and enables a worry-free and hopefully successful performance (figure 13.10).

figure 13.10 – World Cup 1966 - Wembley, 97,000 spectators, homefield advantage?

Strategies for coping with evaluation apprehension

Strategies include:

- Stress management (see page 79 above).
- Mental rehearsal (see page 79 above).
- Selective attention (away from evaluators). See page 94 of AS Revise PE for AQA, ISBN: 978 1 901424 56 0.
- Lowering the importance of the situation.
- Training with an audience present.

Practice questions

1) a) What is meant by the term self-efficacy when applied to sports psychology? 1 mark

b) Bandura suggested that self-efficacy is influenced by four factors. Identify and apply these factors to a sport of your choice. 8 marks

c) As a coach of a sports team, how would you raise an individual's level of self-efficacy? 4 marks

2) a) What is meant by social facilitation and what is its main effect? 3 marks

b) What effects can be experienced by an individual if there is an audience present? 6 marks

3) a) What is meant by evaluation apprehension? 2 marks

b) As a coach of an individual who is affected adversely by the presence of an audience, how would you help him or her to overcome the negative influences? 4 marks

4) Two groups of male sportspeople (of the same age) undertook an arms-length weight hold endurance test. Success at this exercise was measured by the length of time the weight was held. Table 13.1 below shows the average times for group 1 (who did the exercise alone) and group 2 (who did the exercise in the presence of an audience).

Table 13.1 – **time for a weight hold endurance test**

	group 1 no audience	group 2 with audience
average time held in seconds	46.5	50.5

a) What effect (if any) did the audience have on the performance of the exercise? 1 mark

b) How would you account for this effect (or lack of effect)? 4 marks

c) The audience in this exercise (for group 2) was not known to the participants. Explain any effect you think there would be if the audience was known to the group. 6 marks

5) Using examples from sport, explain what is meant by evaluation apprehension and outline the causes of it. 3 marks

CHAPTER 14 – ATTRIBUTION THEORY

Attribution theory

Attribution is the process of giving **reasons** for behaviour and ascribing **causes** for events. For example, the player played badly today because the weather was poor.

Weiner's model

Weiner's model has four attributions, **ability**, **effort**, **task difficulty** and **luck** (see figure 14.1).

As in figure 14.1, these attributions are arranged in two dimensions, **locus of causality** and **stability** (with a possible third dimension, **controllability**).

figure 14.1 – Weiner's model of sports attribution

		LOCUS OF CAUSALITY	
		INTERNAL	EXTERNAL
STABILITY	STABLE	ability 'we were more skilful '	task difficulty 'the opposition are world champions'
	UNSTABLE	effort 'we tried hard'	luck 'the court was slippy'

Locus of causality dimension

Locus of causality is the performance outcome caused by:

- **Internal factors** under the control of the performer such as ability and effort.
  - **Ability** is the extent of the performer's capacity to cope with a sporting task.
  - **Effort** refers to the amount of mental and physical effort the performer gives to the task.

- **External factors** beyond the control of the performer such as task difficulty and luck.
  - **Task difficulty** is the term describing the extent of the problems posed by the task including the strength of the opposition.
  - **Luck** describes factors attributable to chance, such as the weather or the state of the pitch.

Stability dimension

Stability refers to the performance outcome caused by stable or unstable factors:

- **Stable** factors are fixed factors which don't change with time such as **ability** or **task difficulty**.
- **Unstable** factors are factors which can vary with time such as **effort** or **luck**.

In attribution theory, **success** is explained by internal attributions, and **failure** is explained by external attributions. **Future expectations** are related to stability. If we attribute success to stable factors, or if we attribute failure to stable factors, then we expect the same next time.

figure 14.2 – Andy Murray - high achiever

Relationship to sports achievement

- **High achievers** (such as Andy Murray, figure 14.2) tend to attribute **success** to internal factors (such as Andy's incredible state of fitness), and attribute **failure** to external factors (such as the high temperature or strong wind during the match).
- **Low achievers** tend to attribute success to external factors (such as a favourable wind), and attribute failure to internal factors (such as lack of fitness or ability).

- The process of changing attributions is called **attribution retraining**. The point of this is to change a person's tendency to ascribe reasons for success or failure so that it is more like that of a successful performer rather than an unsuccessful performer.
- Attributions affect a sportsperson's **pride**, **satisfaction**, and **expectancy of success**. Some people exhibit **avoidance** tendencies when faced with a sporting situation (they try to avoid participating), and this is called **learned helplessness** (see page 93 opposite).

Controllability, the third dimension

The **locus of control** covers attributions under the control of the performer (and sometimes not under the control of the performer). The locus of control dimension relates to the intensity of a performer's feelings of **pride** and **satisfaction**, **shame** and **guilt**.

- **Pride** and **satisfaction** are maximised if success is attributed to internal controllable factors such as ability and effort, and motivation would be enhanced.
- If **success** were attributed to **external** and **uncontrollable** factors such as luck or the fact that the task was very easy, then satisfaction would be less intense and motivation less.
- If **failure** is attributed to internal controllable factors such as **lack of ability** and **lack of effort**, then the overpowering emotion would be dissatisfaction and motivation would be reduced.

The self-serving bias

- This idea crops up because **successful performers** tend to take credit for success. They do this by **attributing success** to their own overwhelmingly outstanding **qualities** (natural ability, **ability** to respond to the competitive situation), thereby enhancing their feelings of pride, self-worth, and self-esteem. They also tend to **blame external factors** for failure.
- Failure is automatically attributed to **avoid internal** controllable and stable factors (even if such factors may be true). This is the **self-serving bias**, people tend to give attributions to **protect their self-esteem** rather than look for true attributions which would reflect the reality of the situation.
- **Unsuccessful performers** do not always attribute failure to external factors and therefore do not protect their self-esteem. This tends to reduce motivation.

Figure 14.3 summarises the attribution process.

figure 14.3 – the attribution process

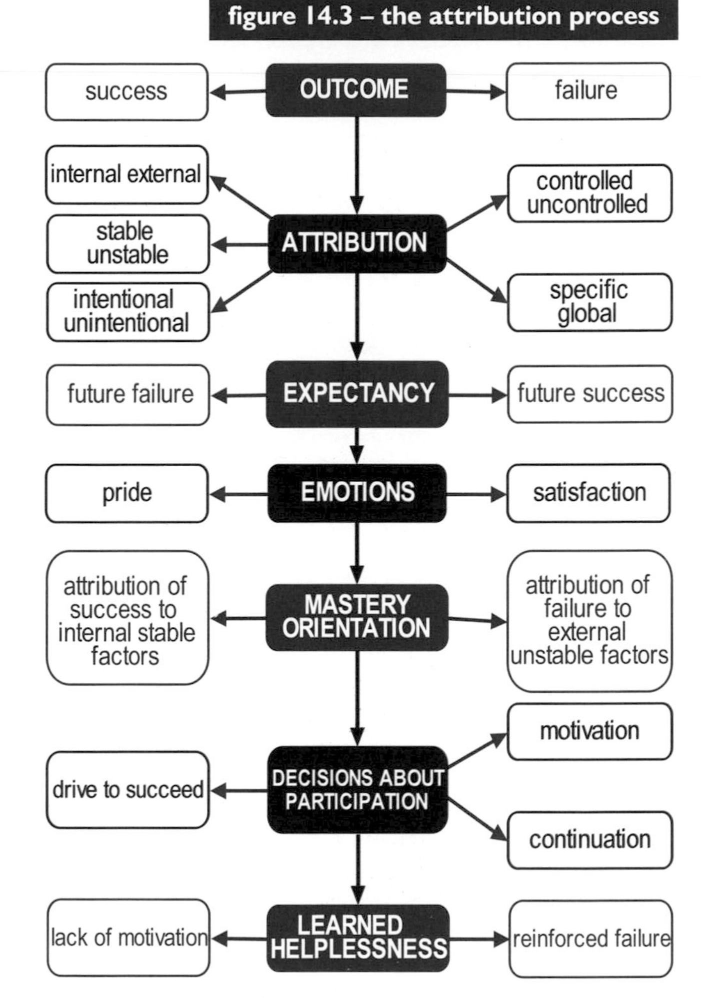

Learned helplessness (LH)

As mentioned in figure 14.3, **repeated failure** (or lack of success) can lead to a state known as **learned helplessness**.

This is explained as a **belief** acquired over time that one has no control over events and that failure is inevitable (for example, if a batsman repeatedly gets a duck, he may feel that he no longer has the skill to succeed at sport). It is characterised by a feeling of **hopelessness** in which a person with the physical potential to achieve highly at sport no longer feels that it is possible for him or her to do so.

This is what is behind the common belief that if you fall off a bike, you must get back on straight away, otherwise you may never do so (figure 14.4).

figure 14.4 – get back on the bike straight away

General and specific learned helplessness

- **General (global) learned helplessness** occurs when a person attributes failure to internal and stable factors, and this feeling of failure is applied to all sports. For example, the comment 'I am useless at all sports'.
- **Specific learned helplessness** occurs when a person attributes difficulties to internal and stable factors, and this feeling is applied to one specific sport. For example, the comment 'I am good at soccer but useless at racquet games'.

Attribution retraining

Figure 14.5 summarises the process which must be undertaken if learned helplessness is to be avoided or recovered from. Following failure, low achievers need to learn to attribute success and failure to the same reasons as high achievers, namely:

- Success should be attributable to stable internal factors.
- Failure should be attributable to unstable external factors.

This would raise the **self-efficacy** of the performer for his or her sport.

figure 14.5 – attribution retraining

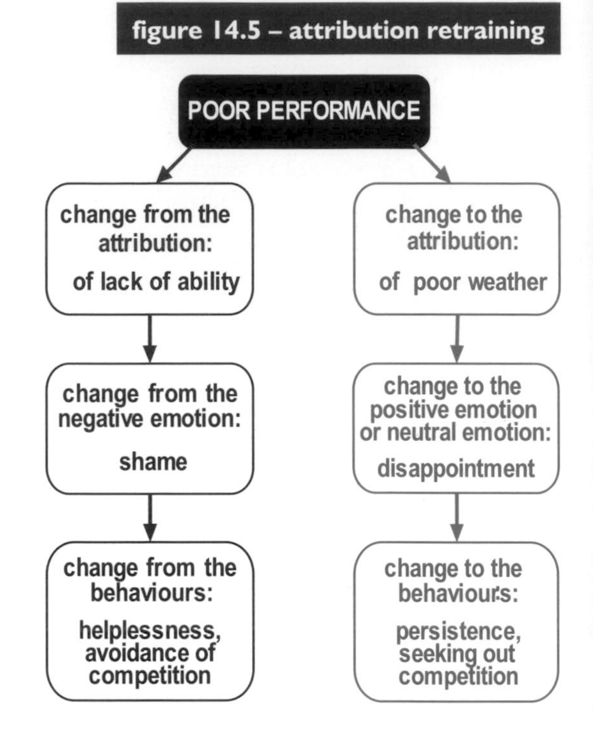

The link between motivation and attribution

Table 14.1 – **motivation, attribution and behaviour**

	high achiever	low achiever
motivation	high motive to achieve success low motive to avoid failure focuses on pride and on success	low motive to achieve success high motive to avoid failure focuses on shame and worry about failure
attributions	ascribes success to stable internal controllable factors ascribes failure to unstable external uncontrollable factors	ascribes success to unstable external uncontrollable factors ascribes failure to stable internal controllable factors
goals adopted	adopts task oriented goals	adopts outcome oriented goals
task choice	seeks challenging tasks and competitive situations	avoids challenge, seeks very difficult or very easy tasks or competition
performance	performs well in front of evaluative audiences	performs badly in front of evaluative audiences

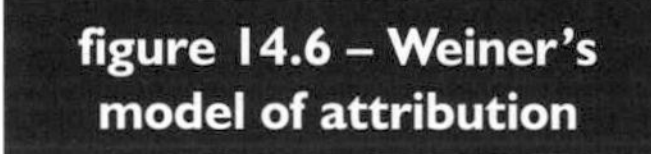

figure 14.6 – Weiner's model of attribution

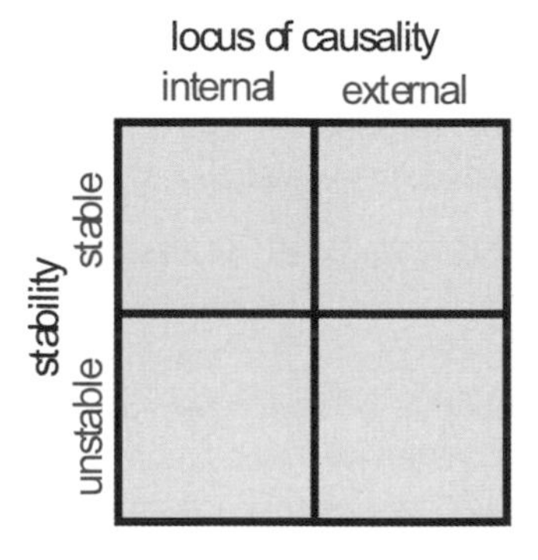

Practice questions

1) a) Figure 14.6 partly illustrates Weiner's model of attribution. Explain the term attribution using a sporting situation. 2 marks

b) Explain the terms locus of causality and stability when applied to attribution theory. 4 marks

c) Redraw the model and place on it relevant attributions for each of the four boxes. 4 marks

d) What attributions would you encourage if your team were playing well but often losing? 5 marks

2) a) Many young people claim to be hopeless at gymnastics. Suggest three reasons why these youngsters might have a negative attitude to gymnastics. 3 marks

b) What is meant by learned helplessness (LH) and how is it caused? 3 marks

c) How would you attempt to attract beginners to a gymnastics class, and then change any negative attitudes? 4 marks

3) Those who achieve little in sport often attribute their failure to factors outside their control and learned helplessness can result. Using examples from sport, explain what is meant by learned helplessness and identify how self-motivational techniques may help to limit the effects of learned helplessness. 6 marks

CHAPTER 15 – GROUPS AND LEADERSHIP

Groups

A **group** consists of two or more people **interacting** with one another so that each person influences and is influenced by the others. A group will have a **collective identity** and a sense of **shared purpose**, and is a **social aggregate** involving **mutual awareness** and **potential interaction** with structured patterns of **communication**. For example, a crowd at a soccer match, a soccer team or parents watching their children swim.

Successful groups:
- Have a strong collective identity in which members have an opportunity to **socialise** and who **share goals**, **ambitions** and **ownership** of ideas.
- Will have members who are able to **communicate effectively** (on the same wavelength).
- Will have strong **cohesion** (see below).
- Have members who **value relationships** within the group.
- Have a **successful coach** or leader who ensures that **members' contributions** to the group are **valued**.

Formation of groups

Tuckman's model for group formation

Tuckman's model says (figure 15.1) that groups are formed in four stages, with a possible fifth stage occurring afterwards. These are:
- **Forming**, in which group members get to know each other, they find out about the task or objective of the group, and they show respect for one another (before starting to work together). During this stage, the coach **tells the group** what to do.
- **Storming**, in which group members argue and compete with each other, and different types of leader emerge. During this stage, inexperienced group members may refuse to compromise, and a team may fail. The coach must **drive the team** through the stage.
- **Norming**, in which group members agree how to work together, and rules are developed with acceptable behaviour defined. Members begin to trust one another, and the accepting of criticism and new ideas are developed. During this stage, leaders emerge and take responsibility, and the coach becomes a **consultant**.
- **Performing**, in which the group works as a unit, group members are interdependent, and the more skilful or experienced members make decisions independently. During this stage, there is consultation (by the coach), leadership is devolved and accepted, and authority and direction are accepted in times of stress. Dissent can be used to improve performance, as members argue and reach agreement on the best way forward at difficult moments.

figure 15.1 – Tuckman's model

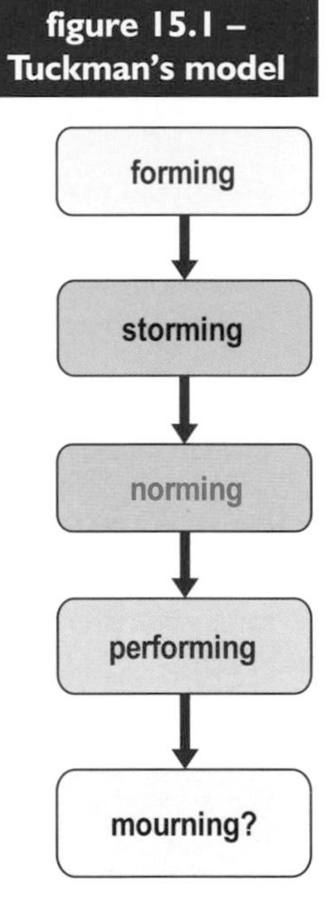

The possible fifth stage is:
- **Mourning**, as a group breaks up and members go their separate ways. This is almost the inevitable eventual outcome when a number of highly independent and articulate individuals are members of a group.

Group cohesion

Cohesion points at the way in which group members **gel** together, or feel **collective affection** for one another, or feel a strong **sense of sharing** whatever it is that the group does. It is the extent to which members of a group exhibit a desire to **achieve common goals** and **group identity**. The two themes of co-operation and co-ordination are strong elements of this idea.
- Sometimes this can mean selection of less skilled but more co-operative players for a team.
- Unfortunately, friendship groups can have negative effects.

Cohesion has both **task** and **social** elements:
- **Task cohesion** is about people who are willing to work together (see figure 15.2) whether or not they get on personally, hence the group would have the potential to be successful.
- **Social cohesion** covers the notion that teams with high social cohesion but low task cohesion are less successful.

Carron's model

figure 15.2 – cohesion is important for some teams

This model (figure 15.3) outlines **four** factors that affect the development of cohesion:

- **Environmental factors** which bind members to a team, for example, contracts, location, age, eligibility. To make cohesion stronger, you should avoid a star system and provide opportunities for socialising.
- **Personal factors** which feature things that members believe are important, and include motives for taking part. To optimise on cohesion, a coach should give opportunities for motives to be realised, and develop ownership feelings and social groupings within the team.
- **Leadership factors** which are about the behaviour of leaders and coaches. Coaches should use all leadership behaviours to influence different individuals.
- **Team factors** relating to the group, including team identity, targets, member ability and role, creation of team short- and long-term goals, and the rewarding of individual and team efforts.

figure 15.3 – Carron's model of cohesion

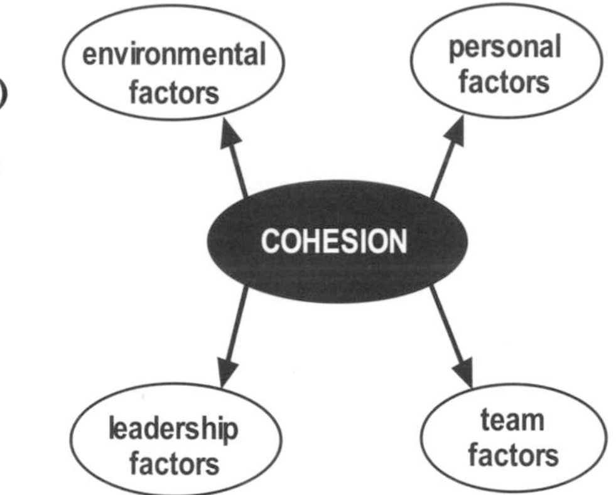

Steiner's model of a group or team

This model states that:

team success
= (potential for success) - (co-ordination and motivation problems)

- **Potential for success** revolves around the issues that usually skilful individuals make the best team, and usually individual success (of team members) correlates with overall team success.
- **Co-ordination problems** (for players) occur if there should be a high level of interaction between players, but one (or more) player is being selfish or aggressive, or if a defence is not working together, and hence overall team performance suffers.

figure 15.4 – social loafing

- **Motivation problems** occur because people seem to work less hard in a group than they do on their own. For example, in rowing, times of winning double sculls are often only slightly faster than single sculls. This is **social loafing**, 'the **Ringlemann Effect**.'
- **Motivational losses** occur because individuals may not share the same motives. This leads to loss of group cohesion, for example, some players may play a game for social reasons, others in order to win.

Social loafing, the Ringlemann Effect

- **Social loafing** is the term which describes the fact that individuals appear to **reduce their effort** when in a group (figure 15.4), and can **hide their lack of effort** amongst the effort of other group members.
- It can be eliminated if the contribution of an individual **can be identified** as with **player statistics** (American football, rugby league, cricket, basketball).
- The **need** for interaction between players varies between sports.
- **Co-operation** between players can be significant in eliminating social loafing.

Sociograms

A **sociogram** is a chart which shows the links and relationships between members of a group. Sociograms also demonstrate how sub-groups are formed within the main group, and the reasons for the existence of subgroupings.

Sociogram example

To establish a sociogram, people (labelled A to Z in figure 15.5) within a group are each asked to list contacts and relationships between themselves and the other members of the group. Individuals are then represented by a circle on the sociogram (figure 15.5), and the contacts and relationships by arrows. As you can see from figure 15.5, one or two individuals are much more popular than others (X and Y), and others are almost completely isolated (without any relationships with others), for example individual Z.

figure 15.5 – a sociogram

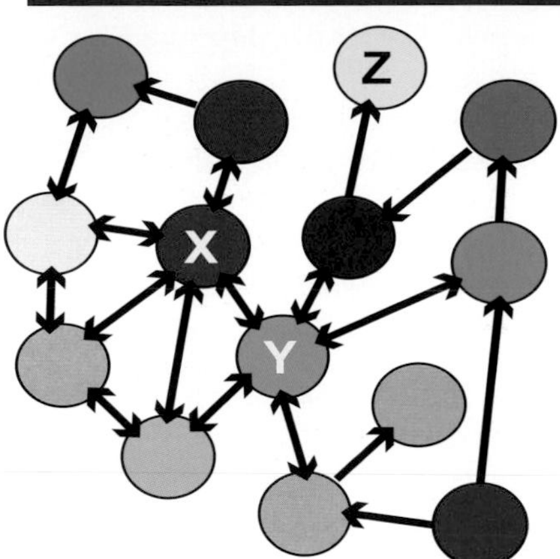

The chart produced will tell a coach whether he would need to help an individual make contacts with other members of a group, which would help **group cohesion** and collective well-being. He would need to develop tactics to **include** such individuals in activities, and to positively reinforce his or her worth to other group members.

Leadership

figure 15.6 – who is the leader of this group?

A leader can influence the behaviour of others towards required goals and will influence effective team cohesion. He or she will also help fulfil the expectations of a team, and will develop an environment in which a group is motivated, rewarded and helped towards its common goals.

- **Emergent leaders** come from within a group because of their skill and abilities or through nomination or election.
- **Prescribed leaders** are appointed by a governing body or agency outside the group.

Theories of leadership

These theories centre around the **nature** or **nurture** debate.

The 'great man' or trait theory

This is the '**nature**' theory, that leaders are born (figure 15.6) not made, and have relevant innate personality qualities.

figure 15.7 – what style of leadership is shown here?

Social learning theory

This is the '**nurture**' theory, in which leaders learn their skills through watching and imitating other people (models). This theory says that leaders are formed throughout life by social or environmental influences.

According to this idea, learning to be a leader starts by observation of a model, then continues by imitation or copying of the behaviour of the model. The effectiveness of this process would depend on the model having high status.

The Chelladurai continuum

The Chelladurai continuum theory covers the notion that there are three types of leader, and that an actual leader may adopt all three of the types in different situations depending on the circumstances. These three types of leader are:

- The **autocratic authoritarian** leader who makes all the decisions.
- The **democratic** leader who shares the decisions (with members of a group or team), and seeks advice from the group itself. He or she will be prepared to change his or her mind based on this advice.
- The **laissez-faire** leader who lets others make decisions and is prepared to go along with whatever they decide.

Martin Johnson (figure 15.7) leads by both example and by his own trait qualities. The following discussion outlines how someone like Martin can lead by his authority, based on his past history as a player.

Factors affecting leader effectiveness

The following **leadership qualities** will determine a leader's effectiveness:

- Ability to communicate.
- Respect for group members.
- Enthusiasm.
- High ability.
- Deep knowledge of the sport and techniques or tactics.
- Charisma.

Figure 15.8 summarises the three broad groups of factors affecting the effectiveness of a leader with any given group or team.

figure 15.8 – factors affecting leader effectiveness

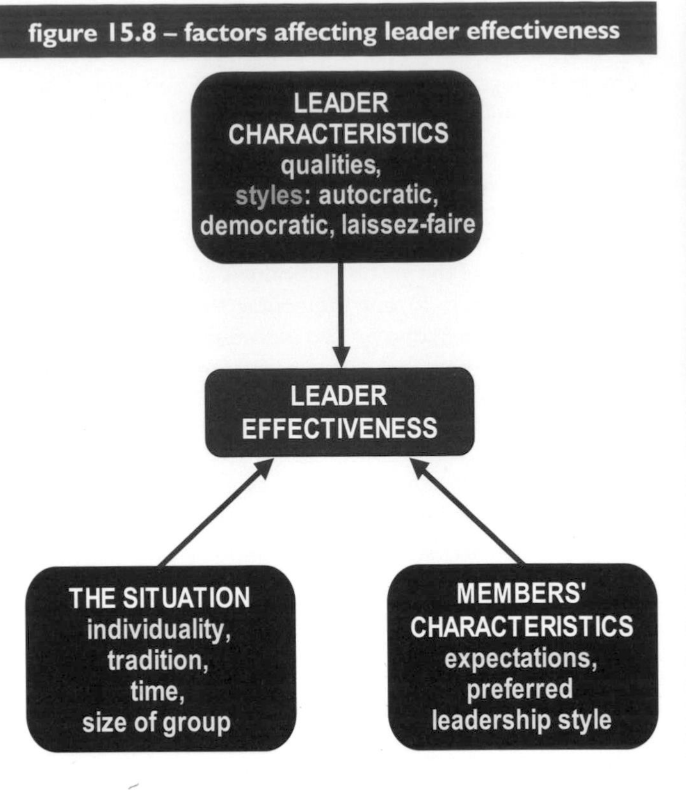

Fiedler's contingency theory

Fiedler's theory states that there is a continuum between:

- **Task-centred leadership**, which would be best for the most favourable or least favourable situations.
- **Person** (or relationship) **centred leadership** which would be best for moderately favourable situations.

Whether or not the task-centred or person-centred approach should be used depends on whether relationships are warm, if the task has a clear structure, or if the leader is powerful and people will do exactly what he or she says. There would also be the pressure of time which might affect the choice of leadership style.

Situational factors within leadership

- If things are going **well** for the team, or things are going **badly** (for example there are poor facilities or no support), then a leader needs to be **task-oriented**.
- On the other hand, if things are going **moderately well**, then a leader needs to be **person-centred**.

- In **team sports**, a leader should be **directive** (task-oriented) and would organise and structure group tasks according to a plan (tactics or game strategy, for example).
- In **individual sports**, however, we would look for a person-oriented leader, who would empathise with athlete problems and be sympathetic to individual difficulties.
- The **size of group** will affect leadership style, since the more members in a group, the less likely individual needs will be taken into account.

- If a **decision needs to be made quickly** (for example in a dangerous rock climbing situation), then an **autocratic** style of leader would be essential to ensure that the correct action is taken immediately (people will need to be told what to do to avoid danger).

- **Tradition** can sometimes play a part in which style of leadership should be used, since within some groups, group members might tend to resent change. Sometimes change is essential, and it would be necessary to be **autocratic** and **task-centred** to implement change (the leader would not try and explain why change is needed, just that it needs to be done for the good of the team).

Members' characteristics within leadership

A good leader will adapt to the expectations, knowledge and experience of group members.

- If members of a group are **hostile**, then a leader would adopt an **autocratic** style.
- If members of a group are **friendly**, then the leader would adopt a more **democratic** and **person-centred** style.

Problems arise if the strategies for preparation used by a leader do not match group expectations (for example, if members of a team do not feel that the proposed strategy will achieve a win in the next match against a particular opposing team).

Chelladurai's multidimensional model

Chelladurai set out the model in figure 15.9, which sets out the links between leader, situation and member characteristics, and required, actual and preferred leader behaviour. All these factors will affect the eventual performance of a team or group, **and** the satisfaction gained or perceived by both group members and the leader him or herself.

The point made by the model is that all the factors discussed above are linked in a real situation.

figure 15.9 – Chelladurai's multidimensional model

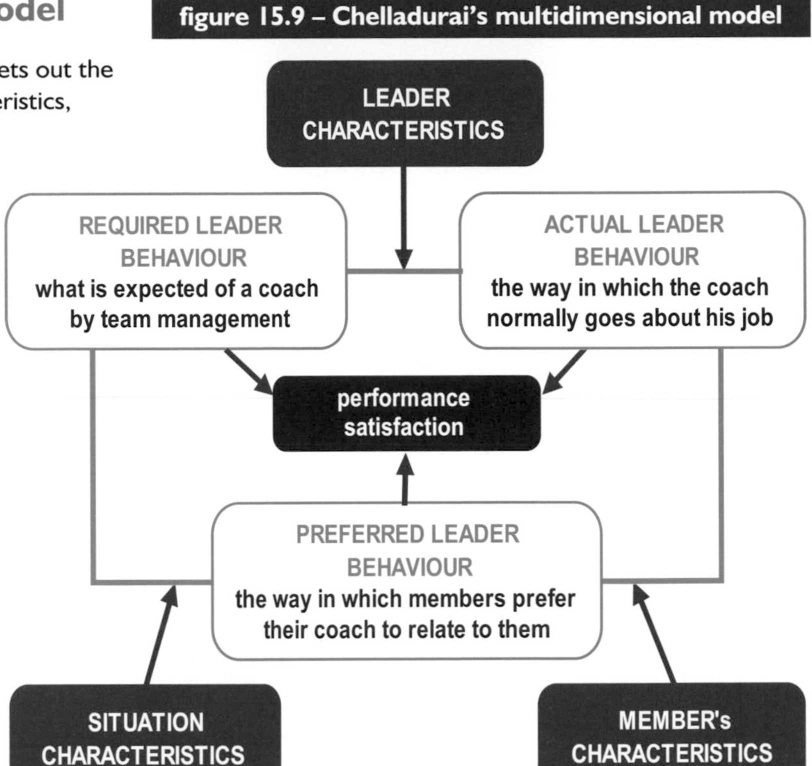

Chelladurai's five types of leader behaviour

- **Training and instruction**, in which behaviour is aimed at improving performance. This type of leader behaviour is strong on technical and tactical aspects.
- A **democratic approach**, in which the leader allows decisions to be made collectively.
- An **autocratic approach**, in which a leader uses his or her personal authority. This type would be least preferred if the leader or coach does not show that he or she is aware of sportspeople's needs and preferences.
- The **social support** approach, in which concern is shown for the well-being of others. This might be preferred by youngsters.
- The **rewards** approach in which a leader uses positive reinforcement to gain the authority of leadership.

Practice questions

1) a) What is meant by cohesion in the context of teams? 4 marks

   b) What factors stop a team ever performing to its true potential? 6 marks

2) a) Explain what is meant by social loafing by using examples from sport. 3 marks

   b) What advice would you give a coach of a team to ensure maximum productivity? 5 marks

3) a) What is meant by a leader and what sort of qualities would you expect to see in a leader within the context of sport? 4 marks

   b) Using psychological theories describe how an individual becomes a leader. 4 marks

4) a) Name three leadership styles. 3 marks

   b) What factors should be taken into consideration when deciding upon which leadership style to adopt? 6 marks

5) Look at figure 15.9 of Chelladurai's Multidimensional Model of Leadership.

   a) Explain each part of the model using examples from sport. 3 marks

   b) Behaviour of the group associated with leadership can be viewed from three perspectives. Briefly name and explain each of these perspectives. 3 marks

   c) Discuss the statement 'Good leaders are born not made', and explain whether you agree or disagree in the light of psychological theory. 5 marks

6) Fiedler's Contingency Model suggests that the effectiveness of a leader can change depending on the situation. Use sporting examples to explain this theory. 4 marks

STUDENT NOTES

SECTION C: EVALUATING CONTEMPORARY INFLUENCES

CHAPTER 16 – CHARACTERISTICS OF WORLD GAMES

Characteristics of World Games

The notion of World Games is broad and can be **multi-sport** or **single sport** and usually involves the **best competitors**, the **elite**, from around the **World**. Such games may be:

- Multi-sport potentially involving all countries, for example, the Summer and Winter Olympic Games, and the Paralympic Games.
- Multi-sport involving several countries, for example, the Commonwealth Games, the African Games, and the Pan-American Games.
- Single-sport potentially involving all countries, for example, the Football FIFA World Cup, the World Athletics Championships, the World Hockey Championships, and the World Badminton Championships.

The characteristics of such global games are:

- They involve **elite performers**.
- Usually from the **whole World**, but can be regional.
- Usually require **qualification** from regional groupings or by standard.
- Most countries staging them will use them as a **shop window**.
- Often highly commercialised with **sponsorship**.
- Often with high **media** coverage (TV rights paid for as part of the finance for the event).
- Development of elite **facilities**, some or all of which will be a heritage for the future.
- Possibly involving large **spectatorship**.

figure 16.1 – global games

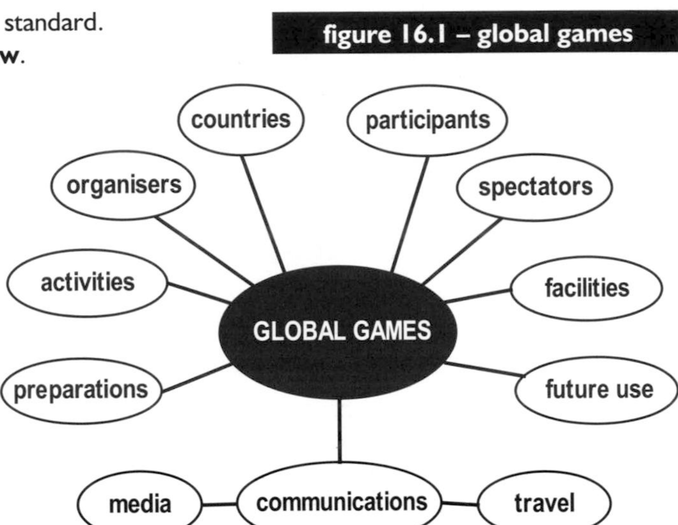

Figure 16.1 outlines the factors involved in staging a global games.

- **Organisers**, the efficient handling of activities.
- **Participants**, the suitability, opportunity, comfort.
- **Spectators**, attendance provision, media provision.
- **Activities**, specified and provided.
- **Facilities**, highest standard with future potential.
- **Preparations**, ready on time.
- **Future use**, forward planning and extended value.
- **Media**, communication and commercial.
- **Travel**, convenient for training and competition.

The host country

figure 16.2 – advantages to a host country

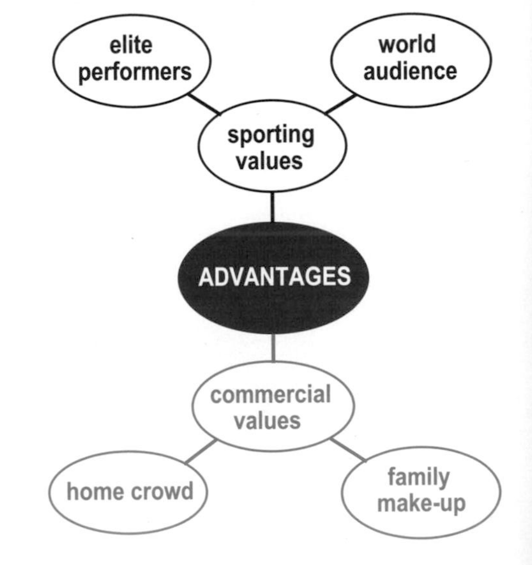

Figure 16.2 summarises the **advantages** to a host country of staging a games:

- **Elite performers'** chance to compete against the best.
- **World audience** enlightening spectators, viewers and nations.
- **Commercial** profit through games ceremonies, merchandising and TV rights.
- The **commercial values** of successful champions.
- **Sponsorship** of performers and events.

STUDENT NOTE

The influence of the USA and of the dependence of the Olympic Games on TV rights – also influenced largely by American interests – is a dominant feature of how the Olympics is allocated and organised. Commercialism, with a huge advertising audience, started in Los Angeles, 1984. This evolved into commercial TV networks owning the broadcasting rights and paying a huge price, but with World-wide advertising.

The socio-cultural factors likely to influence global games are outlined in figure 16.3:

- **Historical**, developmental background and past experience.
- **Social**, well-being of competitors, interaction during games and spectator welfare.
- **Cultural**, opportunity for nations through sport, increased awareness and wellbeing.
- **Political**, a vehicle for harmony or nationalist identity.
- **Economic**, potential national income or debt, useful future usage of facilities.
- **International**, increased national prestige, awareness and wellbeing.

figure 16.3 – socio-cultural factors

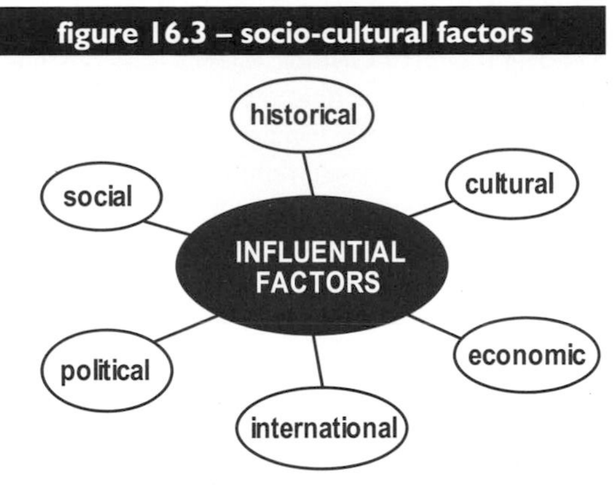

To hold a World championship may be a **shop window** for a country to display its culture and attract business and motivate a society. But recognition can be **temporary** and money spent does not necessarily help those in need in that country.

Similarly, visiting a country to compete may give a performer experience of how others do it, but it is rare if a performer will learn anything permanent from the process. It is difficult for a highly motivated and highly focused individual to learn something of a foreign culture and administration when all he or she is interested in doing is winning his or her event.

If the objective is to hold '**open**' World competition, this may be jeopardised where professionalism has led to a performing elite in some sports, which is little more than a circus. This notion of elitism and high reward has inevitably left us with an illegal drugs industry, with sports medicine and the drug testing organisations too often a step behind.

figure 16.4 – London2012

STUDENT NOTE

The Olympic Games is the most significant attempt to establish globalisation within sport. Therefore you will need to be able to structure an analysis of the Olympic Games, giving points for and against the possibility of successfully achieving sports organisation at World level. This should use examples from various Olympic Games. In this way you can present a feasibility study.

Case study of London2012 as a World Games

Opportunity

The **opportunity** for the society which holds the games – for example **London and Britain 2012** (figure 16.4 and 16.5) – depends on the view it takes of the **facilities** which will be adapted or built to cater for the 28 sports and 11,000+ competitors.

This has been described as the **heritage** to be gained by the people of Britain as reward for holding the Games. However, some facilities will be **dismantled** or **turned over** for other use after the Games. For example, athletes' accommodation will be converted to domestic homes, and the stadium will be reduced in size so that lower numbers can be accommodated for large domestic athletic events.

figure 16.5 – facilities as a heritage

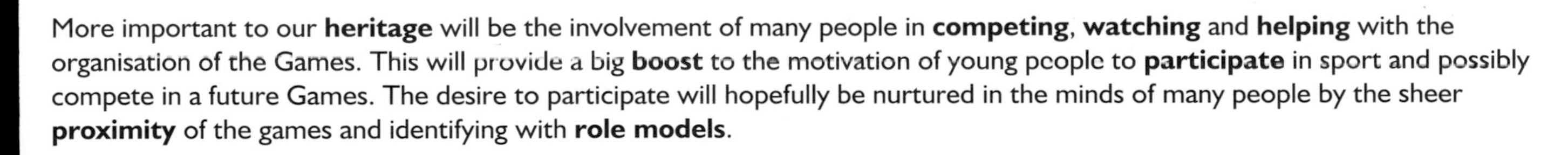

More important to our **heritage** will be the involvement of many people in **competing**, **watching** and **helping** with the organisation of the Games. This will provide a big **boost** to the motivation of young people to **participate** in sport and possibly compete in a future Games. The desire to participate will hopefully be nurtured in the minds of many people by the sheer **proximity** of the games and identifying with **role models**.

Can London2012 enable British sport to move forward? It will be difficult for Britain to improve on 2008!

Government issues

Holding the 2012 Olympic Games is an obvious reason for Britain to join the USA, Australia, and China in a drive to achieve sporting excellence. Reasons for this could be:

- **National pride**, highlight political superiority, prestige and advertising for the host country (shop window?).
- The British Government has a **political motive** for pouring money into sport in the UK.
- Improvement in sporting **facilities**, meeting society's demands for national sporting success.
- The **re-generation** of a whole London district.
- Improvements to trade, economy, tourism, **infrastructure** - transport, housing, hotels.
- A stimulus to a nation faced with excessive obesity.
- Encourages **mass participation** in sport.
- Enables individuals to **succeed** (due to increased provision).

figure 16.6 – Rebecca Adlington, new swim sports star

Impact on the individual

We know how we felt when Rebecca Adlington took on the World and won. Now that the Olympics are '**professional**', the limit of achievement is no longer our cricket and football. Hence we can now produce champion swimmers (figure 16.6), cyclists and athletes as we have rowers, riders and sailors in the past.

This time **all** elite athletes, not just the socially privileged ones, will have the chance to achieve their potential, because there is the funding and organisation to make it possible.

Individuals will be:

- **Motivated** by high competitive drive (i.e. the will to be the best - intrinsic motivation).
- Able to meet **personal goals** - to be number one in the World!
- Able to develop a **career** and to gain recognition or sponsors - extrinsic motivation (rewards).
- Inspired by **role models**.
- **Encouraged** by peer or family.
- GIven the **opportunity**, **pride** or **satisfaction** to represent his or her own country.
- Given the opportunity to **perform** at the **highest** level.

Table 16.1 – **summary of issues affecting World games**

the performer can obtain:	the spectator receives or develops:	commercial interests obtain:
celebrity status	excitement	money or revenue
sponsorship deals	entertainment	advertising
advertising deals	escapism	raised profile
personal satisfaction	fan base	boosts to business
high earning potential	encouragement into sport	association with elite performers
recognition		
respect		

Elite sport development in the United Kingdom

Sporting excellence is the objective of most countries these days and advanced, industrialised countries like the UK, Australia and USA would be looking for a very broad pyramid of opportunity, in which provision for all and self-esteem for all minorities to participate are essential.

To achieve sporting excellence and Olympic success, **disproportionate** funding for sport is necessary. The World tends to place sport high as a barometer of the political and economic success of a country. Hence participation in sport in most countries follows a pyramid model as outlined in figure 16.7, with state funding or support only being available for the top tier (and occasionally for the next to top tier).

The shape of that pyramid depends on the extent to which elitism is operating.

There is a balance between **extrinsic** and **intrinsic** values which leads to professional administrative standards and required levels of sportsmanship.

Sports development pyramid

Each of the five areas of participation - the activity, the performer, the administrator (Governing Bodies), the official, and the spectator - need to be fully 'professionalised' to establish excellence.

The implication is that spectators are going to have to pay a lot of money to fulfil this aim unless television, particularly commercial television, pays the bill.

figure 16.7 – sports development pyramid

elite
national standard
public recognition

performance
coaching & development
done at club & regional levels

participation
increasing leisure options & HRF awareness
promoted via extra-curricular sport

foundation
learning basic skills, knowledge
& understanding, often delivered in
PE programmes in schools

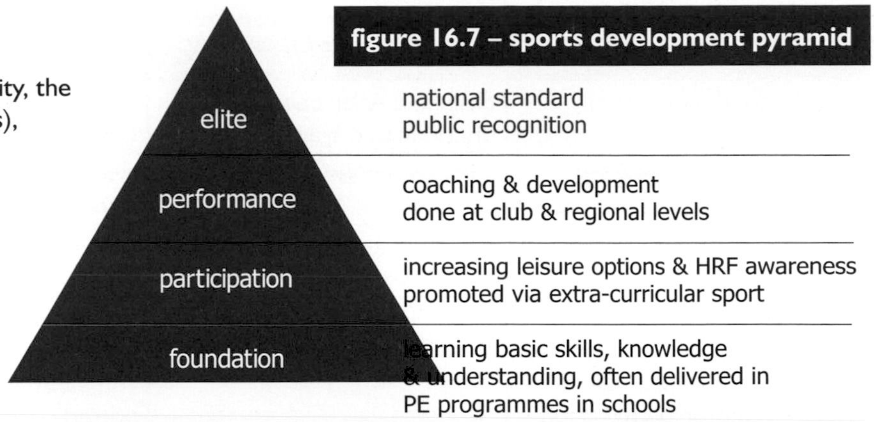

STUDENT NOTE

The pyramid model labels the basic bottom level (figure 16.7) as **foundation** activity in which many people take part in many different broad-based activities. Then some of these people will move on to the next level, **participation**, where particular sports become important to them at the basic competitive level, and they become aware of health, recreation and fitness (HRF) issues. A smaller number of people then become involved at a higher level, which involves training and directed activity where **performance** is improving. From this group would emerge a much smaller group who would have the talent and ability to reach a stage of **excellence** which could be described as **elite performance**. See page 159 onwards of 'AS Revise PE for AQA', ISBN: 978 1 901424 56 0.

This model of funding implies that UK Sport or the English Institute of Sport would only provide funding to those individuals who might achieve a **podium place** at London2012, and, more importantly, would extend the use of the regional centres of excellence, the 12 hubs in the UK, only to those people. Unfortunately, it is very difficult to identify sportspeople in these categories, and so wastage occurs and middle sections of the pyramid miss out.

figure 16.8 – sports development pyramid

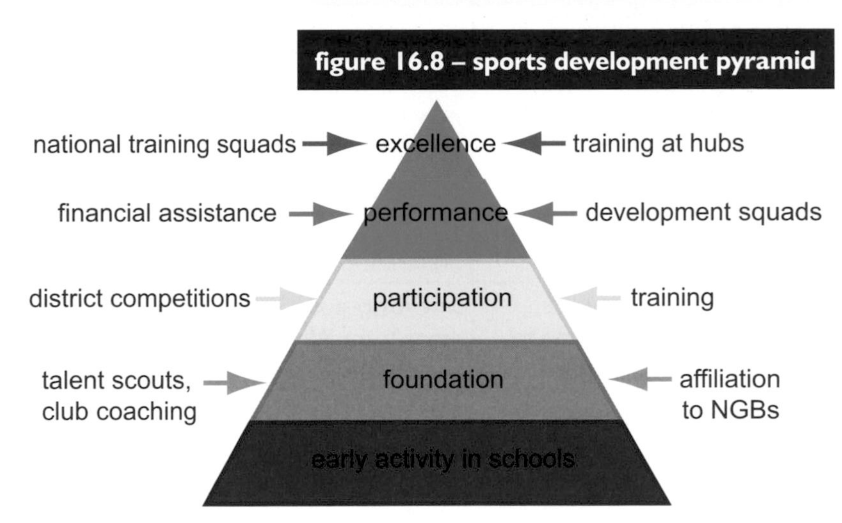

The pyramid model can be extended as in figure 16.8.

The administrative support policy for excellence in sport has already been identified at school level, with the emphasis on sports colleges, gifted and talented programmes and Active Sports.

Barriers to progression

Figure 16.9 outlines four factors which could be **barriers to progression** up the pyramid.

STUDENT NOTE

Issues of gender, race and ethnicity, disability, and social class in sport are discussed on page 161 onwards of 'AS Revise PE for AQA', ISBN: 978 1 901424 56 0.

figure 16.9 – barriers to progression

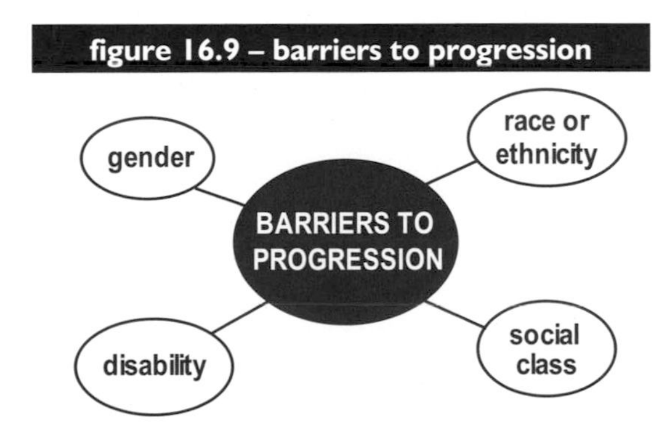

Table 16.2 overleaf summarises the issues which may act as barriers to progression.

Table 16.2 – barriers to progression (SE = socio-economic)

gender	race and ethnicity	disability	social class
women are discriminated against in sport - and in society	black and Asian people discriminated against in society	9% participation in sport (lower than able-bodied)	lack of financial support a big barrier
there are still stereotypical attitudes to female participation	25% soccer premiership players black, hardly any Asians	great success in Paralympics - 2nd in medal table Beijing	parental support important at young age
in Beijing, 45% of participants were female	50% UK athletics power event competitors black	elite athletes funded from lottery same as able-bodied	elite amateur athletes funded from lottery
in Athens 40% of British team were women, in IOC only 14% are women, the glass ceiling applies to female participation	in tennis no black and only one Asian competitor in UK top ten	Sports Aid helps performers in 25 disabled sports compared with 50 able-bodied	participation from lower SE groups about 55% lower when compared to upper SE groups
women's top soccer is still semi-professional	in UK rugby, very few black players	still lack of access to some sports facilities	some activities associated with upper SE status people
before 2007, men's prize money at Wimbledon was more than women's	no research evidence that black Afro-Caribbean people have higher fast twitch muscle, or less subcutaneous fat	age limit for TASS funding raised to 35 compared with 25 for able-bodied	amateur sports have fewer low SE status elite performers
top sportswomen have 14% of income of top men, and find it harder to get sponsorship	hence stereotype of black Afro-Caribbean potential at sport incorrect	low levels of sponsorship	membership of some sport clubs only open to financially independent people
women's boxing, pole vault, triple jump, hammer & weight lifting only allowed since 1987	lack of role models in low black participation sport discourages new participants	lack of media exposure compared to able-bodied sport	low SE group people have less leisure time than upper SE groups
female sport has less social status than male sport	media reflect society's view of black people	media focus on adversity rather than ability	fewer people from low SE groups participate after 16
females get less media space or time than males in the UK	great success from male Asian boxers and cricketers		unless talent identified young, low SE people drop out
women's fitness - hence muscularity - causes media to call into question sexuality	low socio-economic status of many black Afro-Caribbean people prevents participation		
media focus on women's appearance rather than sport			

Practice questions

1) Discuss the characteristics of World games, and explain how participation in such a games will affect a competitor. 10 marks

2) Outline the factors which influence a government to bid for a global games in its country. You may use China or Great Britain to illustrate your answer. 10 marks

3) What benefits will a country gain from staging a global games? 5 marks

4) UK Sport is responsible for managing and distributing a sporting programme. How do the UK Sports Institutes co-ordinate elite sport development within the UK? 4 marks

5) Outline the roles of various agencies or bodies in the UK which have an effect on participation at the foundation level in sport. 6 marks

6) Identify the theory behind the Sports Development Pyramid and explain the intentions behind each section. 6 marks

7) Briefly outline the barriers to progression for a talented youngster to strive towards elite sporting level. How does social status affect progression towards elite sporting level? 10 marks

8) People from ethnic minorities, low socio-economic groups and women, face more barriers in their struggle to reach elite levels in sport than those from dominant groups. Discuss. 14 marks

CHAPTER 17 – THE WORLD CLASS PERFORMANCE PATHWAY

The **World Class Programme** (figure 17.1) is the UK's elite performance structure. It links the most talented with the Governing Bodies structure for development into National Team membership. The Government policy for elite sport is the ultimate opportunity for co-ordinated action in preparation for the 2012 Olympic Games in London.

figure 17.1 – World Class Programme

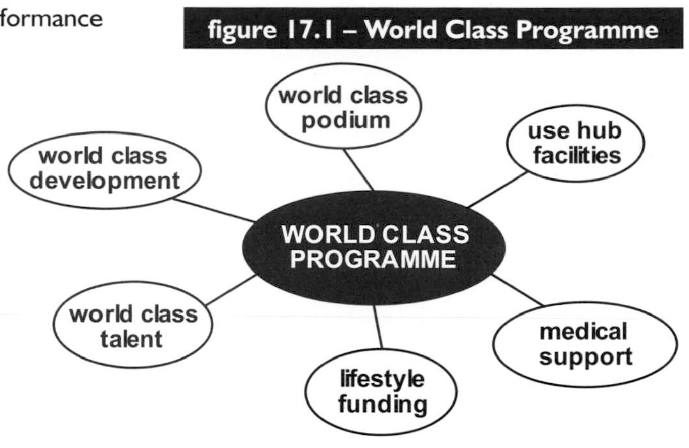

The Governing Bodies still have a major responsibility for their individual sports, but UK Sport is responsible for managing and directing public investment and is a statutory distributor of funds raised by the **National Lottery**. This body is accountable to Parliament through the department of Culture, Media and Sport and UK Sport's aim is to work in partnership to lead sport in the UK to World class success.

UK Sport's goals are given the title 'World Class Performance'.

World Class Programme

The UKSI (specifically the EIS – see page 111 below) is a talent development organisation in that it provides the facilities (the multi-sport hubs) and opportunities for talent to develop. The aim is to produce performers at the elite level of the sport development pyramid, and who will therefore become part of the lottery funded World Class Programme. The WCP has three levels (figure 17.1):

- **World Class Talent** – helping the sportspeople whose talent has been identified to progress towards elite level.
- **World Class Development** – helping talented sportspeople who are competent performers to achieve a competitive edge.
- **World Class Podium** – supporting sportspeople who have medal potential. They should be standing on the medal podium at the next World or global games for their sport – but particularly at the London Olympic Games 2012.

The World Class Programme will then support sportspeople with various services ranging from the use of the hub facilities, the use of the medical support systems run by the EIS, and lifestyle funding (in place of a salary) for those elite athletes on the top level of the programme.

Also, the programme has put in place top quality support people such as strength and conditioning specialists, medical support teams, sports science specialists, and sport psychology experts. These people's job is to advise on most situations facing the aspiring performer.

The main point of this activity is to provide a worry-free environment for the sportsperson to train for up to 6 hours per day for 6 days of the week (allowing for some rest and recovery time!).

The role and purpose of external organisations

STUDENT NOTE

Bodies promoting participation (figure 17.2) are discussed on page 157 onwards of 'AS Revise PE for AQA' ISBN: 978 1 901424 56 0, and are summarised in table 17.1, page 111 below.

UK Sport is subdivided into the Home Country Sports Councils (for example Sport England) who distribute lottery funding to the grass roots of sport, but also to elite sports organisations.

- **Governing Bodies** are still responsible for establishing the rules of their sport, organising national championships, coaching within their sport, and selecting teams for international competitions.
- The **EIS** (English Institute of Sport) is a network of World class support services, which includes nine regional multi-sport hub sites, and an evolving network of satellite centres.
- The EIS runs a **Performance Lifestyle Programme**, which provides supplementary career and education advice and a sports science and sports medicine service.

Opportunity

In terms of sporting excellence, pre-supposing an individual has the talent to achieve excellence, then he or she must have the opportunity provided by facility provision near enough to be feasible for regular travel.

- The '**hubs**' (multi-sports **High Performance Centres**) provided by the Sports Councils and the Institutes of Sport for elite sportspeople, are intended to be located within 1 hour travel time of a million people, and 30 minutes travel time for 250,000.
- What is happening is that **Governing Bodies** are insisting that members of the World Class Performance groups locate themselves near to a hub, so that coaching and medical support can also be provided simply and at less cost.
- Membership of a WCP group or **National Squad** carries great intrinsic and extrinsic esteem (in terms of adulation from the press and people who follow the sport) and ensures high motivation to succeed.

figure 17.2 – bodies promoting participation

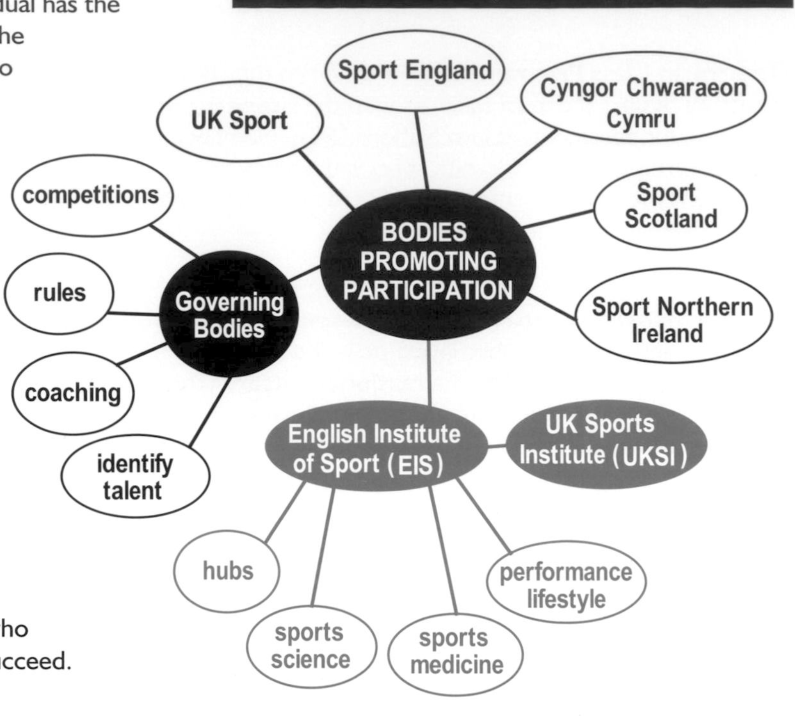

Two programmes warrant special mention.

Talent identification programme

The **Talent Identification Programme** (TIP) was developed by **East Germany** in the 1970s and adopted by **Australia** after their poor showing in the Montreal Olympics in 1976. TIP:

- Promotes the use of a system which is scientifically based in terms of training, diet and sports medicine.
- Gives to elite athletes considerable material benefits, including increased time, professional coaching and the use of top facilities.
- TIP UK is part of the World Class Programme, and promotes the British School Games with its competitive environment.
- The **Talented Athletic Scholarship Scheme** (TASS) is Government funded to support athletes on academic courses.
- Advance Apprenticeship in Sporting Excellence (AASE) targets 16 to 18 year-olds in several games and swimming.

Long Term Athlete Development (LTAD)

The majority of NGBs in the UK use the model of LTAD developed by Istvan Balyi in 2001. The philosophy of this LTAD model is as follows:

- It aims to **retain** athletes for life as well as develop them.
- It hopes to **match** desire and talent of a performer to an appropriate training environment.
- In turn, this should lead to increased retention and increased success.
- It hopes to establish a clear **development** route for athletes.

www.sportscoachuk.org/Investing+in+Coaching/Long-term+Athlete+Development/LTAD+for+NGBs.htm

Structure of the LTAD model

The adoption of the LTAD model by UK Sport is based on its need to see routes from foundation activity into elite sport **in the long-term** for those sportspeople who have been identified as talented enough to reach that level. UK LTAD also provides an underpinning of **Whole Sport Plans** (WSPs - see page 110 below) and **One Stop Plans** implemented by Governing Bodies for their sports.

The model also explains that once an athlete's sporting career is over, he or she should be able or be motivated to continue with some activity based on the athlete's elite sport for the rest of his or her life in the interests of personal health.

An important feature of the model is that it looks at the state of development of the athlete rather than his or her age when setting out the details of what should be done to move on to the next level.

The model will:

- Ensure a systematic and coherent **development** approach for athletes.
- Ensure that competition at a junior level is **not overemphasised**, hence improve retention of potential talent.

The six stages of the late specialisation LTAD model

In the UK programme (figure 17.3), young children are guided from simple, generic movement skills to more complex, sport specific skills. The age at which performers progress through the stages varies from sport to sport.

FUNdamentals, in which:

- **Basic** movement skills are introduced, such as hand-eye-foot co-ordination.
- Skills are **generic** – not sport specific.
- Skills are learnt in a fun and **motivational** environment.
- The aim is to keep children (6-9 yrs) interested and create a **positive attitude** towards sport and physical activity.

Learning to train, the major learning stage in which:

- **Sport specific** skills are learnt.
- The basics learnt at the **FUNdamental** stage are continued.
- Training is tailored to the performer's **maturation stage** (8-12 yrs) and level of growth.
- Players perform in **modified games**, progressing to full games with international rules.

Training to train, in which:

- **Fitness** (aerobic or strength or speed) is developed.
- Training is according to the performer's **developmental stage.**
- There is development of **sport specific movement skills.**
- There is an increased **range and knowledge** of sport specific movements.
- Coaches are encouraged to **monitor players** in this stage, as it is usually around the time of puberty (11-16 yrs).
- Players' bodies are rapidly changing, which may lead to a 'slow down' in their sport development.

Training to compete, in which:

- **Fitness preparation** is optimised.
- There is a high volume and **increasing intensity** of training sessions.
- The sportsperson will continue to develop **sport specific skills**, including tactics, strategies, decision-making skills and technical awareness.
- Training should be **specific** to the performer (16-23 yrs).
- Players learn how to **analyse** their own and others' performances in order to optimise performance.

Training to win, in which:

- **Event specific** preparation is maximised.
- There will be a **high intensity** and volume of training.
- The sportsperson will gain experience in **international**/high level competitions.
- These experiences should be of both **junior** and **adult** competitions (18+ yrs), in order to ensure a seamless transfer from junior to adult level.

Active for life, in which:

- Players are encouraged to **remain** in their sport after retirement.
- An athlete may **change sports** - for example, a shot putter to bobsleigh.
- Retention could be done by gaining **coaching** or **officiating** qualifications throughout their career.
- Athletes are also provided with **playing and contribution opportunities** after their career, such as sport administration or team management, or media involvement.
- There should be a movement away from the intensity of competitive sports and into more **recreative** activity options such as jogging, walking (hill walking?), swimming or cycling.

figure 17.3 – LTAD model

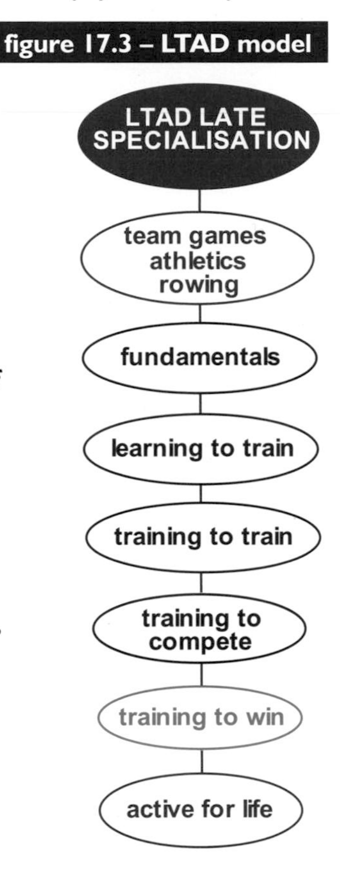

There will be variation of the ages at which the different stages should occur depending on the sport or stage of talent development of the athlete. The model identifies the sports of athletics, most team games, and rowing as being applicable. In this case, talent may sometimes not emerge until 14 to 18 years of age with a correspondingly later age at which specialisation takes place and subsequent development to elite level.

Early specialisation model

For example, it is usual for young people who show talent at swimming, gymnastics or trampolining and diving, to do so when very young, sometimes as early as 8 to 10 years of age. This requires **early specialisation** (figure 17.4) since peak performance will be also expected early. In this model note that it is important not to miss out the early stages even if a young person is ready to quickly move on. It will just be undertaken alongside other stages or more quickly depending on the athlete.

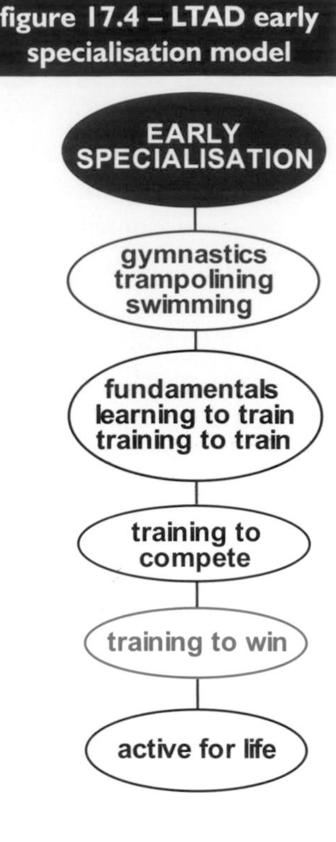

figure 17.4 – LTAD early specialisation model

This early specialisation model therefore combines the first three modules of the late specialisation model into a single period, reducing the time period over which they are developed.

Governing Bodies and Whole Sport Plans (WSPs)

In 2008, Sport England established a new strategy based on the headings, **grow**, **sustain**, and **excel**. This strategy aims to:

- Have 1 million more people doing more sport by 2013.
- Decrease by 25% the drop-out from sport for those participating at the age of 16.
- Develop LTADs alongside NGBs for the elite.

Whole Sport Plans (WSPs)

Sport England also require **Governing Bodies** to produce a **Whole Sport Plan** for their sport. The WSP would look at the whole sport from grass roots to elite in the context of grow, sustain and excel. On the basis of the plans to achieve the targets outlined above, the NGB is in effect applying to Sport England for funding to fulfil their plan. A single grant would then be awarded for the four year Olympic cycle, during which period the outcomes of the plan would be monitored by Sport England.

- An important part of the WSP is the provision of coaches (within the UK coaching framework - see below) to develop talent (**excel**), improve satisfaction (**sustain**), and encourage participation (**grow**).
- The Youth Sports Trust is linked to the '**grow**' target via the '**five hour sports offer**' weekly target for participation in some sort of physical activity by children in full time education.
- A WSP must include sport equity targets for under-represented groups (see '**barriers to progression**' on page 105 above).
- Future funding will depend on how well an NGB achieves its targets.

Other bodies and structures

figure 17.5 – sports coach UK

Sports coach UK

Sports coach UK was established in Leeds in 1983, and had an aim to increase and improve the level of coaching in the UK. This organisation works with sports councils, NGBs, schools, further education and higher education institutions, and awarding bodies across the country. Sports coach UK is a major participant within the UK coaching framework.

Sports coach UK provides a central resource of strategic and technical expertise, advice and support, and publishes a range of material relevant to coaching and sport under the publishing title 'Coachwise'. It also works with funding agencies to integrate coaching development into local authorities and sports agencies.

The UK Coaching Framework

The **UK coaching framework** is a country-wide plan begun in 2008 intended to bring the UK up to World number one standard in coaching by 2016. This framework will:

- **Enhance** the quality of coaching at all stages of coaches' development (for children, players and athletes).
- **Provide** active, skilled and qualified coaches to meet demand.
- **Lead** to sustained and increased participation.
- **Lead** to improved performances in sport underpinned by clear career structures for coaches within a professionally regulated vocation.

The British Olympic Association

The **BOA** aims to maximise the potential of all GB athletes in forthcoming summer and winter Olympic Games. It provides special services to elite athletes in order to ensure success in future Olympic Games. Services provided include:

- Olympic training and preparation camps.
- Sports science and medicine.
- Professional development for medics working with athletes.
- Research and rehabilitation after injury.
- Athlete preparation for elite sport, particularly in strength and conditioning.
- Team management programme to provide Olympic awareness.

National lottery funding for elite athletes

The National lottery was launched in 1994, and the funding for sport is distributed by Sport England (or home country councils).

STUDENT NOTE

National lottery funding for sport is discussed on page 140 onwards of 'AS Revise PE for AQA', ISBN: 978 1 901424 56 0.

National lottery funding for athletes who are on the World Class Performance Plan is the basis for the success of our amateur sportspeople.

Sports Aid

Sports Aid aims to help talented young athletes via support from individuals, corporate partners and grant-giving trusts. The funding takes two forms:

- The **Sports Aid grant** is awarded via NGBs, who must nominate athletes with the highest potential for success. Priority is given to athletes aged between 12 to 16, with the talent for high level performance, but with limited means. These grants make huge differences for talented individuals who have the ability to succeed in their chosen sport but cannot afford coaching, travel or equipment.

- **TASS** is the **Talented Athlete Scholarship Scheme**, which is a government funded programme which represents the links between sport and higher and further education. It hopes to develop sporting talent and success in the 16-25 year-old age range. For example, Carnegie Centre for Sports Performance and Well-being is a TASS hub institution.
  Successful applicants for TASS scholarships will receive between £1000 and £3000 to assist with coaching and equipment costs, as well as educational expenses. TASS athletes also receive a package of core sporting services which include coaching, sports medicine, sports science, strength and conditioning training, and lifestyle management.

Table 17.1 – **summary of functions of external bodies organising sport in the UK**

English Institute of Sport	Sport England	British Olympic Association (BOA)	National Governing Bodies
managed by Sport England	producing an active nation through sport	independent organisation without government control	competitions
network of support services	distributes lottery funds	support for TeamGB at games	officials and referees
nine multisport hub sites	focus on sport participation	planning for Olympic Games	selection for World Games
many satellite sites	provide seamless pathway from school to community to elite performance	promotes interest in Olympic Games and movement in Britain	maintenance of rules and discipline
supports > 2000 performers	work with NGBs to ensure TIP systems in place	with NGBs selects people for Olympic Games	promote sport throughout the UK and internationally
sport science support	link with NGBs over WSPs	planning for preparation to OG	attract sponsorship
physiology	include sport-equity	planning acclimatisation for OG	maintain TIP schemes
biomechanics	work with sports coach UK	runs programmes to assist athlete training	provide financial support
strength and conditioning	work with YST (5 hour offer)		selection for Sports Aid
sports medicine	work with YST to produce high quality coaching		selecting people for World Class Programme

English Institute of Sport	Sport England	British Olympic Association (BOA)	National Governing Bodies
medical screening	with NGBs attract volunteers	funds for OG used for:	selection for TASS funding
nutritional advice	establish sport club structure	athlete travel	access to hubs
sports massage	1 million more in sport by 2013	kit and equipment	training high level coaches
podiatry	25% less drop-out at 16	preparation camp	special development squads
performance lifestyle programme	help deliver 5 hour sport offer	funding from corporate sponsorship and appeals	access to high quality equipment
talent identification	improve TIP systems	role in delivering London2012:	sports science support
talent selection	increase in sport satisfaction	ensure success at 2012	provide lifestyle support
talent confirmation		viable London Institute of Sport	provide mentors
Olympic/Paralympic development	investing another £1bn before London2012	promote Olympic ideals across Olympic programme	information about competitions at all levels
talent transfer	helps athletes to find jobs which fit in with training		partnership with BOA, UK Sport

Practice questions

1) Explain how the structure of sporting organisation in the UK is able to develop talent. 5 marks

2) Describe the administrative system underpinning elite sport in the UK and account for its structure. 4 marks

3) Briefly identify and describe what you think UK Sport is doing to satisfy the needs of elite British performers. 4 marks

4) Describe a talent identification programme implemented by a UK governing body of a sport. 5 marks

5) a) Explain the philosophy of the Long Term Athlete Development model in use in most elite sports in the UK. 3 marks

   b) Briefly outline the difference between the two strands of the LTAD model as it is used in practice. 3 marks

6) Describe the main aims of the following organisations in relation to elite sport: National Governing Bodies, the British Olympic Association, Sports Aid, and Sport England. 8 marks

7) Identify the respective roles of government and lottery funding in the development of elite performers. 6 marks

8) Discuss how the UK coaching framework can achieve its aim to take coaching in the UK towards being the World number one by 2016. 4 marks

CHAPTER 18 – DEVELOPMENT and SPREAD of RATIONAL RECREATION

Popular recreation

It is important to understand the structure and function of popular recreation as it existed in pre-industrial Britain. Some of these recreations continued in rural society well after industrialisation, and others have been revived today as ethnic festival occasions.

The emergence of rational recreation was very much triggered by pupils and staff at upper middle class schools as they converted mob schoolboy sports into a controlled format. This controlled athleticism was seen to be a vehicle for desirable values and a way of life for respectable society.

Sport in pre-industrial England

The rise of **aristocratic and popular sports in England** reflected the influence of the Roman conquest on the existing Ancient British Celts and subsequent waves of invaders including the Anglo-Saxons and Vikings. By the time of the Norman Conquest, many folk activities existed, but the Norman aristocracy imposed their own activities, which divided sporting pastimes into **aristocratic pursuits** and **folk games**. Aristocrats indulged in such pastimes as 'par force' hunting, which combined most of the attributes of the killing of 'game', while the **folk games** emerged as religious festivals. These festivals were imposed on older pagan customs and became holy day celebrations and wakes. At this time, violent annual mob games existed in many towns and blood sports remained part of a cruel public ritual.

figure 18.1 – rural upper class pursuits

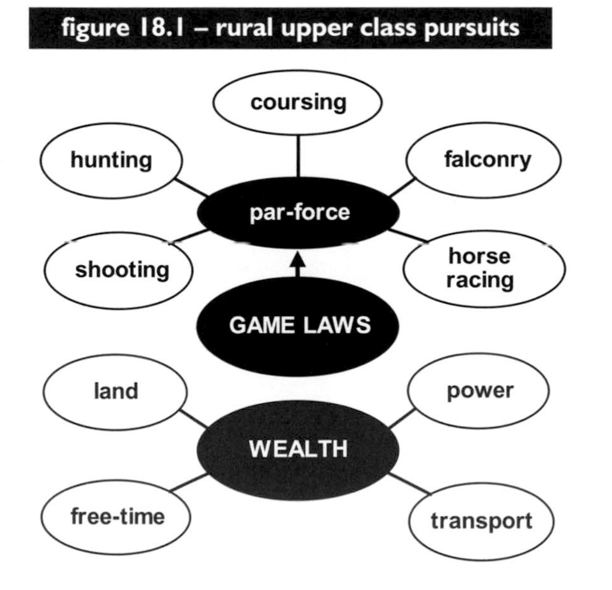

figure 18.2 – hunting as a sport?

figure 18.3 – falconry as an upper class pursuit

Many such activities continued until the end of the 19th century. In feudal times, **popular** sports were only possible with the sanction of the **clergy** and often the involvement of the landowners.

Rural upper class pursuits

The rural upper class (figure 18.1) had **power**, **land ownership** and **wealth** which allowed them to engage in activities (figures 18.2 and 18.3) controlled by the game laws as and when they liked without interference from the public. Gradually, aristocratic constraints were relaxed to include an emerging county gentry.

Popular recreations

The culture of the English lower classes before the late 19th century was linked with social conditions and formed the characteristics of their recreation and pastimes (figure 18.4) – in so far as there were any!

Popular recreations

- They were **occasional** (figure 18.4) because there was limited free time.
- They were **local** because there was limited transport.
- They were **uncoded** (figure 18.5) because the peasantry was often illiterate.
- They were **ritualised** because of the influence of older pagan and existing church influences.
- Any recreations of a sporting nature were often in the context of village fêtes or **fairs** held on holydays.
- The activities were often **violent and cruel**, (figure 18.6) because life was hard and harsh at that time.
- **Wagering** was a primary feature of life at this time, and wagers would be made on the outcome of any contest.

figure 18.4 – popular recreations

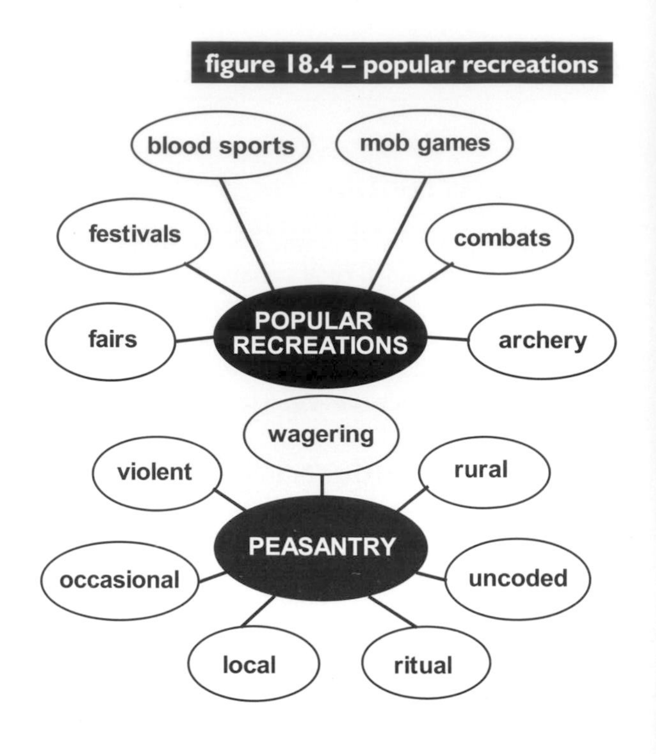

Many of these activities have survived both at an aristocratic and popular level, but many have been either curtailed or reformed. Nor is there the clean separation between the two groups (upper and lower classes) within our present democracy.

Among the **upper class sports**, coursing is pretty-well banned in this country, hunting is now legally restricted and shooting is strictly controlled.

figure 18.5 – mob football as a lower class pursuit

figure 18.6 – bull baiting, brutal but exciting

figure 18.7 – archery as preparation for war?

- Popular recreations like **baiting** have long since been made illegal.
- **Festivals** are more respectable.
- **Archery** (figure 18.7) has changed from military combat practice to a codified target sport.
- And mob football has only survived in rural areas which escaped the impact of reform.

The **socio-cultural influences** which brought about the evolution of the various pastimes of the middle ages are summarised in figure 18.8.

The changes which led to modern versions of existing sports will be explained later with the focus on the mid 19th century development of **public school athleticism** and **rational sport**.

figure 18.8 – socio-cultural influences

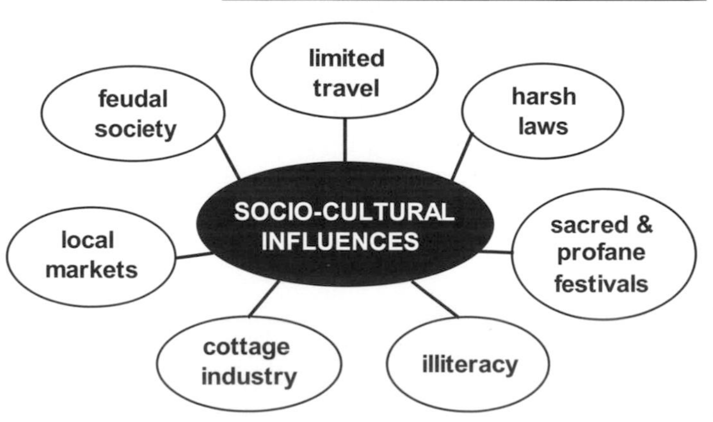

Emergence of rational sport as a product of the industrial revolution

Changes in society

The development of **physical education** and **sport** reflected changes in British society. Hence we place **social and cultural** changes in the context of elitist **institutions** like the **English public schools**.

The major changes which occurred in society influenced participation in sport today. We will now discuss how society changed during the period over which the industrial revolution occurred, as it influenced **development and change** in English institutions.

The early 19th century marked the beginnings of **three social revolutions** in England:

- The **agrarian revolution** which involved the gradual movement of workers from the countryside to the larger towns.
- The **industrial revolution**, which gave increased power to the middle classes, better wages for the industrial working class and greater prosperity for the country at large.
- The **urban revolution**, which marked a massive rise in the population, as industrial and commercially well-placed towns grew in size and national significance.

Popular and rational recreation

These two strands of development towards modern sport had the characteristics identified in figures 18.9 and 18.10.

Popular and rational recreation are not totally different. They both involve **physical activity**, they are both **competitive** and they are both **enjoyable** and **fulfilling**. They both have features of **ritual** and **festival** and both have elements to be seen in modern sport.

STUDENT NOTE

The social revolutions in England during the 19th century are discussed on page 144 onwards of 'AS Revise PE for AQA', ISBN: 978 1 901424 56 0.

figure 18.9 – characteristics of popular recreation

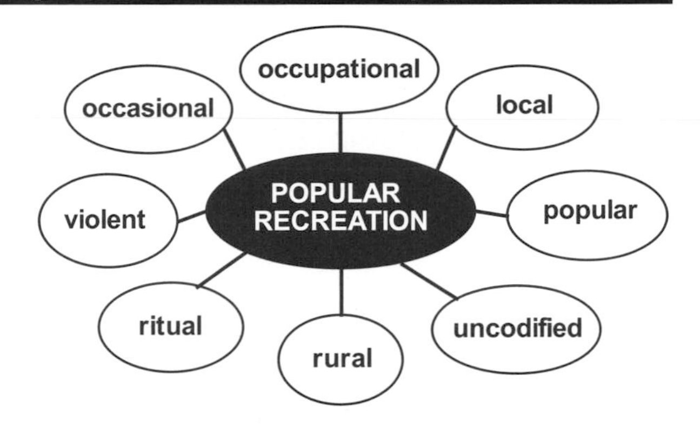

figure 18.10 – characteristics of rational recreation

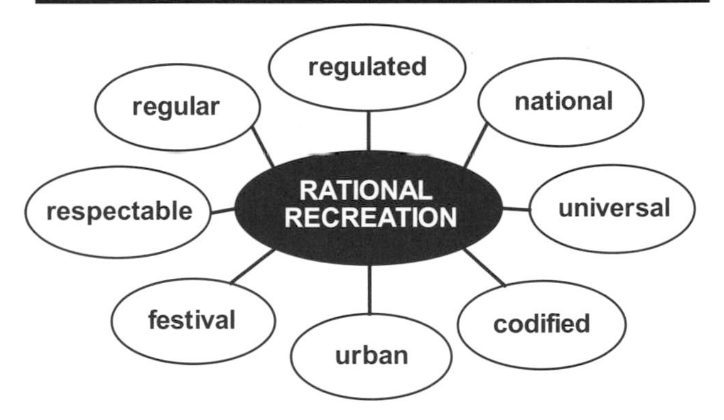

Table 18.1 – **the cultural factors which influenced the conversion of popular sports into rational sports**

popular	rational
agrarian	industrial and urban
feudal	emergent middle class
limited travel	railways
illiterate	elementary education
cottage industry	factories
payment in kind	wages
limited free-time	regular free-time and the Saturday half day
markets	shopping centres
harsh laws	law and policing
church festivals	muscular Christianity - athleticism
fields and rivers	parks and baths

Nineteenth century public schools and athleticism

The **characteristics** of the 19th century public schools included the facts that they were for the **sons of the gentry** and they were **boarding**, **fee paying**, and **non-local** establishments.

STUDENT NOTE

The 19th century public schools are discussed on page 144 onwards of 'AS Revise PE for AQA', ISBN: 978 1 901424 56 0.

- The non-local feature of these schools was very important in that the developments that occurred in the schools became spread across the nation.
- There were also scholars from poorer families and by the 1870s the number of schools had increased to accommodate an emergent middle class.
- There was a delay before similar selective high schools emerged for **upper and middle class girls**.
- By the end of the nineteenth century, there was public or grammar school access for wealthy and bright boys and girls with an active policy of **athleticism** (**goodness**, **manliness**, **restraint** and **discipline**), and the **size** and **provision** to promote it. Other reforms also occurred, a broader curriculum, reduced flogging and control of school sport by the Sixth Form.

The role of ex-public schoolboys in the development of rational sport

Activity development

We can use examples of different activities to **explain** how development occurred. The main popular example is of mob football which tended to differ in each school:

- Eton played a field game and a wall game.
- Rugby School played a handling game.
- Harrow and Charterhouse played a so-called dribbling game.
- Local conditions (the availability of large grassy areas or pitches, and whether or not the areas were bounded by fences or walls) at each school largely determined these differences.

When the boys left school for **Oxford or Cambridge** Universities, they had already established an acceptable combination of the rules in public schools to produce a **set of rules** which allowed them to play at their university college. From there it was necessary to produce unified rules and a stringent organisation for competitions **between** university colleges, and finally a set of rules for **inter-varsity** games and contests, with the reward of **blues** for representation.

figure 18.11 – inter-school cricket by 1851

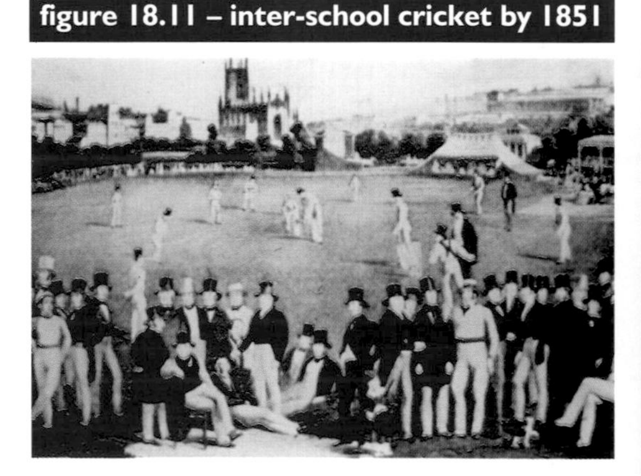

A large number of these boys returned to teach in the public schools after graduation, and spread the new rules to the next generation of schoolboys. Hence inter-school matches (figure 18.11) and competitions were held according to the new unified rules, and the word was spread.

The gentleman amateur

- The university college competition structure and the inter-varsity structures remained an elite development and represented the foundation of the **gentleman amateur**. When graduates left university, they entered various careers including industry, the church and the army, and they took their amateur sport with them throughout Britain and the Empire.
- Hence **cricket** was the first sport to be taken by former **Oxbridge** students into the British Empire.
- They initially promoted it amongst themselves, **expanded** to take in the middle classes in their community, and finally took amateurism to the working classes as a **reforming vehicle**. Hence it became **respectable** for the middle and working classes to participate in the new games and sports, since it was what the upper classes spent their time doing!
- As the schools and society changed to meet the energy and reforming zeal of Victorian England, so the lesser gentry and **industrial middle class** presumed the right to public boarding school education. They were not allowed into the Clarendon Schools and so they built new schools with extensive sports facilities in attractive spa towns and other wealthy areas. They were linked by the new **railway** system.

Middle class developments

- The middle classes were not only wealthy and industrious, they wanted the status previously reserved for the gentry and they felt that the **public schools** would at least give that to their sons.
- Meanwhile, with some upper class women gaining access to Oxbridge, these women opened boarding schools for their daughters with a **girls' high school** opening in every major town (figure 18.12).

figure 18.12 – lacrosse as a girls' game

- For example, a group of university graduates discussed the rules of football. They accepted the divide between the two codes of association and rugby, and established the **Governing Bodies** of the Football Association (FA) in 1863, and the Rugby Football Union (RFU) in 1870.
- The notion of the **gentleman amateur** continued, while several games had acknowledged the place of the **professional** performer.
- In cricket and association football, the professional player and club were controlled by middle class administrators, who accepted the code of **physical endeavour and moral integrity** as the basis of all modern games and sports. Hence the nineteenth century public schools had a major part to play in the development of most modern day sports and games.

Some cultural changes, such as working class free time, elementary education and the emancipation of the lower class female, took more time. But the cultural changes were under way, and perhaps sport led the way.

The historical development of professional sport

Popular recreation is normally centred on the **lower classes**, with **aristocratic** or **gentry** sports co-existing alongside peasant sports. Normally, **patronage** by the gentry not only determined whether the popular activities and **festivals** flourished in a community, but it was also why they were allowed to continue well after levels of industrialisation and urbanisation had increased. Figure 18.9 above (page 115) summarises the characteristics of popular sport in Britain before the 18th century.

The key factors were:

- The significance of **wagering**.
- The **limited free time** available to the urban lower class and agricultural labourers.
- The **minimal pay** for workers who were on the bread-line.
- The **lack of transport** except for the wealthiest classes.

As a result, the **occasional festival** and fair offered the chance to **earn money prizes** through sporting competition to young people with talent and bravery. If they were good enough, they could increase their income by travelling to different fairs and wakes to compete in combat sports like single stick play and wrestling or running events. In addition to prize money, there was always **wagering** where you could risk money on backing yourself to win or lose!

The prize fighter

Prize fighting is chosen as a case study because it involved **professional** performers by the end of the 18th century. The sport gave the opportunity to win large sums of money, and involved the upper class and the peasantry in a partnership in which high standards were achieved. Pedestrianism followed similar lines, but we confine our discussion to prize fighting as a case study.

Prize fighting

Prize fighting (figure 18.13) dates back to the 13th century when there were gladiatorial schools, relics of the Roman Conquest, where individuals were prepared to defend themselves and compete in 'sword and buckle' contests. By the time of the Tudors, there were so-called professors of defence, who formed a company called **Masters of Defence**. This was the cradle of the **Noble Art of Self Defence**, which came to prominence in the 18th century with **James Figg** opening the **Academy of Boxing** in London in 1718. As a Master of Defence one had to be able to defend oneself against all-comers at swordplay, cudgels, quarter staff and grappling. He would also be employed as a tutor to fashionable young 'dandies' and aggressive 'dualists'.

figure 18.13 – bareknuckle prizefighting

Prize fighting

When **Jack Broughton** (figure 18.14) became champion, he changed the rules of the prize ring to establish **pugilism**, limiting the contest to **bare-knuckle** punching and throws. The tradition of teaching the gentry resulted in '**sparring**' being developed and '**mufflers**' (the precursor of modern boxing gloves) for protection.

figure 18.14 – Figg and Broughton

Wagering in prize fighting

With **wagering** taking place, there was always an element of **corruption**, and when the Duke of Cumberland lost heavily because Broughton was unexpectedly beaten by Jack Slack, he used his influence to drive the sport underground. From this time, the 'Fancy' had to run the gauntlet of police and magistrates. Right through to the 1830s **huge crowds** were attracted to major fights and fortunes were won and lost.

Excellence

There are **two** separate notions of **excellence** within these developments:

- The **talented individual** (from a peasant background) managed to compete in festivals and win prizes, but this tended to be occasional as work and survival came first.
- There was a **professional elite**, whose talent was such that they could earn a good living through challenge events and **wagering** successfully.

Development of elite amateur sport

Elite levels of sport evolved because:

- School and even house teams displayed excellence.
- **Blues** were awarded to the best players at Oxbridge, many being outstanding players who played for **British** teams.
- The former pupils took **amateur games** to a level which rivalled the best professionals.
- Elite sport was organised for **gentleman amateur** sport initially, but eventually the gentlemen themselves **changed the amateur code** to allow **working class males** to compete in organised sports at a high level.
- Former public schoolboys helped to organise and compete in the early **Modern Olympics**.
- The standard of coaching was such that Lyttelton and Foster were playing county cricket for Worcestershire while still at school, with several of their group going on to play for England.

As a product of public school graduates, rational sport was initially an exclusive development by the male upper and middle class and is normally described as the **Gentleman Amateur** period. Oxbridge sportsmen initially took the games to members of their own social group, forming games clubs and sports associations and eventually National and **International Governing Bodies**. These clubs and organisations were 'amateur' and **excluded the people** of the lower classes, who only had popular festivals and professional opportunities to participate in sport.

The **FA** was formed by these gentlemen and the early soccer sides (like Sheffield) were all **gentlemen**. The FA Cup was won by old student clubs or urban gentlemen's clubs. Similarly, the early Athletic Clubs admitted **middle class gentlemen** who established and developed athletics and gymnastics.

Exclusion

These middle and upper class gentlemen were the new elite performers and the **lower classes and women were excluded**, leaving the prize fighters and pedestrians to make a living by competing in front of crowds. Opportunities for the lower classes and all women remained at an occasional festival level. Additionally, the lower classes needed to work for a living, and so had no **time** for this sort of thing.

Democratisation of sport in British society

The people running sport at this time promoted the notion that the **positive use** of 'free time' for the **workers** would **take them out of pubs** and allow them to play rational games, which had strong **physical** and **moral** values.

Hence games and sport became **codified** and **regulated**, **regular**, **respectable** and **rational**, and the **numbers of people** participating expanded rapidly (figure 18.15, note the industrial city centre setting and the large number of spectators).

figure 18.15 – association football

- The **Saturday half-day** and increasing **free time** (for factory workers) increased playing and training opportunities.
- The emergence of a **powerful middle class** came about together with a supportive commercial class.
- The '**early closing movement**' was achieved by shop assistants, with a subsequent development of **mid-week football** leagues.
- The **transport** revolution, particularly the growth of the **railways** from the 1850s, was closely linked with increased wealth and more free time.
- The **turn-pike system** improved roads and facilitated travel by carriage and stage for the wealthy. Eventually the bicycle (figure 18.16) allowed organised groups to cycle for sport and pleasure. There was also a second-hand trade in bikes.
- **Omnibuses** (buses) influenced the development of **suburbia** in very large towns.
- The **church** supported organised sport which was seen to have moral and health values. This was not only for the middle classes but also for commercial class youth, in the form of the YMCA and YWCA.
- **Benevolent** Quaker industrialists, Mechanics Institutes, Working Men's Clubs and Sunday schools promoted improved working class work conditions, **recreation and sport** (as well as education).

figure 18.16 – cycling in the 1890s

The notion of the **gentleman amateur** continued throughout the nineteenth century in some sports, but **Governing Bodies** gradually reformed their rules to change the class and gender **definition of amateurism** to a regulation based on **no financial gain**.

STUDENT NOTE

The crucial point concerning this '**amateur**' period was the element of purity of the morality of competition with others on an equal basis. This was to be unsullied by payment, wagering or corruption. Therefore participation had to be only by those who could afford to perform without payment, and who were the wealthy members of an upper or middle class in society.

The professionals

Meanwhile, towards the end of the 19th century, several games had acknowledged the place of the lower class **professional performer**, especially in cricket and association football.

Cricket engaged members of the lower class as groundsmen, but they were also chosen because of their ability as players and often fulfilled the role of **coaches** for gentry children. With games becoming **rationalised** and **regularised** in a society which was increasingly industrial and urban, the **standard of play** became important as a crowd attraction.

As a result, full-time professionals began to compete with the best amateurs (figure 18.17) and so were increasingly **paid according to their talent** and **crowd appeal**.

figure 18.17 – old-boys' association football

The professionals to date

It was not until the 20th century that professionals were able to outplay the best amateurs, and much later that professionalism became attractive to the middle classes in most sports.

From the end of the 19th century and up to the 1990s in some sports (examples would be tennis, rugby union and athletics), amateur and professional sports developed separately. The middle classes were administrators, agents and promoters, the working classes were participants, and the upper classes were sponsors or patrons. Examples of the attitude of administrators to performers included:

- The maximum wage in football (£8.00 per week in 1950, and only ended in 1961).
- The definition of amateurism in athletics, which excluded the possibility of earning any money through sport until the 1980s.
- The exclusion of rugby league (and therefore **potentially** professional) players from **any** part in rugby union until the 1990s.

Nowadays, the professional performer can emerge into almost any sport (from whatever background). Income from TV, media and sponsorship is sufficient to support professionals in most sports. Although administrators and agents are still middle class, so are most performers, and the attitude towards performers has become more concerned with excellence than relative income.

Practice questions

1) What were the main characteristics of popular recreations in England before the development of rational sport? Give examples of activities where you can. 4 marks

2) a) Describe the characteristics of popular recreation and discuss the socio-cultural factors which determined them. 8 marks

b) Discuss the changes which occurred in 19th century British society and the effect these had on the most popular sports and games by 1900. 10 marks

3) How was the 19th century class system in the UK reflected in the development of cricket? 5 marks

4) The development of rational recreation was very much the result of Britain becoming an industrialised society.

a) Using figure 18.18, explain the characteristics of an AAA Athletics Meeting. 4 marks

b) Describe amateurism as it concerned Track and Field Athletics towards the end of the 19th century. 4 marks

figure 18.18 – the AAA championships 1870

5) What do you understand by the terms codified, regulated, and respectable in relation to rational recreation? 6 marks

6) Discuss the changing attitude to sport in the elite 19th century public schools and its effect on the emergence of amateur sport in the UK. 14 marks

7) What influence did 'non-local' admission to the public schools and universities have on the development of rational sport? 6 marks

8) Explain the 'full expression of athleticism' as found in leading public schools towards the end of the 19th century. 6 marks

9) Why were Oxford and Cambridge Universities able to make such an impressive contribution to elite sport in the late 19th century? 6 marks

10) a) Describe and explain the effect that the Industrial Revolution had on sport after 1800. 5 marks

b) Explain why these social changes led to the formation of National Governing Bodies. 3 marks

c) Describe the role that National Governing Bodies play in the organisation of sport. 4 marks

11) Describe the transition from the traditionally amateur approach to a more professional approach over the last 30 years. 6 marks

CHAPTER 19 – THE CONTRACT TO COMPETE, DEVIANCE and the LAW

The contract to compete

The **contract to compete** is an **unwritten** code within sports where participants agree to '**do their best**', to strive to win, to play within the rules, and to do this with a degree of sportsmanship. Playing to win is said to be a good thing as long as it is within the '**spirit of the game**'. This implies that a person should allow his or her opponent to do the same, and not be unduly upset if that opponent wins. Respect is to be given to the rules, to opponents, and to officials attempting to administer a contest. The whole thing should be undertaken within the spirit of '**fair play**'.

Fair play is an idea developed from Victorian attitudes and ethics about amateurism, athleticism, and the taking part that is important.

Sportsmanship and gamesmanship

figure 19.1 – sportsmanship / gamesmanship

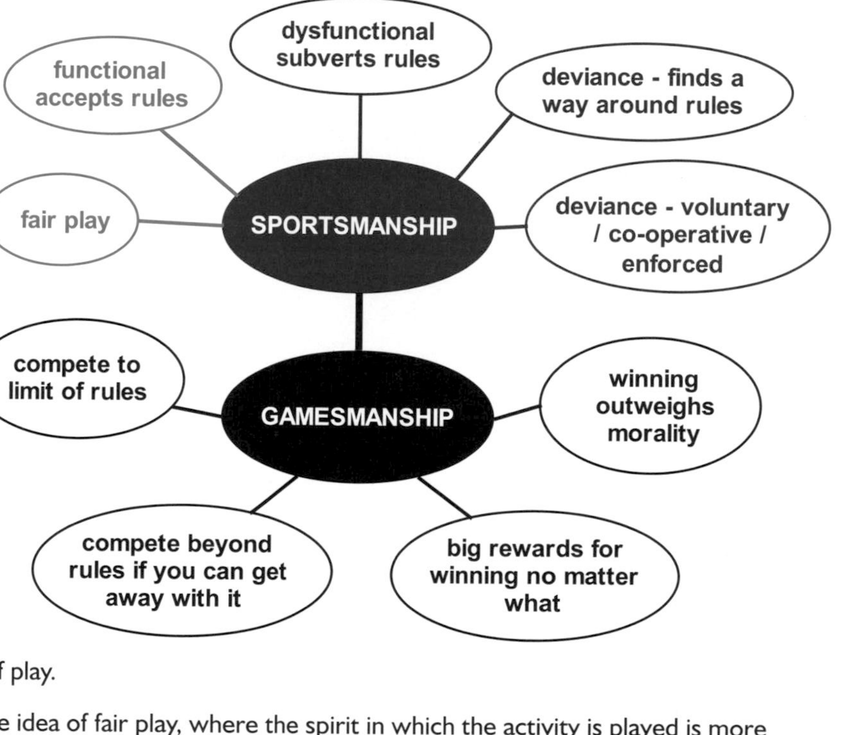

Sportsmanship

Sportsmanship is not just what you play, but how you play in a sport. If the sporting activity involves competition, then it should always be performed with a **spirit of sportsmanship**.

In sport, we have problems of **violence** on the field and the use of **performance enhancing drugs** (PEDs). This tells us that the ethic of **fair play** is under attack. Without fair play, sport as a noble pastime is doomed. It is possible to look at games on the television or during school sport and test the behaviour of performers. The behaviour will vary from the high point of players making moral decisions to the other extreme of deliberate violence against others. **Fair play** will exist as long as you at least accept the referee, but it's better if you accept the rules of play.

- Perhaps there can be no true sport without the idea of fair play, where the spirit in which the activity is played is more important than a '**win-at-all-costs**' attitude?
- Sportsmanship is **functional** if the rules of a game or sport are accepted, or the decisions of a referee or umpire are accepted, and **dysfunctional** if a performer has no regard for others or deliberately subverts the rules of a game in order to gain advantage (figure 19.1).

Gamesmanship

Gamesmanship is the term which describes behaviour outside the rules of a sport or game which aims to gain advantage over an opponent, and has been defined as: '**the intention to compete to the limit of the rules and beyond if you can get away with it**'.

Some professional performers and coaches maintain that '**you get away with what you can**', an admission that potential rewards, millions in sponsorship and wages, can outweigh moral considerations.

Gamesmanship is driven by a '**win-at-all-costs**' attitude and shows no regard for the well-being of the opponent.

Examples of **gamesmanship** are:

- A boxer or fighter thumbing the eye of an opponent.
- A soccer player deliberately fouling an opponent with the aim of getting him or her off the pitch.
- A rugby player stamping on an opposing player.
- A cricket team 'sledging' their opponents when batting – extreme verbal banter – destroying confidence and concentration.

The Olympic Ideal

The **Olympic Creed** was and is an ideal hope for human behaviour when faced with sporting adversity or success. It was put forward in 1908:

*'**The most important thing in the Olympic Games is not to win but to take part, just as the most important thing in life is not the triumph but the struggle. The essential thing is not to have conquered but to have fought well.**'*

*The **Olympic Charter** states '**Olympism is a philosophy of life, exalting and combining in a balanced whole the qualities of body, will and mind. Blending sport with culture and education, Olympism seeks to create a way of life based on the joy found in effort, the educational value of good example and respect for universal fundamental ethical principles.**'*

These statements revolve around the fact that athletes should be free to participate irrespective of race, colour or creed. Mass access to sport requires that **constraints** upon cultural and sub-cultural groups should be removed. But in order for minority groups to have equality they must also have **access** and **provision**. **Access** can be denied by a numerically superior culture, self-imposed cultural constraint, and economic and topographical limitations.

The major issue at the beginning of the modern Olympic movement was the **exclusion** of racial minorities from existing opportunity, or the failure to **extend provision** to all. **Olympic Solidarity** programmes and the various IOC commissions are responsible for education and provision in areas of need, which are funded these days by income from television rights.

Deviance and performance enhancing drugs or products

Deviance

The term **deviance** describes behaviour in which people find a way around the rules, however they are framed. This behaviour can be institutional, group specific, or individual. Deviant behaviour could be one of three possibilities:

- **Voluntary**, the performer decides to take drugs.
- **Co-operative**, the performer decides to take drugs, because all his friends are doing so.
- **Enforced**, a former East German swimmer took drugs because her coach gave them to her.

Deviance in sport concerns the **intention to cheat** as part of deviant behaviour, and includes aggression and violence among competitors and spectators, as well as the issue of doping.

Positive and negative deviance

In sociological terms, deviance means the variation of behaviour from the norm (what is normal). This can be upwards (**positive**) or downwards (**negative**) deviance.

Examples of positive deviance include training through injury, adopting a 'no pain, no gain' attitude which implies an 'over' commitment to sport.

For example, it used to be a common occurrence within rugby union, to continue 'playing through' an injury in the interests of the team as a whole. This behaviour has largely disappeared with the advent of substitutions, but used to be the major reason for the ending of a promising career in the sport.

Violence in sport

This issue arises when acceptable **aggression** (assertion) in sport becomes **violence**.

Violence is normally where aggression goes beyond the agreed codification in that game or activity. There is an additional dimension, in that acceptable aggression in the activity may not match up with the laws of the land and so players can misunderstand their **legal** position. But spectators certainly need to recognise that no matter how much they get worked up, their violence is measured in legal terms.

Figure 19.2 summarises the issues affecting player violence.

figure 19.2 – aggression and violence in sport

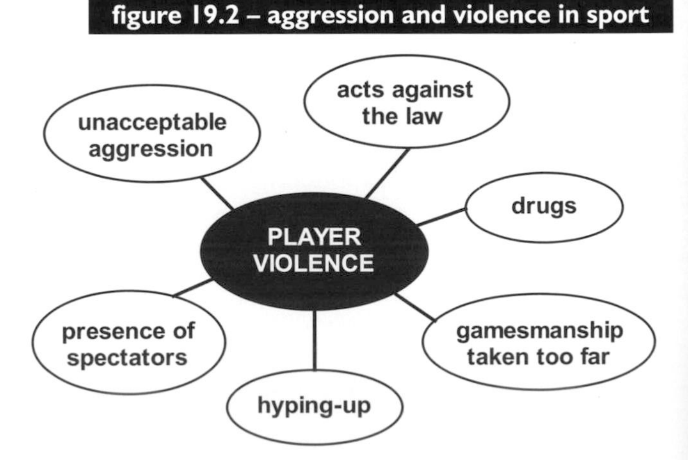

Player violence

Physical aggression and an unacceptable level of **verbal abuse** may be identified as part of player violence:

- The presence of spectators can increase player arousal.
- Many games require players to be **hyped-up** to perform at their best, making aggression and outbreaks of violence more likely.
- More recently, the use of **drugs** may have increased this tendency.
- On the other hand, some sports require calmness and focus. For example, darts, snooker, dance and gymnastics, and players in these sports are less likely to be violent.
- **Gamesmanship**, aimed at putting an opponent off, can be equally unacceptable.

Aggression by **sports performers** is a part of their sporting life. The need to be competitive and the **frustration** felt at failure can lead sportspeople to be violent as an extreme expression of this aggression. The level at which aggression becomes violence varies according to the **activity**.

For example, boxing involves punching an opponent, which would be violence in any other sport. In this case, it is argued that the essence of boxing is '**the art of self-defence**' and that boxing has its own code of acceptable behaviour with a referee to see that this is observed, as well as the safety precaution of gloves. There is also a difference here between amateur and professional boxing and also regulations for junior competitors as against seniors. This rules difference also is relevant to a variety of other activities and games, such as tag rugby with young children.

Causes of violence in sport

The **causes** of violence among players are summarised in figure 19.3.

- **Players** will be violent for the reasons outlined above.
- The **crowd** response to player activity (chanting, booing, name calling) can affect player tendency to violence.
- The confrontational nature of most top professional games (the **gladiatorial** influence) can increase the tendency to violence.
- The **popular** nature of some sports can lead to player expectation of violence as part of the game culture.
- The presence of a **large number** of spectators and the significance of victory can increase the **emotion** of a sporting occasion, and again make violence more likely.
- The failure of sports **administrators** to adequately punish players who are persistently violent can cause players to cynically commit further violent offences on the field.

figure 19.3 – causes of violence in sport

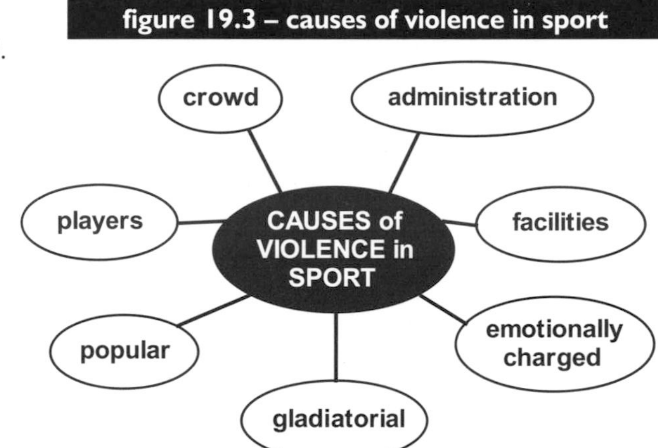

The **solutions** lie in the code of behaviour being part of the tradition of the activity from school onwards and the quality of control by officials (figure 19.4) during the game. Officials should include an explanation of their action. The increased use of **TV play-back** at agreed times can help. Punishments by controlling bodies should be seen to be fair and consistent, and should therefore fit the offence. But the essential element is the attitude of each player.

figure 19.4 – referees have the power to punish

Spectators and violence

Spectators get very emotionally involved, desperately wanting their side to win. They often direct this emotion at players on the pitch, and also at opposition supporters. This can lead to violence on the terraces and on the streets, but can also involve extreme verbal abuse. In such instances the law is probably being broken, but access by the stewards and the police is not possible because of the crowd effect. The **facilities** of a stadium, in respect of the mixing of the fans of opposing teams, can be a cause of spectator violence particularly in professional soccer.

Hooliganism

The dominance of a youth culture, where gangs identify with a professional football club and are prepared to fight an opposition group in a chosen place, is a frightening extension of **soccer hooliganism**. Although there is a strong working class peer group culture associated with soccer, this has, occasionally, involved middle class male groups. The media can encourage **confrontational** situations by highlighting players' comments about opponents and giving these hooligan gangs publicity.

There are numerous **causes** in what is naturally an **antagonistic** and often **frustrating** situation. For example, the tendency towards violence by a supporter group is linked to whether or not their team is winning. Supporters of a winning team are more likely to be benevolent and good natured, whereas supporters of a losing team often turn to violence, particularly in 'derby games'.

This has been explained as a form of social deviance:

- Caused by being in a crowd, where there is **confinement**.
- High emotion and the likelihood of **shared aggression**.
- Particularly if **alcohol** has been consumed.
- There is also an element of **depersonalisation** that a crowd gives an individual, where it is 'easy to be lost in a crowd'.

In the case of hooliganism, the question arises as to whether these are **hooligans at football** or **football hooligans**. In the case of the former, the **solution** lies in the conditions and control needed to prevent this antisocial behaviour. If, however, football **makes** them behave as hooligans, then one must look at the behaviour of the players and the causes of frustration.

Solutions

Measures (figure 19.5) which have been taken to **reduce** the chances of spectator violence are:

- **Segregation** of home and away supporters.
- The introduction of **all-seater stadia**.
- Increasing the **'family'** concept.
- Increasing the number of **stewards** and **police**.
- Ensuring that **alcohol** cannot be bought or brought into grounds.
- Detecting trouble using **CCTV**.

In addition, campaigns like '**kick racism out of football**', sponsored by major soccer clubs, player and Governing Bodies, can defuse unacceptable racial aggression.

figure 19.5 – prevention of hooliganism

The drug issue

The **reason** sportspeople take drugs (PEDs) or other nutritional ergogenic aids is to attempt to gain an advantage over other competitors or players. Some drugs are against the law and others against sporting regulations, but young people can be attracted to these **unethical** and **dangerous** substances because their heroes and **role models** are presumed to have taken them.

- Thus taking drugs ceases to be only a personal decision. This is part of the **win ethic**, the willingness to win at all costs, or simply a desire to excel in something as an unbridled ambition (see figure 19.6).
- The International Olympic Committee and International Sports Authorities view drug taking as **cheating**, where it is deemed totally unacceptable for the unscrupulous to be allowed to take unfair advantage. Let's not forget the Olympic oath sworn on behalf of all participant States.

figure 19.6 – performance enhancing products

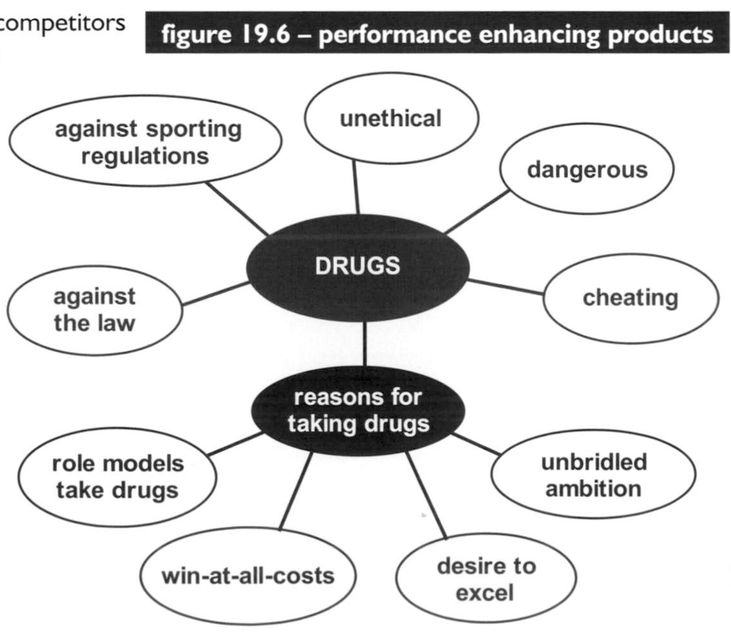

The Olympic oath

> **'In the name of all competitors, I promise that we shall take part in these Olympic Games ...without doping and using drugs in the true spirit of sportsmanship.'**

figure 19.7 – possible solutions to drug abuse

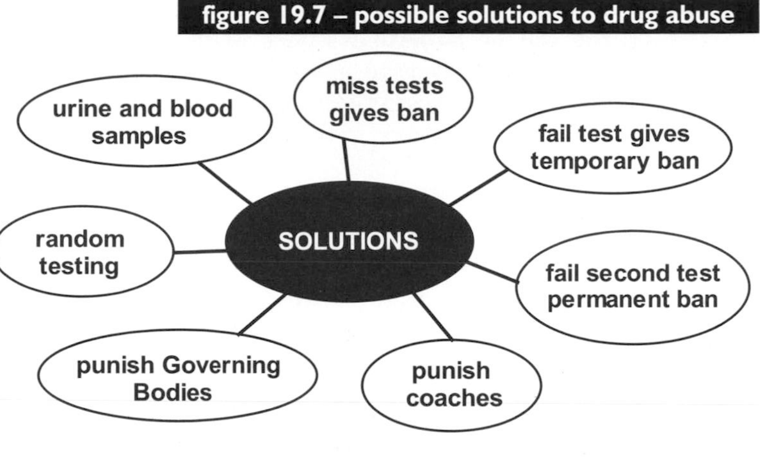

Testing

Testing for drugs (figure 19.7) is subject to **stringent** procedures for supervising **sample taking**, where urine and blood samples are now being taken. The procedures for observing the taking of urine samples were made all the more rigorous after two male winners in the Athens Olympic athletics programme were found to be using prosthetic (false) genitals and a hidden storage bag for the production of their sample.

STUDENT NOTE

You will find a discussion and table (4.4) of the categories and effects of the various drugs used in sport on page 37 above.

- The **British Olympic Committee** and **UK sport** have a widespread **random drug testing programme**.
- To miss two of these random tests results in sanctions and to miss for a third time produces an automatic one year ban.
- This happened to Christine Ohuruogu – World and Olympic champion in track and field athletics.
- This was in spite of her passing many other tests during the period when this was happening. She was forced to miss the 2006 season during her ban.

- Under the **WADA** rules brought in January 1st 2009, athletes in all Olympic sports are required to state 3 months in advance their locations for 1 hour per day, 7 days a week.
- This is the time during which random testing could take place.
- This is called the '**whereabouts rule**' and this rule has provoked anger from tennis players, such as Andy Murray, Rafael Nadal and Roger Federer, who feel that the European Union privacy law has been breached.
- In season, testing normally takes place after competitions or matches.

Punishment

Punishment can be by a temporary ban on performers, with usually a second offence involving the most serious drugs leading to a permanent ban. Some sports have punished coaches and have the power to confront guilty officials. Also there are examples of the punishment of Governing Bodies as in weightlifting (where the whole national team will be suspended if a drug positive is found on just one weightlifter), as well as putting pressure on transgressing governments.

Policies adopted by **Governing Bodies** to reduce drug taking by sportspeople include liaison with other Governing Bodies so that a unified approach is made. This has led to the initiation of **educational programmes** for players and coaches, while government bodies, like **UK sport**, provide resources for research into more effective testing.

WADA

The **World Anti-Doping Agency** (**WADA**) is the World body set up in 1998 tasked with enforcing the international regulations on doping or drug taking. WADA aims to bring together governments, the IOC, international Governing Bodies and National Governing Bodies (NGBs) to sort out the difficulties posed by athletes performing on the international stage. This issue was brought to a head at the Athens Olympics 2004, when two of the host nation's best athletes went missing just before the games and a compulsory drug test. These athletes faked a road accident and sought hospitalisation falsely in order to avoid taking the test. The same athletes had a record of going missing from international training venues just before the IAAF drug testers arrived – and even being found registered under false names in hotels so that their whereabouts could not be definitely fixed.

Innocent or guilty?

Great care has to be taken when testing takes place. Britain's Diane Modahl failed a test in 1994 just prior to the Commonwealth Games of that year. It was later discovered that her urine sample had undergone changes while being stored in the testing laboratory, and she was cleared of the doping offence. She then sued the British Athletic Federation for their mishandling of the situation. This led to the eventual near bankruptcy of the BAF and the destruction of Diane's athletic career. Although she was reinstated, she was unable to regain the fitness and excellence needed to compete at elite level.

The athlete passport

WADA has introduced the '**Athlete passport**' which contains an on-going collection of an individual's urine and blood profiles which have so far been collected and tested during the international athlete's performance lifespan. Samples are stored and then made available for retro-testing when appropriate. It is projected that future profile collection could include endocrine information. For further information go to: www.wada-ama.org/en/dynamic.ch2?pageCategory.id=870

For or against doping in sport?

Although most **top performers** would say that performance enhancing drugs (PEDs) should not be allowed in sport, it is almost certain that many such performers are **actually using** such drugs.

Some people feel that it would be better to avoid the costs of testing, of developing new tests for new drugs, and of defending the subsequent court battles, and that therefore we should allow drugs to be used in a controlled manner.

The fact that **detection** of drugs depends on the **efficiency** of the testing procedure, and that some countries and sports have little or no such procedure, means that the playing field is relatively bumpy for top performers.

The argument to allow drugs (in a controlled manner) would:

- **Remove** dangerous substances (known to inflict harm on participants).
- **Allow** people to take drugs in a controlled manner.
- Allow everyone to compete on a **level playing field**.
- Create the possibility that **more records** would be broken by greater amounts, and therefore create more spectacular sport for spectators.

Unfortunately:

- Some people would **not be prepared to take drugs** - so there would not be a level playing field after all.
- The **dangerous side effects** of many performance enhancing products are known and inevitable.
- It would be assumed by some coaches and athletes that success would **not be possible** without drugs, and peer pressure would force people to **participate in illegal programmes** against their better instincts.
- The **cost** of taking some substances would be substantial, since the costs of developing new and effective drugs would have to be borne by someone.

What about the notion that sports should be about the testing of one performer against another (or team against team), with the best, most talented and best prepared athlete winning?

The law and sport

In the early years of rational sport, the people who established the Governing Bodies and controlled the activities and games were the **upper or middle classes** who also established the **law of the land**. Hence there was little direct conflict between the law of the land and the codes in amateur sport.

The first problems arose when reforms to professional sports came into conflict with the **upper class** who controlled them. The clearest example of this was in the Prize Ring, where the Duke of Cumberland accused Broughton of throwing his fight with Jack Slack. Cumberland's reaction was to take it to the House of Lords in 1750, and attempt to invoke a ban on the Prize Ring.

The important point to make is that laws in society and laws in sport were not always 'reformed' **at the same time**. Because the codes adopted by sports bodies were private, there was a conservative retention of traditional rules long after national legislation had been reformed. The argument stressed is that the **field of play is a private venue**, separate from the real World and in some cases blood sports like pigeon shooting continued despite local politicians objecting to the 'carnage'. At the end of the 19th century, middle class urban sensitivities were often ignored, particularly when the rural gentry were involved. The relatively unsuccessful banning of fox hunting in England (today) shows how a social elite can find ways round the law.

Sport law

However, the traditional argument for exclusivity has been gradually lost as sport law has been forced by legal representation to exist within international law:

- The **Bosman ruling** on the employment of professional players has resulted in sport law being superseded by employment legislation.
- As regards violence in sport, the UK Crown Prosecution Service has the right to prosecute players and spectators for violence in football grounds as well as outside.
- Significantly, this legislation also applies to officials, leading to problems of accusations of bribery.
- Also referee responsibilities became no longer in the sole control of Governing Bodies of sport, but open to an interpretation by law.
- The legislation arising from the **Hillsborough disaster** is a major example of how responsibility in sport is now answerable to international law and no longer contained within the jurisdiction of a specific club or sport.

Rule enforcement

Rule enforcement is usually down to the officials who are responsible for ensuring that players abide by the written rules of a sport or game. If players fail to do this, then officials have the duty and power to punish players as necessary. For example, David Beckham was sent off during the 1998 World Cup Argentina game when he deliberately kicked another player.

As mentioned above when talking about the contract to compete (see page 121 above), there are unwritten 'rules' that determine how a player should behave during a game, covering fair play, sportsmanship, and sporting ethics.

The need for the law in sport

Whilst it would be nice to believe that individuals who participate in sport always adhere to the rules, there are many who try to gain personal advantage from the sports they play. Thus, in recent years, sporting laws have become more and more common.

Figure 19.8 outlines the areas in which the law may impact on sport.

figure 19.8 – the law in sport

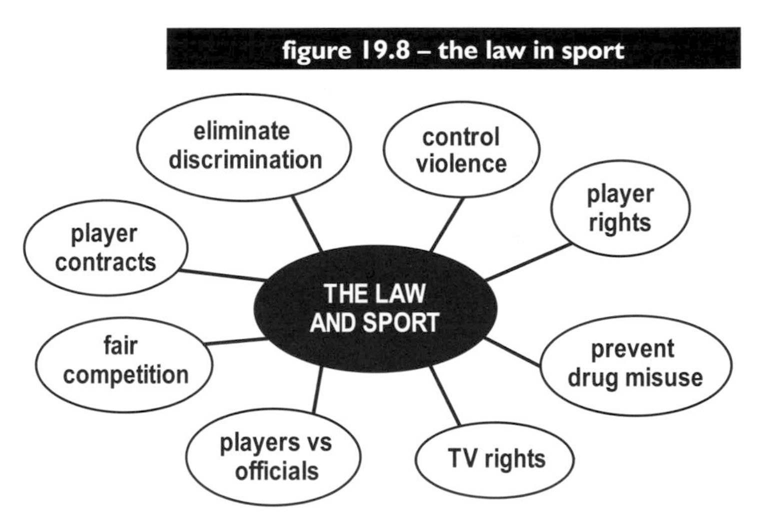

- **Fair competition** can be related to teams' actions surrounding a game, and it is important that teams start on a level playing field, and if this does not occur, the responsible team should be made accountable for their actions.

- **Player contracts** are concerned with ever-increasing wages in professional sports. It is important that players have legal documents which ensure wages are correctly paid. Equally, clubs require such documents in order to ensure players meet the demands laid out within their contracts.

- **Violence control** is relevant to actions made both off and on the field of play, for example, players injuring other players with deliberate intent, and hooliganism and crowd control.

- **Eliminate discrimination** concerns an extremely important type of law. It is illegal for any club to disallow an individual to become a member of an institution on the grounds of colour or race.

- **Players' rights** is related to players' contracts. It is now legal for players to leave a professional soccer club for no transfer fee once a player's contract has expired.

- **Drug misuse**. By taking drugs to enhance performance, players are essentially cheating in order to gain the upper hand over their opponents. Thus, it is against sporting regulations to take performance enhancing drugs (PEDs) such as anabolic steroids, although not against the law of the land. Hence testing procedures need to be foolproof in the case of a performer being banned for taking such drugs, since a person's right to earn a living is being removed in the case of a drug ban. This is what happened in the Diane Modahl case discussed above on page 125.

- The issue of **television rights** is especially relevant to football, as large revenues are generated in this way. Clubs are arguing that it is unfair that the Premier League negotiates TV rights for premiership games (in the premiership as a whole), and some clubs believe it is their right to organise their own TV deals.

- **Players vs officials**. It is now law that officials take responsibility for the reasonable care of players. For example, the case of Smolden v Whitworth (1991), in which a young rugby player was permanently paralysed when a scrum collapsed during a bad-tempered game. It was later ruled that the referee had not acted with competence, and thus was liable for the player's injuries.

Practice questions

1) Sportsmanship and gamesmanship are two opposites. Explain the differences between the two in a game of your choice. 6 marks

2) Explain what is meant by 'a contract to compete'. Describe ways in which gamesmanship breaks this code. 7 marks

3) Give reasons for spectator violence at professional association football matches. 5 marks

4) Hooliganism has affected football over the past 40 years.
   a) Define the term 'hooliganism' and discuss the reasons why it might occur. 4 marks

   b) What steps have been taken to reduce the incidents of hooliganism in Premiership football? 3 marks

5) Discuss the problem of illegal drug-taking in sport. Focus your answer on one performance-enhancing drug. 14 marks

6) The taking of performance enhancing drugs is a serious issue in elite sport.
   a) Outline the major steps in the drug-testing procedure that may face an elite level performer. 3 marks

   b) In 1998, the head of the IOC (Juan Antonio Samaranch) told a newspaper that 'substances that do not harm an athlete's health should not be banned and should not be considered as a case of doping'. Discuss this statement. 6 marks

7) Explain the differences between sport law and national law and discuss how this has changed. 8 marks

CHAPTER 20 – COMMERCIALISATION and TECHNOLOGY in SPORT

The media and commercialisation

figure 20.1 – media and sport

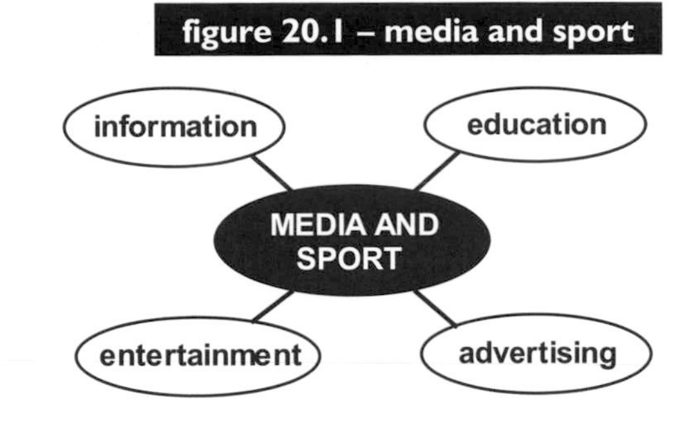

The impact of the **media** on modern life has grown enormously over the last 30 years, and now gives each household **global** coverage.

- Television now holds the attention of virtually every household.
- The internet has had a colossal global effect on news, data and time.
- The tabloid and broadsheet press is getting less influential.
- Sport coverage through the media has expanded alongside portrayal of general World events.
- The professionalisation and high level of play of World sport is closely linked to media portrayal.

Roles of the media

The roles of the media, generally and in terms of sport, are **fourfold** (see figure 20.1).

- The basic function of the media has always been to give **information**. Radio and television give immediate **results, event descriptions** and **rankings**.
- **Education**. The media **inform**, **advise** and **critically analyse** issues through explanation, discussion and debate. Terrestrial and satellite TV have **quality documentaries** which give coaching advice, explain the risk of drug-taking, and give post-event discussions on games.
- **Entertainment**. A TV programme will give experience and pleasure to an armchair spectator almost equivalent to the live event. Attending live events is expensive, hence the popularity of screens in pubs, clubs or parks near to the venues (Henman's Hill/Murray's Mound at Wimbledon for example).
- **Advertising**. The selling of products associated with sport is a major media aim, for example, a tennis player wearing a certain make of headband, sports shoe or shirt. Each club in both rugby and soccer displays sponsors' names on its shirts. Electronic billboarding around an arena is aimed at the cameras. Advertising breaks on TV (although usually coincident with a break in play) attract large sums from the products being advertised.

The impact of the **media on sport** is extensive. They can **promote** balanced, active, healthy lifestyles and lifelong involvement in physical activity. This is via the people it presents, the way these people act and the messages they give. These messages could be given in children's programmes as well as in adult news and documentaries.

Hence the media's **selective** use of visual and written material can have a major influence. Most important is the **balance** of the message, not just the hero worship of sports stars, but help in recognising the **problems** as well as the pleasures of achievement. The media can give insight into the effort needed for success, and a belief in the ideal of fair play.

Sponsorship and advertising

The so-called **'golden triangle'** (figure 20.2) links **sport**, **sponsorship** and the **media**.

figure 20.2 – the media golden triangle

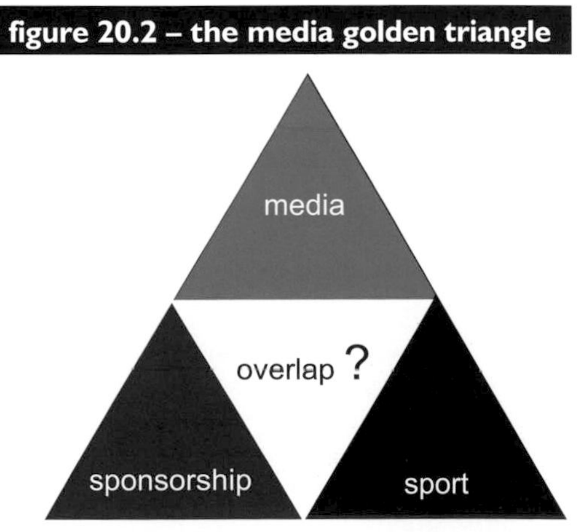

A sponsor will expect to promote its products by using a performer's image in return for financial support. A contract will be commercial and dependent on the star status of the sportsperson. If the status falls, so might the sponsorship. An example of this is Tiger Woods and his portrayal by the media after his 2009 personal difficulties. These difficulties had nothing to do with his status as World leading golfer, but caused several sponsors to withdraw support.

Also, the media use their power to sell products with players acting as clotheshorses. This can put fashion and behaviour before performance. An example of this is the range of clothing worn by Rafael Nadal, down to the 'Rafa' logo on his tennis shoes. Presumably he has to wear this gear regardless of whether or not it would be the best equipment for the job.

Advertising and the sports star

Figure 20.3 contains a summary of how advertising affects the sports star.

However, the **motives** of the commercial media differ from sport motives, even though some products may be seen to help sport in other than financial ways.

In the face of the recent recession, several companies have withdrawn sponsorship because profit is their central motive.

figure 20.3 – advertising

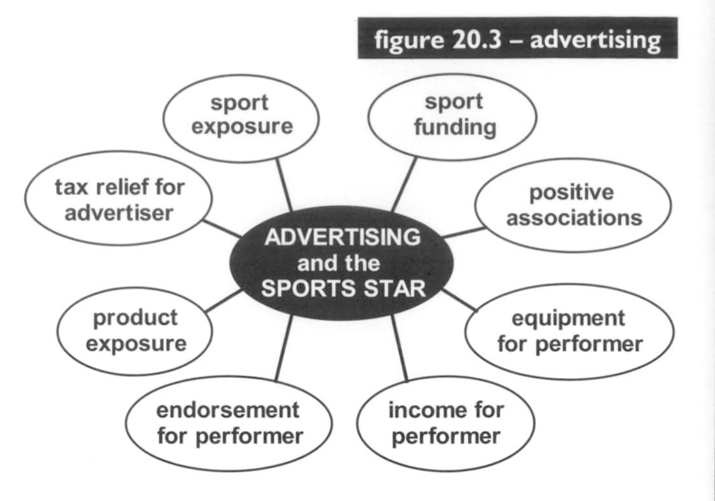

Table 20.1 – **positive and negative aspects of media coverage of sport**

positive aspects of media coverage	negative aspects of media coverage
players or teams gain revenue from sponsors	sponsorship companies usually only focus on high profile players or teams
sponsorship can provide teams with improved facilities and/ or equipment	sponsors can control event timings to suit peak-viewing times
teams or players gain publicity and promotion	players or teams can be restricted as to what products they can use
sponsorship can elevate new sports into the limelight via media publicity	sports can be overrun with sponsors – thus losing the nature of the game
more money for grass-roots teams	NGBs forced to alter rules to make games more exciting - in order to generate sponsorship interest
	more exciting events given priority over other sport

The commercial value of sport

The commercial value of sport is reflected in its profit making potential. Sponsors inevitably focus on revenue or product returns, and so communicate with and sell to as large an audience as possible. The key motive is the association of a company or product with a successful sport or sportsperson.

This means that high profile sport is targeted, which means professional sports which either attract a large number of active spectators or a huge, relatively passive audience on the TV.

Sponsorship and female sport

As male sports attract larger audiences, female sports tend to lose out both in the newspapers and on television. This is because men's games are seen to be more exciting, skilful and popular. This could be because of the differences in sheer physique between the sexes, or because of male testosterone driven competitiveness.

Hence sponsors do not invest as much money in women's sport unless the female athlete can be turned into a sex symbol – for example, Maria Sharapova, figure 20.4.

figure 20.4 – Maria Sharapova

The professional sporting event

- The **live game** is always the central interest for the spectator, and advertising is only a by-product. But with television and the printed word, there is the opportunity of reinforcing the impact of the product through **repetition**.
- The sporting event is the fundamental attraction, and the return advantage to the sport is the considerable sponsorship deals that exist. Popularity of the sport and its individual participants, means that people will buy a sponsor's product.

- In professional British soccer, **commercial funding** has been a huge financial bonus. However, this wealth has been mostly accumulated by the successful clubs, and hence the bidding war for the best players is usually won by these same clubs. This means that relatively few clubs will continually dominate the game.

- The players consequently become part of the advertising procedure, and receive huge amounts of endorsement money as well as inflated wages. However, this is a fragile existence as it only lasts as long as these particular players are successful in the public eye.

- As a direct result of its commercial nature, an event itself accumulates further features which were originally not part of its sporting element. For example, **mixed zone interviews** with managers, coaches, performers (captains and goalscorers), and officials (third or fourth match referees). These interviews have become an expected part of the proceedings, and have led to players being coached as to their performance in the interview itself.

- International events often have to programme and timetable their activities according to the USA media requirements for advertising breaks and prime (USA) time viewing.

Sports management and Governing Bodies

Commercialism of major sports has led to huge managerial development, where the clubs themselves need to employ specialists to handle financial affairs, and players need managers and agents as 'professionals' to get the players the best deal.

figure 20.5 – cricket as a new game

- A further issue is that players in major sports teams have become '**superstars**' as a result of **media coverage**. This has meant that players' role model status has dramatically increased. As a result, managers are responsible for ensuring that their players behave in a sensible and appropriate way, since a big chunk of income via sponsorship depends on the image of the team.

- A major incident in which commercialism affected how a whole sport was governed and how rules were dramatically changed was the Australian revolution.
- This was instigated by **Kerry Packer** with his link between commercial television and advertising. This changed the whole commercial nature of cricket as a sport, with coloured kit and a white ball played at night under floodlights. This new game appealed to the working man (since it was not played during the working day), and was made more exciting, shorter, and decisive (figure 20.5).

- This was shortly thereafter followed by Rugby League which changed its nature from a winter game to a summer game in response to Kerry Packer's commercial (TV) needs, and the rugby league superleague was born.

The effect on spectators

While focus is often between the **sporting organisations** and the **performers**, it is important not to ignore the effect of commercialism and the media on **spectators**.

Herein lies the biggest marketing ploy of commercial companies as the major objective of the advertising process is to have a positive impact on the largest number of consumers as summarised in figure 20.6.

figure 20.6 – spectators, sponsors and the media

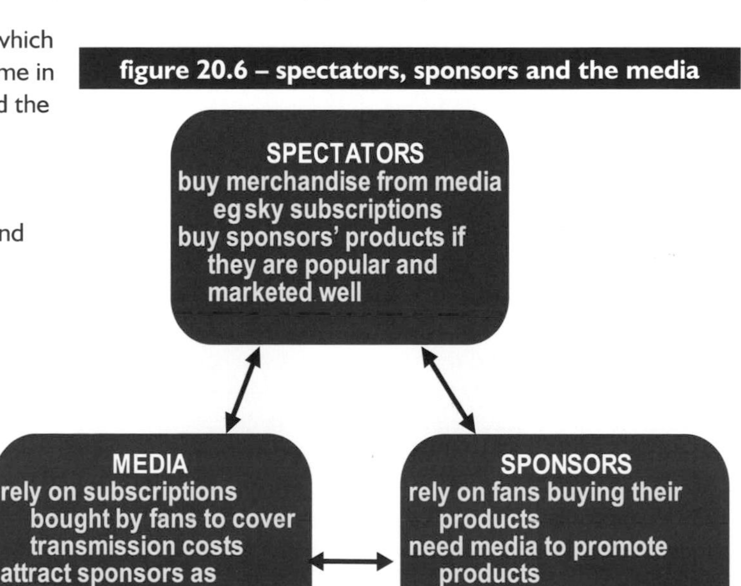

Technology in sport

Technology has had a massive impact on sport during the past twenty-five years. The development of kit, equipment, playing surfaces, facilities and ergogenic aids are examples of this. Video analysis and software programmes to analyse team and individual performances and assist TV match officials are more recent developments.

Modern technologies are used to engage elite performers, officials, coaches, spectators and armchair TV audiences with instant replay, statistical information and the excitement of record breaking performances.

Kit and equipment selection and design

Specialist clothing

- Lycra sports clothing **reduces air resistance**.
- Swim hats reduce drag on the head.
- Compression clothing (figure 20.7) will **increase venous return** and $\dot{V}O_{2max}$ during **high intensity exercise**. Recovery is improved and DOMS reduced.
- Special **shark suits** for the swimmers - **reduce drag**.

figure 20.7 – compression clothing

The shark suit dilemma

At the 2009 World swimming championships, almost every race produced a World record swim (from 50m fly to 1500m freestyle).

The suits being used were essentially wetsuits with four characteristics:

- High **compression**, hence **better venous return** and **recovery**. The suits took up to 40 minutes to get into, causing problems with check-in and warm-up.
- **Teflon coated**, so that the **drag was reduced** by between 2 and 5%.
- **Air trapping** which gave the suit extra **buoyancy** and caused the swimmer to have less surface in contact with the water (more body showing above the water surface), and hence **less drag**.
- The **cost**, at up to £1000 for three or four swims. This means that there was a financial penalty placed on non-elite swimmers without National support.

The suits have been banned from the end of the 2009 season - will World performances fall?

figure 20.8 – specialist protection clothing

Protective clothing

Protective clothing ranges from wetsuits to winter sports clothing, hikers' outfits, and specialist protective clothing needed in many of the sports listed below.
Protective clothing reduces the risk of injury from impact, playing surfaces and environmental conditions depending on the nature of the sport, for example:

- Fencing (figure 20.8).
- Ice hockey.
- Field hockey.
- Cricket.

This kit is expensive and therefore its cost will restrict the opportunity for participation among the majority of the population. This makes even cricket and hockey games in which only the middle classes (and above!) can take part at the non-elite level. Hence the base of the sporting pyramid will be substantially reduced compared with sports like soccer or athletics (running!).

The implications for coaching and facility provision are that these factors also will be expensive and therefore scattered thinly about the country (fewer people participating will not be able to fund these factors at the same levels as soccer or athletics for example).

Equipment

The design of kit and equipment must meet the requirements of the sport for which it is intended. However, experiments are regularly made by manufacturers to sports shoes, for example:

- Multiple spikes to track shoes.
- Thickness of sole for rock climbing boots and throwing shoes.
- Studs on soccer and rugby boots (length and number).

Examples of other items of clothing:

- Strength of the material in rugby shorts and shirts.
- Stretchability of material used in tennis or athletics wear.

figure 20.9 – Super Roo bike

Example of improvements in bike technology

Australian **track cyclists** were World Track Champions for the three years from 1995-1997 and owed much of this to their **Super Roo carbon fibre cycle** (figure 20.9). This bike was developed via scientific evaluation of cycle design and weighed around 5kg. The best riders in Australia were allowed to train on **personally adjusted** aerodynamically designed models for various international track and road events. This was a commercially funded venture which led to outstanding Australian performances at that time.

Top cycling countries have invested in this technology, and Britain has taken advantage of the new concept, resulting in **British victories** in the 2008 Beijing Olympics and the World Track Championships.

figure 20.10 – Oscar Pistorius, blade runner

Oscar Pistorius

Advances in technology have also aided paralympic athletes such as Oscar Pistorius. Using his 'Cheetah Flex-Foot' blades, Oscar has run 26 world record performances. In 2008 he started an amazing debate within the athletics community by petitioning to be able to compete at the Beijing Olympic Games, against able-bodied competitors.

He won his appeal that overturned the IOC decision not to allow him to compete in Beijing but did not achieve the qualifying time. However, the blades have been proved to enhance sprint running speeds by 15-30 percent which possibly could give him an unfair advantage over able-bodied athletes.

This case raises issues about equity of performers and performance as well as technology. The degree to which able-bodied performers should or should not be able to use the same technology as Oscar to improve their competitiveness in the international arena, is an unanswered question.

Playing surface - indoor or outdoor?

Over the last 30 years synthetic playing surfaces have spread throughout the World. These surfaces have reduced the element of chance, speeding games up and rewarding skill.

For example, tennis players preparing for a hard court tournament, such as the US or Australian Opens, know that the hard playing surface will hardly change from one venue to the next and hence their matches will be more predictable.

Some sports have retained their natural playing surfaces. For example, cricket played on grass can have cracked, fast or slow surfaces, and grass tennis courts can be threadbare or lush. Playing surface variables such as this affect speed of play, elements of surprise, and reward skill.

Table 20.2 – **advantages and disadvantages of synthetic playing surfaces**

advantages of synthetic playing surfaces	disadvantages of synthetic playing surfaces
more frequent use in spite of weather	hard surface which could lead to chronic injury
consistent playing surface	increase bounce of soccer ball
no divots which could affect play	less skill differentiation between top and average performers
maintenance costs low	installation costs high (but comparable with modern hydroculture in grass surfaces for professional soccer)
good draining surface	

Note that the PFA have banned the use of synthetic surfaces for top league soccer. Perhaps players like the inconsistency of muddy grass surfaces during winter.

figure 20.11 – the new Wimbledon

Facilities

Facilities have become very sophisticated with retractable playing surfaces, variable seating configurations, and complex hydroculture and under-pitch heating systems for grass surfaces.

Indoor stadia are exemplified by the shiny new retractable roof for Wimbledon centre court (see figure 20.11). This roof can cut out unpleasantly cold, blustery and wet conditions to give still air and ambient adjustable temperatures. This provides comfort for players, spectators, officials and coaches, and **consistency of playing conditions** for players.

Video analysis

figure 20.12 – Hawkeye in action

Video developments that help in officiating have been extremely important technological aids.
For example the use of video replays in cricket and rugby to confirm decisions. Hawkeye (tennis, cricket and snooker) and the Snickometer/Hot Spot technology (cricket) have allowed commentators, viewers and listeners to sit in on controversial or questionable judgements made by officials.

Not only is the Hawkeye Officiating System (in tennis figure 20.12) vital for ensuring that high pressure points do not fall prey to umpiring mistakes, it brings the fans closer to the action. Spectators watch alongside their heroes and heroines on court as Hawkeye shows whether a ball was 'in' or out' on stadia big screens. This gives great entertainment value.

Unfortunately, it is impossible to provide this system to all courts even in grand slam tournaments. Players on outside courts still have to deal with unchallenged umpiring mistakes. Also, when inexperienced players get the opportunity to play on centre court they often lack the experience of when to use their Hawkeye challenges effectively.

Technique analysis

Apart from the simple digital camera, there are many software systems which analyse and compare technique. Some of these look at body positions, angles and speeds and also provide frame to frame comparison between the performer and a technical model (figure 20.13).

figure 20.13 – technique comparison software

Video analysis reinforces, supports and develops technical skills and so provide coach and elite performer with a mechanical tool that can enhance performance in the long-term.

Positional software

Other systems look at the movement of players during a game, enabling strategy and tactics to be monitored by a coach.

Prozone

Prozone uses up to 12 fixed cameras and sensors around a pitch or playing area. This analyses the positions and speeds of players at up to 10 times per second (10 Hertz). In 2009, 14 premiership soccer clubs used the system.

GPS applications

A **GPS** (global positioning system) device contains a small receiver chip that links to an array of satellites orbiting the Earth to give position and speed of an object.

- **GPSports** have developed a system in which a device carried (strapped to the torso) by a player is monitored for position by GPS technology.
- Some sports allow the devices to be worn during competitive games (for example, hockey).
- GPS data can be linked to programmes such as Google Earth to create simulation of course terrain. For example, cyclists can ride a course without actually being there. Race plans can be prepared from this visualisation process. Indoor GPS applications include links to heart rate monitors and even video to gain a better picture of an athlete's performance.
- The main use so far has been to highlight to a player where on a pitch his activity has been, and how his pitch coverage compares with other players operating within the same tactics.
- As with any technology, accuracy of data is sometimes questionable and cost is a major issue.

Technical ergogenic aids

These are devices used to analyse technique and the mechanics of a movement, or monitor essential factors of a performer's activity:

- **Force plates** can be inserted into the ground at the take-off area for a long jump or high jump, or in the space in a track immediately after a sprint start. This enables the patterns of force made by a foot striking the plate to be determined, which can tell a coach the precise way in which the foot is active during its strike with the ground, and enables him or her to assess whether **changes in foot posture** are required.
- **Pedometers** are wrist-worn devices used to detect footfall, and a coach will use this information to assess **stride length** or total energy output.
- **Heart rate monitors** are fairly old technology, which can be strapped to the torso or worn as a watch-like device on the wrist. Hence heart rate can be observed by the performer during training or competition to ensure that HR operates within a predetermined training zone.

Loughborough University Sports Technology Institute

Sports technology institutes such as Loughborough, recognise the growth in the commercial markets for high tech kit and equipment to support the development of elite performers. An example of a current project is:

- Reassessing how **footwear** can be made to match the **shape and mechanics** of feet on an individual basis (figure 20.14). The foot is scanned to capture its shape, then footfall is analysed (using forceplate technology). This indicates exactly how the foot lands and moves, and leads to the construction of personalised footwear, whose aim is to make movement more efficient and improve performance.

figure 20.14 – Dan Hipkiss - with specially moulded boots

Practice questions

1) Outline the positive and negative features of sponsorship for the sports performer. 6 marks

2) What is the role of the media in promoting healthy lifestyles and lifelong involvement in physical activity? 5 marks

3) World Championships are organised by the International Federation of that sport. Discuss how external factors (such as the media) may influence the organisation, structure or management of these events. 7 marks

4) Sport, sponsorship and the media are all interdependent on each other for their success and popularity. Discuss. 7 marks

5) How has commercialisation influenced recent Olympic Games? 5 marks

6) Discuss the arguments for and against television coverage of sport. 6 marks

7) Discuss the notion that sports performers are only as good as the technology that supports them. Use examples from global sports to support your answer. 14 marks

8) Some sports have changed to make them more suitable to media coverage.
   a) Identify four ways in which a spectator can benefit from the application of technology in sport. 4 marks
   b) Discuss two disadvantages that these technologies might create. 2 marks

INDEX

F

G

H

I